D0445947

The Enough Moment

ALSO BY DON CHEADLE AND JOHN PRENDERGAST

Not On Our Watch: The Mission to End Genocide in Darfur and Beyond

The

Enough
Moment

Fighting to End Africa's
Worst Human Rights Crimes

John Prendergast *with* **Don Cheadle**

Three Rivers Press / New York

Copyright © 2010 by John Prendergast

All rights reserved.

Published in the United States by Three Rivers Press, an imprint of the Crown
Publishing Group, a division of Random House, Inc., New York.
www.crownpublishing.com

Three Rivers Press and the Tugboat design are registered trademarks of
Random House, Inc.

This work contains brief excerpts from the following articles: "Obama's
Opportunity to Help Africa" by George Clooney, David Pressman, and John
Prendergast, *The Wall Street Journal*, November 22, 2008; "Obama Can Make
A Difference in Darfur" by Jim Wallis and John Prendergast, *The Wall Street
Journal*, April 13, 2009; and "At War in the Fields of the Lord" by Ryan Gosling
and John Prendergast, ABC News, March 1, 2007.

Grateful acknowledgment is made to Omekongo Dibinga for permission to
reprint his poem "Honorata."

Library of Congress Cataloging-in-Publication Data
Prendergast, John, 1963–
The enough moment : fighting to end Africa's worst human rights crimes /
by John Prendergast with Don Cheadle.
p.   cm.
1. Human rights—Africa.   2. War crimes—Africa.   3. Crimes against
humanity—Africa.   4. Social movements.   5. Political participation.
I. Cheadle, Don.   II. Title.
JC599.A35P74 2010
364.1'38096—dc22   2010007642

ISBN 978-0-307-46482-8

Printed in the United States of America

Design by Elizabeth Rendfleisch

Map on page vi by Ellen McElhinny
Maps on pages 174–175 by The Enough Project

10 9 8 7 6 5 4 3 2 1

First Edition

We are not guaranteeing the end of all human rights crimes in Africa if you follow the advice in these pages. And we certainly do not claim to possess all the answers to the complex problems we address here. But we can be sure that if war criminals everywhere face an ocean of people with Braveheart-like commitment standing up in support of peace and human rights, the odds improve that the world will be a better and safer place for millions of people. So we dedicate this book to all the folks on the front lines of this fight, and to a future in which these most heinous human rights crimes no longer exist.

John and Don
May 16, 2010
Los Angeles, California

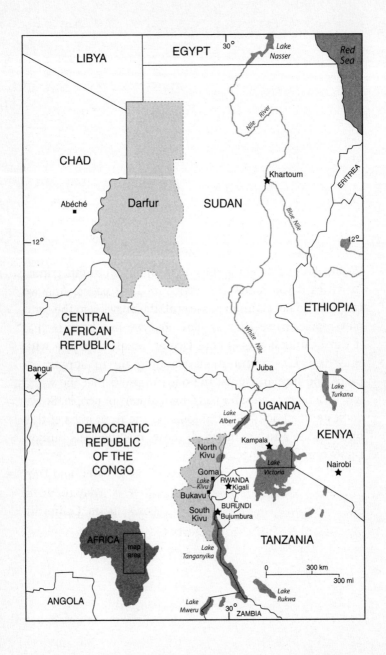

Authors' Note

We believe this book should be a living document, so we've created a place online—www.enoughmoment.org—where you can connect with others, see how to get involved, watch inspiring videos, write letters, sign petitions, and get real-time updates on what's happening in the countries and crises we discuss. There's a wealth of information there, including some amazing Enough Moments from Upstanders around the world. Share your Enough Moment with others, and read the inspiring things people are doing every day all over the world in the fight to end Africa's greatest human rights crimes.

A portion of the authors' earnings will be donated to the Enough Project (www.enoughproject.org) at the Center for American Progress in its efforts to end the human rights crimes discussed in this book.

Contents

Introduction

Don and John and the Enough Moment

Dateline, Las Vegas.

It is a few hours after the successful conclusion of another Ante Up for Africa charity poker tournament to raise funds and awareness for Darfur. Two years have passed since our first book, *Not On Our Watch,* was published. But it is the immediate future that consumes us on this boiling Las Vegas night: there is an impossibly short time before our next book is due to the publisher. If you are not reading this, it didn't happen. The tape recorder is turned on . . .

JOHN PRENDERGAST: Buddy. The deadline for this book is coming at us like a runaway train, and we have the grand total of a vague outline. Some people hate endings. I seem to be unable to cope with beginnings.

DON CHEADLE: Well, nothing concentrates the mind like a crushing deadline. But, frankly, I really hate committing anything to tape.

JOHN: The post–Richard Nixon Syndrome? I can take lots of notes, and we can shut this thing off . . .

DON: Naah, let's play through. It seems surreal that our last book came out two years ago.

JOHN: My God, my life is careening by. I'm a dinosaur, man.

DON: A fossil.

JOHN: A museum exhibit. So the idea here is that part of this book we can talk through, and part of it I can write. Our conversations can be the narrative spine that links the chapters together, the Mississippi River that winds its way through the middle of the book and keeps everything flowing. Branching off our conversations will be stories and testimonies of Upstanders from the wars' front lines, from amazing everyday activists, and from celebrities and other prominent folks, as well as everything you ever wanted to know about why genocidal tactics and other human rights crimes are used and how we can stop them. Geez, I have the sudden, chilling feeling that it won't work.

DON: Of course it will work.

JOHN: Who are you, the conductor of the *Titanic* string band?

DON: So can we hit rewind and tape over some of the parts of this conversation we don't like?

JOHN: How many times a day do I wanna just hit the rewind button, extract my foot out of my mouth, and re-record? What a great thing to have in life. A much more pressing issue, however, requires reiteration. This publisher is gonna have to send the literary bounty hunters after us to get this book, brother, if we don't get our act together.

DON: Umm, I thought you were kidding about this deadline?

JOHN: (Silence)

DON: This is the mother of all Hail Marys.

JOHN: We are going to redefine the concept of Hail Mary.

DON: No, this is the exact definition of a Hail Mary. I'm sure there's an opt-out clause in the contract.

JOHN: Or at least some kind of extension based on incompetence or desperation, for which we qualify and will no doubt utilize more than once on this one. So much pressure. Is that tape really rolling? Can you check?

DON: It's rolling. I pressed start. Someone had to take charge.

JOHN: Oh, it is moving . . . Oh, God . . .

DON: That tape is a metaphor for something. If we were real writers, we'd think of something insightful to write here.

JOHN: Real writers? I'm the nomadic son of a frozen foods salesman, and you're Iron Man's accomplice. I hope people aren't expecting too many fancy metaphors from us. But we do have a purpose here that we've been talking about for the last few months now. The essence of our discussions has been this concept of the "Enough Moment."

DON: Yeah, after all the "Never Again" speeches by all of these politicians, as genocide and other horrible human rights crimes continue, and all this attention for Darfur and the Congo and other places, we can't just sit by and not respond to them. Enough is enough.

JOHN: Exactly. So the point of writing another book is to focus on this concept of the "Enough Moment," when a potentially perfect storm is gathering for real action in response to some of the worst atrocities in world history. For the first time we've seen the creation of an anti-genocide constituency, around Darfur, while the genocide was still happening. For the first time a global effort is being developed to counter rape as a war weapon, with the tip of the iceberg in the Congo. And for the first time we have a young people's movement forming to protect other young people half a world away who are being forced to become child soldiers, in the attempt to stop the Lord's Resistance Army. These are three of the most heinous and despicable ways to fight a war, and the objective of this growing movement is to eradicate their use from the face of the earth.

DON: And helping to fuel all these efforts is this incredible new engine: these social networking tools. Every day there are new innovations. You learn from a sixteen year old what the new thing is.

JOHN: And we aren't done yet. Finally, we have an administration in Washington, a cabinet full of people who have really made a mark in their previous positions as vocal human rights advocates, as anti-genocide crusaders.

DON: From the president to the vice president to the secretary of state to the UN ambassador. We have had interactions with all of them, and we could see it firsthand, that all of them have been committed to doing much more to bring these nightmares to an end.

JOHN: And though we might have been inclined to give them a pass during the first year and a half on the job, by now they've all had sufficient time to adjust to their executive branch jobs and really live their principles. So if there ever were one, this is the Enough Moment, potentially, for these human rights issues. And that's just on the macro level. There is also the micro level, the individual level. Anyone who has stepped up to become an advocate for other people in less fortunate circumstances has had his or her own personal Enough Moment. These Enough Moments originate from all kinds of things. Like when you see a picture that personalizes someone's suffering, or you hear a story, or someone tells you about a particular issue.

DON: Or you see a movie, a TV show, or hear a song, and something registers. It could be for a million different reasons that it registers.

JOHN: You may have had a teacher or an experience as a kid that triggers some level of compassion and desire to act. Or it could have been a parent, or a role model.

DON: You heard the bell toll.

JOHN: Yeah, it's like in that Sinatra/Denzel movie, when the chip gets switched on . . .

DON: Oh, yeah, *The Manchurian Candidate*, but in this case the light gets switched on for good instead of evil.

JOHN: The light goes on, and you are like, okay, now I gotta go and do something. I can no longer be a bystander. I have to become an Upstander, to use Samantha Power's term. What I am going to do I may not know immediately, but I know

I must do something. So these auditoriums full of people who show up for events and film screenings, for people who buy books like this, for people who come to rallies and demonstrations, for folks who get online and sign petitions and write letters to public officials . . .

DON: They all have had some kind of Enough Moment that led them to decide to be part of something bigger for something beyond themselves.

JOHN: It is fascinating to explore what makes people care about these issues. I think some people have their Enough Moment because they genuinely are driven or touched or affected by the suffering of others, and they feel in some way, shape, or form that there is some kind of responsibility . . .

DON: Cosmic responsibility . . .

JOHN: The concept of being my brother's or sister's keeper. And I think some people are driven by an imperative that is found in any faith to reach out and provide assistance to those less fortunate. Action is very clearly an essential element of any faith. I was just at a service on Sunday, and the sermon was all about the imperative to work for peace. And then, of course, there is the common security threat—you know, if we don't deal with some of these issues, then they might bounce back on us. Whether it is terrorism, disease, or environmental degradation, the issue of enlightened self-interest also can be the catalyst for involvement.

DON: It will always be my hope that people will care beyond themselves, and they will want to do more. That's going to be an imperative a lot more quickly than we think it is, as some of these problems that seem so far away are going to rebound back here on us. So we are going to need to link arms with people all over the world against a greater common enemy involving environmental destruction and the ensuing lack of resources, water, and food. I mean, we cannot continue to waste as we have as a world and expect that there will be no consequence. So you need to be able to flex the muscle of altruism and humanitarianism and brotherhood and fellowship in a very necessary way. Or you know, get a bunch of guns, and hunker down and hope you got enough people with you that you can stave off the masses when they come to try to take your stuff, because it's one or the other—stand apart . . . united we . . .

JOHN: Hang together, or all hang separately.

DON: Exactly. Any one of those concepts. So I think that people will come to the realization that it's not just necessarily saying "I want to stop genocide in Sudan" but rather "We HAVE to stop genocide. We have to stop rape as a war weapon, or it will spread and some day rebound directly on us."

Ultimately, what are we doing this for? What's the point? What's gonna make some senator get off his ass, walk down the steps, get in his car, drive to the White House, and say, "No, I gotta get in now. No, move, I gotta talk to the president now." "What's the problem, senator?" "This is the problem, and we have to do something about it now."

What is the gear that has to be shifted to make that happen? There has to be a political benefit to taking meaningful action for some politicians. How do we translate altruism into something that is maybe less idealistic and more visceral for the people we are asking to act, so that there is a reward, a real reward, and a recognition, for being an Upstander?

Because we, as ordinary citizens, can feel good just knowing that we have done something, that we have tried to do something. But I don't think that is always what motivates politicians. I think there are many more people that they have to answer to, and there is sort of a bottom line in all the policies they put into place that has a big quid pro quo element to it and a big concern with staying in that seat of power for as long as they can. So in order to break through the barrier of inaction and inertia that exists in halls of power in D.C. and around the world, we're gonna have to be more creative in going beyond the usual reasons why people care.

JOHN: Recently I was in Washington, and we had an event with a group called Invisible Children, which is an organization led by young people and focused on stopping the recruitment of child soldiers by the Lord's Resistance Army of Uganda. We were having a lobby day.

So we get the word out, and we have no idea how many people are gonna be willing to fly or bus or drive to D.C. to be part of this thing on behalf of kids half a world away. Frankly, I'm thinking a hundred or so will straggle in on their own dime. I mean, they're students, so this kind of unanticipated expense isn't easy to absorb.

So I arrive at the auditorium that morning, and what do you know: there are 1,500 young people already there from all over the country, ready to descend on Capitol Hill. The number of congressional cosponsors for the legislation we had worked on quadrupled in something like six hours, because there is a light at the end of the tunnel. The bill ended up having the most cosponsors of any freestanding bill on Africa ever.

DON: When you and I went to northern Uganda a few years ago, nobody in the United States had even heard of the Lord's Resistance Army.

JOHN: It's incredible. So the point is that we have these growing people's movements focused not on responding to the symptoms of human rights abuses but on ENDING genocide, on ENDING child soldier recruitment, and on ENDING rape as a war weapon. And we finally have a group of people in government whose careers have in part been committed to ENDING these scourges as well.

DON: And we need to remind them every day of their commitment.

JOHN: You ain't kiddin'. But the news gets even better. It turns out that when political will is generated, and it is combined with smart, game-changing, inspired, effective policies, wars can end, and problems can get solved.

DON: You're always talking about "blood diamonds."

JOHN: Yep, perfect example. A multifront movement was created that sought an end to the connection between diamond purchases and terrible human rights abuses in places like Sierra Leone, Liberia, and Angola. When the political will was generated and consumer pressure got hot enough, corporations and governments did the right thing and filtered blood diamonds out of the interational market. And now, less than a decade later, all three of those countries are at peace.

DON: When you look at this history, the possibility for transformation can be dramatic. But supporting that transformation requires focus, attention, commitment, drive, and innovation.

JOHN: And imagination. People have to believe peace and justice are possible, and they have to imagine the roadmap required to get there. It was an Enough Moment for those countries and that issue. Now the time has come for the Enough Moment for the issues you and I have worked on together, some of the most dramatic human rights issues of the last century: genocide, child soldier recruitment, and rape as a tool of war.

CHAPTER ONE

Enough Is Enough

Building a People's Movement Against Genocide,
Child Soldier Recruitment, and Rape as a War Weapon

A human wave in support of the world's most forgotten people is building. We're not surfers, but we love how surfers describe the perfect wave. The wave builds to a crescendo, you're in awe of it, you approach and ride it, and it carries you safely home to your destination. The formation of this human wave was not predicted. A decade ago, few people even knew what a "Darfur" was, how our cell phones directly contributed to making Congo the most dangerous place in the world to be a woman or a girl, or who the "invisible children" of Uganda were. Ten years ago, an event regarding genocide or other crimes against humanity would have attracted perhaps a dozen or so hardy souls, wearing their sandals and psychedelic t-shirts, prepared, if necessary, to break out into a stanza or two of "Kumbaya."

But today a strange and beautiful cocktail of hope, anger, citizen activism, social networking, compassion, celebrities, faith in action, and globalization are all coming together to produce the beginnings of a mass movement of people against these crimes and for peace. And this is happening at the very time that an American administration is populated by a number of people who have been the leading elected officials to have stood up against genocide, child soldier recruitment, and rape as a war weapon. We call the sheer possibility inherent in this confluence of factors the Enough Moment, and it means that our feeling that Enough Is Enough might actually get translated into real action for change.

These are three of the great scourges of our world, of our time. Genocide, mass rape, and child conscription are the most deadly and diabolical manifestations of war, with the gravest human consequences imaginable. Nearly 10 million fresh graves have been dug as a result of these tactics in East and Central Africa alone over the last twenty years, and countless millions of refugees have been rendered homeless. Sudan and Congo, in fact, are the two deadliest conflicts in the world since the Holocaust.

The stakes remain enormous. And this is by no means an Africa-only phenomenon. The kinds of tactics used by warring parties globally are increasingly targeted at civilian populations who are usually defenseless and largely disconnected from the perpetrators of the violence. As a result, the ratio of civilians to soldiers who die at times runs as high as nine to one. Because of this targeting of civilians, over 100 million people died violent deaths during the twentieth century's wars and genocides. This exceeds the death count of all pre-twentieth-century wars and massacres combined.

At this juncture of human history, and because of the distortion and delay in Africa's own historical trajectory created by the European colonial era, it turns out that the global epicenter of this kind of targeted violence is currently playing itself out on African soil, with weapons that come largely from America, Europe, and Asia. And these are therefore the places most in need of a global people's movement and smart U.S. policies to ensure an appropriate global response in support of peace.

This is also the continent we know best, and we have committed ourselves to making a difference there.

The Enough Moment

In times of tragedy the United States of America steps forward and helps. That is who we are. That is what we do. . . . When we show not just our power but also our compassion, the world looks to us with a mixture of awe and admiration. That advances our leadership. That shows the character of our country.

—PRESIDENT BARACK OBAMA[1]

Strong and true words indeed from President Obama. But words unmatched with deeds can sometimes be worse than no words at all. Politician after politician, and UN resolution after UN resolution, have made promise after promise to end these crimes without doing what is necessary to give their words teeth.

But now a politically potent constituency forming through mass campaigns is raising awareness of these crimes, and it's time to translate intention into action. There is an increasing opportunity to democratize our foreign policy-making and to widen and deepen people's stake in international issues. We've finally got a president and a cabinet that have made huge pledges to act. Before they took office in 2009, President Obama, Vice President Biden, and Secretary of State Clinton were all major anti-genocide campaigners in the U.S. Senate, as was U.S. Ambassador to the United Nations Susan Rice in her previous think tank capacity. They all have formidable track records, demonstrating that being a bystander has never been an option for them. Now in the executive branch, they have the opportunity to act.

Now is the time to make this our collective Enough Moment—the day when we say "Enough" to the atrocities happening to our brothers and sisters in these war-torn regions. We have the opportunity to say "Enough Is Enough" and have these words become something tangible.

Historically, when we have decided that we are indeed our brother's and sister's keepers, we have acted. There are cases around the world of this resolve, such as global efforts to stop genocides in Kosovo and in East Timor. Africa has its own examples:

- When a genocide was about to occur in northeast Congo in 2003, the world said ENOUGH and stopped it from happening by deploying a European-led force to protect people and disarm militias.
- When terrible wars fueled by blood diamonds ripped Sierra Leone, Liberia, and Angola apart, the world said ENOUGH and stopped buying the blood diamonds, which helped cut off the fuel for the war, providing the opening for the wars to finally end.
- When South Africa was ruled by a racist white supremacist government that put Nelson Mandela in Robben Island prison for decades, the world said ENOUGH, and governments imposed—at the request of the people of South Africa—biting comprehensive sanctions until the racist system and government were dismantled completely and Mandela was freed (and elected president).

Now it is the moment to say Enough death in Darfur. Enough rape in the Congo. Enough children turned into fighting machines in northern Uganda and the surrounding region. Enough.

JOHN: There are so many great examples and great stories in Africa that people hardly know anything about. There was this kid, Arnold, that I met on my last trip to Congo, who had been forcibly recruited a few times as a child soldier, but he escaped and he is now going to university. He went through all this counseling, and he recently started his own nongovernment organization (NGO), Youth and Human Rights, advocating for the importance of justice and accountability. Instead of succumbing to the crushing circumstances he had endured, the kind of trauma that would destroy most of us, and then instead of being a bystander, Arnold decided to stand up and be a leader. That is utterly remarkable.

DON: It was amazing when we were making *Hotel Rwanda*. In one of the scenes where women were being brutalized, a lot of the extras had actually been through it in real life. And I just remember asking one of the women, "How could you go through it again like this, even in a movie scene?" And she said, "It's very important that the story be told again, and in the right way. And I want to be part of that." And I was like, "Wow."

JOHN: That is a strength that is just immeasurable, man. I remember this one Darfurian fellah that Samantha Power and I met on our first trip together into the rebel-held areas of Darfur. One night early on in our trip, out under a thousand stars, with everyone in their sleeping bags, this gentleman began telling us the story of Darfur and why his people are fighting for freedom. With a flashlight and his finger, he illustrated everything with drawings and diagrams in the sand. He spent hours on the nuances, the grievances, the rationale for what he argued is a just war in Darfur. The people in Darfur, he

told us, are not helpless or passive victims. Most are struggling, indeed, but many are fighting for their rights and for
peace. Under that starry canopy, he was telling us that there are
REASONS for the conflict in Darfur, and therefore there
are SOLUTIONS that the Darfurian people are trying to
contribute to by supporting the rebellion with their sons and
their sustenance. And the reason he said he was risking his
life to travel with us is because the solution won't come without telling the real story of Darfur to America and the world,
and he is hoping that enough people in what seemed to him
to be an indifferent world will stand up and lend a hand in the
solution.

The good news is that over the last few years, there have
been huge rallies, large numbers of people joining advocacy
groups, lobby days, petition drives, massive postcard and
letter writing campaigns, major congressional interest, and
bold pronouncements by all the major candidates for president in 2008. And even our previous book became a top-five
New York Times bestseller. It's still available, by the way. I'm
just saying.

DON: Please focus.

The task is clear. We as caring citizens need to catalyze
and build an even bigger and stronger people's movement
for change. We need to assemble an unusual coalition and
force better policies through popular demand. The political will for real change will come from the bottom up. This
is our chance. There may never again be an opportunity
like this. We must seize this Enough Moment, and seize
it now.

Why This Book

Africa is a continent full of promise, with identifiable solutions to these human rights crimes. Genocide has, in some places, been successfully prevented or ended. Child soldier recruitment has, in some places, been stopped, and the children affected have been rehabilitated. Rape as a tool of war, in some places, has been neutralized. Wars have been resolved. Understanding that there are answers is empowering. Demonstrating that the answers usually involve partnerships between Frontline Upstanders in the war zones and Citizen Upstanders in the United States and around the world is crucial to showing that there is a connection between the activism of ordinary citizens and the ending of wars and massive human rights crimes.

If we can build a broader and deeper people's movement against these kinds of crimes against humanity, our political system will become more motivated and effective in responding to and ultimately in preventing these crimes. Unless there is a political cost for inaction, we will get inaction. The growing people's movement is attempting to create a political cost for inaction, for lip service, for turning away from people in need of a hand. We hope to see a world where the penalties for committing these atrocities are so severe and the diplomacy to prevent them so deft and automatic that their recurrence becomes a subject relegated to our museums and history books.

We want to ring the bell for the seven-alarm fire that is raging in Africa's deadliest war zones. The 10 million deaths in the countries on which we are focused is a modern-day holocaust that demands a response. This book is the call to your Enough Moment.

People's Movements

If we take a hard look at the last century, we see both politicians and great ideas come and go. But the ingredients that time and again have really changed the world are the people's movements we know so well: the women's movement, the civil rights movement, the labor movement, the peace movement, the environmental movement, the anti-apartheid movement. They all show how change is possible—even when conventional wisdom is stacked in opposition—when organized groups of people come together around an issue they care enough about to move aside the forces of the status quo.

Finally, for the first time ever, we have a popularly based anti-genocide movement. We have a growing chorus of voices focused on stopping the destruction of women in the Congo. There is a renegade, underground phenomenon, called Invisible Children, that is sweeping through college campuses and that is dedicated to finding a solution to the child soldier travesty in northern Uganda and the surrounding region. Building the scale and scope of these efforts provides a unique and historic opportunity to help alter the course of history in those areas.

When we hear about Africa, it is often in the context of war, genocide, or famine. These phenomena are not inevitable. They can be stopped, and even prevented. Enlightened government policies focused on solving these challenges have proven successful. Unfortunately, so much of the effort and resources are focused on the shocking symptoms of war, leading to multi-billion-dollar outlays for emergency aid and military observers. There needs to be an equal emphasis on dealing with the causes led by competent peace processes, which are perhaps the most cost-effective tool we have in the international arsenal for dealing with crises. The truth is, though, government action in support of address-ing the causes that will lead to an end to these crises will be deployed earlier and be more consistent only when there is a larger and deeper people's movement focused on ending these tragedies.

We need to shift the paradigm away from simply respond-ing to the symptoms of these wars to focusing on ending them. The best way to end genocide, child soldier recruit-ment, and rape as a war weapon is to end the wars in which these strategies run wild and to impose a significant cost on those who utilize these deadly strategies.

This is where you come in. People's movements have two functions: to place pressure on our government to care about these kinds of issues that are often at the bottom of the list, and to ensure that our government is actually pursu-ing lasting cures for these crises, rather than just treating their symptoms. In other words, we don't want just action. We want smart action.

There are reasons why the world hasn't "saved" Darfur. The genocide there raged long beyond the time it could have been stopped. The reason is that the governmen-tal policies that were pursued regarding Darfur were not focused on ending the crisis. Instead, the policies mostly addressed only the symptoms, which they treated with hu-manitarian aid and peacekeeping forces, for which billions of taxpayer dollars have been and are being spent. This symptoms-based approach represented a failure of nations like the United States, but it also represented the Darfur anti-genocide movement's early overemphasis on UN peace-keeping troops, when the emphasis should have been on a peace deal backed by serious consequences for continued human right crimes.

Humanitarian aid is a necessary bandage, provided to keep people alive and address their acute emergencies pre-sumably while solutions are being sought. Peacekeeping forces are sent in primarily to observe and report on the actions of the parties to a conflict or a ceasefire, sometimes before a peace deal has even been signed. Inexplicably, it usually takes years of a crisis burning before there are systematic attempts to END the crisis that generate the need for aid and peacekeepers. That is what the people's movement must do: demand that government and UN policies be designed to focus early on dealing with root causes and ending these crises in a sustainable way. This Enough Moment today may be the best chance we will ever have to do so.

The people's movements against genocide, child soldier recruitment, and rape as a war weapon are composed of people from all walks of life and from many different motivations. Students, faith-based groups, and a diverse constituency of concerned citizens throughout the world have come together to express the sentiment that the destruction of human life on the basis of identity, gender, or age is simply not acceptable in the twenty-first century.

Significant constituencies are being constructed for each of these major human rights crimes:

- The anti-genocide movement for Darfur (also marked by efforts to prevent further crimes throughout Sudan) continues to advocate in the United States and in other countries, and Humanity United's Sudan Now campaign was constructed in mid-2009 to reenergize advocacy efforts of the movement and take them to the next level.
- There are rapidly expanding worldwide efforts to protect and empower the women of eastern Congo, who are subjected to violence more extreme than anywhere else globally. (The V-Day campaign led by Eve Ensler and the Enough Project's Raise Hope for Congo campaign work on parallel tracks and cooperate closely.)

- Similar efforts have been expended to protect the children of northern Uganda and the surrounding region (the How It Ends campaign spearheaded by a partnership between Invisible Children, Resolve Uganda, and Enough) who have experienced the highest abduction rates in the world at the hands of the Lord's Resistance Army.

In 2007, Gayle Smith and John founded the Enough Project to contribute to catalyzing this movement to focus on ENDING these kinds of human rights abuses rather than just responding to their symptoms with humanitarian aid, peacekeeping forces, and "Never Again" speeches and press releases. The Enough Project and other groups are attempting to create foreign policy literacy and trying to move the discussion beyond just getting involved to actual participation in tactics and strategy for change, especially when the "right" way is not always so clear. The objective is to not just shed light on the big policy solutions but to also help people understand why, and give people the tools for participating in an informed way. We want a smarter movement because compassion and dedication have exponentially more impact when they are applied strategically.

"What distinguishes the Enough Project is that it doesn't say, 'Hey, we've built this house, come and live in it with us,'" notes Karen Murphy of the organization Facing History and Ourselves. "Instead, Enough is showing people how to build it out, make it stronger. People feel prepared, inspired, successful, ready to take on something. Belonging is an essential human need. Enough provides that for these causes. You inspire people to say 'I want to belong to that,' or 'I want to do that,' and even 'I can do that.' People make this essential connection because they are informed and feel like they are part of something."

"Obama's Opportunity to Help Africa"

—George Clooney, David Pressman,
and John Prendergast, *Wall Street Journal*,
November 22, 2008

Rahm Emanuel, the White House chief of staff, recently reminded us that in the midst of crisis, there is great opportunity. For Congo and Sudan, we see three big reasons for hope.

The first is China. Because of China's nearly $9 billion investment in the oil sector in Sudan, and its recent $5 billion deal for Congolese minerals, China increasingly has a vested interest in peace and stability in these two countries. President Obama could send a powerful message and take a meaningful step by sending a high-level envoy to Beijing, early in his first 100 days, to explore ways to work together to help bring peace to these African countries. With all that divides the United States and China, these are issues we can and should unite on.

The second reason for hope is the [president] himself. Mr. Obama has offered the world a renewed American commitment to global citizenship. In both Congo and Sudan, as is the case in countries around the world, there is an extraordinary eagerness to see this global phenomenon engage positively in their crises. However intangible, the president-elect's ability to inspire and lead is as real as any other point of leverage. He can make the case for peace to those controlling the flow of money and munitions into Congo and Sudan. And he can raise the cost of continuing the status quo through multilateral measures to economically and politically isolate the spoilers.

The third reason for hope may be the most potent of all. The American public, especially our younger generation, is increasingly interested in what happens outside of our borders, and particularly in Africa. While we have all participated in our own way in building an advocacy movement around Darfur, it has been the high school and college students who have made Darfur a political issue too important to be ignored, and who are now preparing similar campaigns for Congo. It is these same young Americans who voted in large numbers for the new president. They are now ready to be led by a President Obama to build a safer world and a safer Africa.

Why Activism Matters

By mid-2009, many critics had looked at Darfur's continuing crisis and pronounced activist efforts aimed at stopping it a failure.

Not so fast.

Activists helped put the issue on the map for politicians on both sides of the aisle in Congress and on the presidential campaign trail in 2008, forcing them to address a situation that would have otherwise been lost in a sea of competing domestic and foreign policy priorities. But activists have done much more than simply garner attention for this cause.

Let's look at what has actually been accomplished in part due to activist efforts:

1. **Saving Lives:** It is no exaggeration to say that hundreds of thousands of Darfurians are alive today because of the anti-genocide activist movement. In the absence of the extraordinary global effort to shine a light on what is happening in Darfur, the death toll would have been far higher. Look back in history—to a time when there was *not* a mobilized and active anti-genocide constituency—at what the Sudanese regime did in southern Sudan during the twenty-year war there: tens and sometimes hundreds of thousands of

southerners perished each time the regime cut off access for humanitarian aid, until the death toll reached two and a quarter million. There was never a strong enough public outcry in the United States or elsewhere to force politicians to confront the Sudanese regime in a way that would prevent large-scale deaths. But now, because of the globalization of the genocide prevention movement, it is impossible for the Sudanese regime to cut off the flow of aid in Darfur without a huge international outcry from activists, journalists, and governments. In the spring of 2009, when the regime threw out over a dozen aid agencies from Darfur, the response was swift and united, and although many of the groups weren't allowed back in, the lost capacities were in part replaced as quickly as possible by other groups, thus avoiding a large increase in death rates. Additionally, activist-driven initiatives on the ground in Darfur—such as pressing for the establishment of focused patrols allowing women to collect firewood in the absence of a substantial peacekeeping presence around displaced camps and providing solar cooking stoves to reduce the number of trips outside protected areas—continue to save lives and reduce the rate of sexual violence.

2. **Supporting Peacemaking:** At the beginning of the Bush administration's time in office, before the Darfur war erupted, many Christian organizations, human rights activists, and committed members of Congress pressed for a robust response to the deadly north-south Sudanese war. Particularly in response to the faith-based constituency, the Bush administration led a complex and protracted peace process that resulted in the Comprehensive Peace Agreement (CPA) in 2005 ending that war. Furthermore, Darfur activist efforts around the time of the 2006 Washington, D.C., rally resulted in President Bush's sending a top diplomat to attempt to negotiate an end to the Darfur war. However, the negotiators' poorly conceived proposals and hurried

negotiations left the resulting deal dead on arrival. These two examples—though only one resulted in an actual peace deal—of activist-led pressure triggering government-led peacemaking efforts are promising illustrations of what activists have already helped to achieve for Sudan.

3. Indicting War Criminals: The Bush administration's strong opposition to the International Criminal Court nearly doomed an effort by the United Nations Security Council to refer the case of Darfur to the court. However, a major push by activists and congressional allies led the Bush administration to step aside and let the referral pass. The resulting investigation has led to an arrest warrant for President Omar al-Bashir and other officials charged with war crimes and crimes against humanity, an important step toward real accountability.

4. Deploying Peacekeepers: Despite consistent pledges by Sudanese government officials that they would never allow UN peacekeeping troops in Darfur, over 15,000 troops were sent to be part of a UN and African Union combined force attempting to provide some measure of monitoring and protection to Darfuri civilians. Woefully inadequately equipped, this peacekeeping force was ill fated from the start as it was sent to keep a peace that didn't exist. Activists were able to generate the necessary political will to get troops authorized and deployed, but in the absence of a peace deal, the effectiveness of the peacekeepers remains compromised. Nevertheless, many Darfuri civilians have been protected from further attacks simply because of the presence of these peacekeeping forces, directly attributable to activist pressures.

5. Removing Genocide from Stock Portfolios: A student-led activist initiative spearheaded by the Sudan Divestment Task Force and supported by the Save Darfur Coalition has resulted in numerous institutions' selling their stock holdings of companies doing business with the Sudanese government and thereby helping indirectly to finance genocide. As of the Spring of 2010, over 60 universities and colleges have divested, along with 27 state pension funds and 23 cities.

Activism does matter. We know that ultimately the conflicts in Africa will be solved because of the efforts of African people themselves. But the rest of the world has a major role to play in promoting solutions. Our roles as interested citizens and activists are to urge our political leaders to invest in achieving peace and ending human rights atrocities and to remind these officials that doing so is in the political and strategic interests of the United States. These crises are complex, and they will not be solved quickly or without sustained negotiations and engagement between multiple parties. We must resist the temptation to jump at overly simplistic or ineffective solutions and proceed with appropriate humility, while continuing to act with the knowledge that our efforts as activists are a crucial component to achieving peace and ending human rights abuses in Africa.

In towns and cities around the United States hang banners that read: "Darfur, A Call to Your Conscience." They are spot on. Responding to the crises of genocide, rape as a war weapon, and child soldier recruitment is fundamentally about our responsibility to affirm our belief in the value of human life and call on our government to promote policies that reflect our nation's core values. The Save Darfur Coalition pulled together 180 organizations, and it has been at the center of keeping grassroots constituencies informed and active. On the student side, the Genocide Intervention Network oversees the student anti-genocide organization STAND as well as the Sudan Divestment Task Force, and it helped focus young people's attention on the issue. Working with the Enough Project, these organizations were joined by many other localized groups—such as Jewish World Watch, the Massachusetts

Coalition to Save Darfur, and the San Francisco Bay Area Coalition to Save Darfur—as well as faith-based organizations—like the National Council of Churches, the National Association of Evangelicals, the American Jewish World Service, and Religious Action Center for Reform Judaism—in the quest to bring an end to the suffering of the people of Sudan.

The increasingly interconnected nature of the world means that the well-being and security of Americans are inextricably linked to the lives of people thousands of miles away. Terrorism, insurgencies, organized crime, drug trafficking, infectious diseases, environmental crises, refugee flows, and mass migrations can spill over into neighboring states, destabilizing entire regions. Our world is often like a gigantic spider web: touch one part of it and you set the whole thing trembling.

It is increasingly understood that failed states or ungoverned regions can become incubators for extremism, terrorist recruitment, and other cross-border threats. The United States cannot afford to ignore these crises. But it shouldn't ignore them anyway because achieving peace there could lead to positive spillover effects in the surrounding countries.

JOHN: More than anything else, it has been people's movements that have altered the course of history. When you look back at the last century of American history, and our interaction with the world, the real shifts have usually occurred in response to growing tidal waves of popular resistance or support for some kind of monumental change. So an interesting argument here is that with most of these movements, there were huge social forces arrayed against change and in favor of the status quo.

DON: Yep, all these movements faced tremendous resistance, but to varying degrees, they have succeeded. An advantage today is that we'd be hard-pressed to find anyone who would say that he or she is for child soldiers.

JOHN: We don't have a bunch of K Street lobbying firms in D.C. supporting genocide.

DON: Not openly anyway . . .

JOHN: Whoa, whaddya mean?

DON: I mean you don't have to be explicit in your "complicit." Special interests often dictate relationships among governments and/or corporations, and the result is silence or inaction in the face of some of the worst human rights crimes.

JOHN: Ahh, I see. That's true, and that is precisely why we have to recruit as many people as possible to make as much noise as possible. We can't have any illusions. This is a battle. There are forces that would use the most inhuman tactics to maintain power or to make money. You know, when we were working with some senators to introduce a bill on the Congo's conflict minerals, the electronics industry spent $15 million to try to kill the bill before it was even introduced. But all those letters and e-mails and calls from voters convinced the senators to move ahead anyway. And now we have a bunch of senators who have become champions on this issue because it is right and because they heard from their constituents that the issue matters. This is a fight. And it is winnable.

CHAPTER TWO

Enough with the Misconceptions

Africa as a Continent of Hope and Upstanders

JOHN: To have your Enough Moment, you have to know that your efforts are not in vain, that there is the potential for success. We want people to know about the success stories of countries that have transformed from seemingly hopeless cases to peaceful democracies, sometimes very quickly.

DON: Right. You want to know that you aren't throwing your efforts into a hole.

JOHN: And by telling the stories of Sierra Leone, Liberia, Angola, Mozambique, South Africa, and many others, we can demonstrate that increased activism by concerned citizens, finally combined with the right policies, can actually make a difference. In fact, activism has made a difference in so many things.

DON: It really has. Each of these conflicts was supposedly intractable, but the right combination of actions and interventions actually had an effect, moving the bar, in a very substantive way.

JOHN: So one of the things we want to do with these successful cases is to demonstrate that these issues like genocide, crimes against women, and child soldiers are not hopeless and that there are solutions.

DON: At the end of the day, let's say you convince me—if I'm Joe Public—to write this letter to my senator or attend that rally. And I make a real commitment to this cause, and I even make a donation even though I'm struggling, and I put in some energy and some time. And let's say our efforts are able to bring about a ceasefire, and the African boy in the refugee camp gets to go home, and he is able to have access to clean water, and there is a school nearby that he can go to. What's to say that the conflict isn't going to come storming back, and we aren't going to have to do this again in two years?

JOHN: That's exactly why we're writing this chapter. We need to demonstrate how the success stories don't just stop wars but actually transform societies. We want people to know that these kinds of problems are solvable and that these countries and people's plights aren't hopeless at all.

The Untold Story of Africa

There is a lingering, omnipresent phenomenon that helps paralyze individual and global responses as we contemplate what to do about Sudan and Congo. It is the widespread belief that Africa is a hopeless continent, filled with war and famine and basket-case countries marked by tribal divisions and aging dictators.

While it is true that there are still some countries in

Africa that are trapped in cycles of conflict and crisis, and this book is dealing directly with the biggest ones, the larger truth is that the majority of the continent is largely peaceful and striving to build democratic institutions and traditions. If we don't combat this perception of Africa as a hopeless continent, we will have much more trouble rallying support for our cause: ending the human rights crimes that occur within the context of the remaining conflicts, and preventing future ones.

From the headlines and the occasional television show, Africa sure *seems* hopeless. But remember the media mantra: If it bleeds, it leads. And if Hollywood's rendition of Africa were any guide, certainly we would think of Africa as a huge chasm of despair and savagery. Let's look at four movies and contrast the image being presented with the reality today of the country being portrayed. While it is positive that these kinds of movies are being made to highlight otherwise obscure crises, in the absence of more elaborate postscripts at the end of the films, as you'll see below, they can help feed stereotypes of Africa as a hopeless place:

1. **Leonardo DiCaprio stars in *Blood Diamond* (2006),** which depicts Sierra Leone as a hell on earth, with drug-crazed child soldiers who hack off people's limbs. Some of that actually happened in the 1990s and early the following decade. But it would have been good if at the end of *Blood Diamond* there had been a more elaborate postscript informing the viewer that Sierra Leone today is not only a country at peace but also a country that boasts positive economic growth rates and democratic elections that reflect the will of the people. The postscript could also have added that some of the rebel leaders who press-ganged the kids into military service and forced them to commit terrible atrocities are now facing justice for their crimes. And perhaps most importantly given the theme of the movie, the postscript could have educated

viewers that Sierra Leone's former blood diamonds are now, for the most part, clean diamonds, no longer fueling one of the most violent wars in African history.

2. **Nicholas Cage plays the lead role** in a movie called *Lord of War* (2005) about an arms dealer who sells some of his merchandise in Liberia, which is depicted as a land of savage violence that Cage's character at one point proclaims "God has forsaken." Liberia's civil war was indeed violent. But again, at the end of the film, it would have been better to add a postscript explaining that Liberia is a country now at peace. In fact, it has held democratic elections that resulted in the first elected female president—Ellen Johnson Sirleaf—in all of Africa, a president who is regularly invited to Europe and North America to lecture about how to heal divided societies. The postscript could have said that thousands of former child soldiers have gone through rehabilitation programs and that the man most responsible for the violence, the former president Charles Taylor, is now in The Hague on trial for crimes against humanity.

3. **Forrest Whitaker portrays the Ugandan dictator Idi Amin's** reign of terror in *The Last King of Scotland* (2006). Indeed, Amin was right out of central casting as one of postcolonial Africa's most murderous strongmen. But again there was no postscript at the end of the film explaining that Uganda is a country that has emerged from this period to see peace consolidated in the center and south of the country. There was no postscript explaining that the north is stabilizing now that the Lord's Resistance Army has been driven out of Uganda into the surrounding region. Without a postscript, most of the movie viewers wouldn't know about Uganda's successes with economic growth and HIV/AIDS reduction and its robust press and civil society sector. Most of Uganda has moved far beyond those dark days of Idi Amin.

4. A certain actor by the name of Don Cheadle portrays hotel manager-turned-rescuer Paul Rusesabagina in *Hotel Rwanda* (2004). The film realistically depicted the most dark and extreme moment in the country's history by using Paul's story. Though the film was phenomenal in educating people about the genocide, it would have been even more helpful if there had been a longer postscript at the end of the film letting the viewers know that Rwanda—a mere decade and a half after the genocide—is now a country that is for the most part at peace internally, though unresolved Rwandan issues bleed across the Congolese border and rebound negatively on the people there. A postscript could have referenced the positive, ongoing work regarding postgenocide justice and reconciliation—as well as the diversity of legislative representation, with the highest percentage of female parliamentarians in the world—helping to lay the groundwork for the possibility of a different future in Rwanda if transparency and inclusivity are stressed.

The point here is that Africa is NOT a continent of despair, or hopelessness. Scratch a little beneath the surface, and there is much hope. Most of Africa is at peace—democratizing and growing economically. To us, Africa's capacity for transformation seems limitless.

Is Africa Really that Different?

In fact, Africa is not only full of hope but its history actually isn't all that different from the rest of the world's history, which by contrast did not have twenty-four-hour cable news coverage of every problem experienced. Most African countries have been independent from European colonial rule for only fifty years or so. Let's not forget, before we judge Africa as different, that Europe fought its own wars of state formation for five centuries—from the Renaissance to World War II and the Holocaust—to determine its borders. And it still isn't finished: There is continuing instability in the Balkans and on Russia's periphery.

And where was the United States fifty years into its independence? Well, among other things there was a massive ethnic cleansing campaign against Native Americans. Look at this account of an attack by English Puritans led by John Mason in Connecticut on the Pequot Indians: "Those that escaped the fire were slaine with the sword; some hewed to peeces, others run through with their rapiers, so they were quickly dispatchte, and very few escaped. It was conceived they thus destroyed about four hundred at this time. It was a fearful sign to see them thus frying in the fyre, and the streams of blood quenching the same, and horrible was the stincke and sente thereof, but the victory seemed a sweete sacrifice."

There was also, of course, a transatlantic slave trade that led to the abduction of 30 million Africans who were sold into bondage, a phenomenon that helped catalyze America's economic juggernaut. At fifty, the United States hadn't even yet fought its own Civil War, one of the bloodiest conflicts in history.

It turns out that Africa is just going through its wars of governance and state formation at a later period in history than Europe, North America, and other continents because of the interruption of its natural historical cycle due to colonialism.

Africa's own course of state building was grossly undermined by Europe's colonization of the continent, leaving legacies of economic exploitation, slavery, and elitist governments that require much more work to overcome. Additionally, Africa has had to deal with major weapons dumping by China, Russia, and the United States and with having their tribulations catalogued on CNN for all the world to see, and judge.

And we need to tell the story of the genocide survivors of Sudan, the rape survivors of Congo, and the child soldier survivors of the Lord's Resistance Army, and tell people that it is their turn to rise now.

If we accept the notion that wars can be resolved in Africa, that Africa is not different from the rest of the world, and that Africa is full of transformative examples of hope, then the effort required to give peace a chance becomes a whole lot more viable, and even attractive.

COUNTRY UPSTANDERS:
African War to Peace Success Stories

LIBERIA

Not too long ago, to even mention Liberia was to evoke images of some of the worst atrocities in the world: drugged-up child soldiers, wide-scale use of rape as a weapon of war, and brutal battles for control of natural resources like diamonds and timber. Today, however, Liberia is at peace, having held democratic elections that brought Ellen Johnson Sirleaf to the presidency.

When Charles Taylor, a former Liberian cabinet official and escapee from a U.S. prison, invaded northwest Liberia in 1989 with a few hundred fighters, he was quickly able to mobilize much of the country against the regime of a U.S.-supported dictator named Master Sergeant Samuel Doe.

Taylor's invasion was the beginning of years of brutal conflict. He broke chilling new ground in his use of children as weapons of war, whom he would drug, indoctrinate, and use to commit brutal atrocities. Pro- and anti-Taylor factions perpetrated horrific atrocities on the civilian population while fighting for control of Liberia's substantial natural resources. Eventually, anti-Taylor elements began to coalesce. These rebel factions brought additional pressure on Taylor, as did his indictment for war crimes in June 2003 by the Special Court for Sierra Leone—a tribunal jointly administered by the United Nations and the government of Sierra Leone. Facing mounting international pressure to step down and courageous internal human rights organizing, often led by women (see the extraordinary 2008 documentary film *Pray the Devil Back to Hell*), Taylor departed for exile in Nigeria on August 11, 2003. A week later the factions signed a peace agreement that paved the way for a transitional government and a UN peacekeeping mission. A two-year transitional period cleared the way for disarmament, the return of refugees and displaced persons, and national elections.

It was never predetermined that Liberia would successfully emerge from war. A heroic combination of goodwill, good governance, and good luck helped Liberia to manage its transition. Donor governments like the United States brought significant sums of aid to the table, thanks in no small part to an active and organized Liberian Diaspora community that effectively pressured Capitol Hill. Fed up with the looting of reconstruction aid by the fighting factions, international donors devised a new system to administer aid transparently, putting international experts and respected Liberian civil servants jointly in control of those parts of the government that had been funnels for corruption. After Liberia's first free elections, Ellen Johnson Sirleaf, a former World Bank official who had supported Taylor but was later imprisoned by him, became the first democratically elected female president of an African state.

ELLEN JOHNSON SIRLEAF, LIBERIAN UPSTANDER

President Ellen Johnson Sirleaf is known in Liberia as "the Iron Lady" for her iron will and determination, qualities that are well reflected in her career. Johnson Sirleaf became Liberia's first female minister of finance in 1979, just before Doe's coup. She avoided the fate that met most of Liberia's ministers when Doe executed thirteen of them on the beach after seizing power. Johnson Sirleaf spent the Doe years in and out of Liberia, with stints at the World Bank, Citibank, and the United Nations. But in 1985, when she turned her criticism toward Doe and his associates, she was imprisoned and threatened with rape. She went into exile for more than a decade.

When Charles Taylor launched his assault on Liberia in 1991, Johnson Sirleaf initially supported him, a decision that would prove controversial. But she went on to oppose Taylor, and she later contested the 1997 elections, coming in second. Once he became president, Taylor charged her with treason, forcing her once again into exile. As one supporter put it to the BBC, "It would have been much easier for her to quit politics and sit at home like others have done, but she has never given up."[2]

Following her own election, she pledged to bring the "motherly sensitivity and emotion to the presidency" needed to heal the problems that plague Liberia after years of violence and warfare.[3] She has continued to fight graft by firing corrupt officials and demanding transparency in contracts, and she has appointed experienced women to run the ministries of finance, justice, and commerce.

SIERRA LEONE

Children as young as eight being forcibly conscripted by rebels; women getting their arms cut off because they voted for the wrong presidential candidate; diamonds being traded for guns to perpetuate war. This was Sierra Leone, a small, coastal country in west Africa, about half the size of Illinois, in the 1990s. When all was said and done, over 50,000 people had been killed, and 4,000 people had their arms or legs cut off by rebels. And yet nearly ten years later, Sierra Leone is at peace. The warlords that were behind its conflict are either on trial or are deceased, and its people are picking up their lives to rebuild. How did this happen?

Sierra Leone's war lasted ten years, and its main victims were the civilian population. In 1991 when the war began, there was large-scale opposition to the government because of deep corruption, but the rebel Revolutionary United Front (RUF) that sprung up quickly became unpopular itself. Rather than mobilize popular support, its two main leaders—ex-junior army officer Foday Sankoh and his former colleague, warlord rebel leader and future president of Liberia Charles Taylor—were a deadly duo, intent on gaining personal power and monetary gain for themselves at any cost. Sometimes in collaboration with units from the national army, the RUF raided villages to loot for food and goods, and they killed uncooperative civilians in very brutal ways, such as using machetes to behead local chiefs.

Far from mindless violence, these were deliberate, rational strategies used by the RUF's leaders to gain power. The brutal killings and raids—called "population-clearing guerrilla tactics" by military strategists—spread fear like wildfire, causing civilians to flee from their homes in droves. One in five people in Sierra Leone—1 million in total—became homeless as a result of the war, either forced to flee to other areas of the country or to neighboring Guinea or the Ivory Coast. (One of those 1 million was Ishmael Beah, the extraordinary author of *A Long Way Gone*.) The RUF was then able to operate out of the newly emptied villages and stage attacks on the next area.

Finally, the international community, led by the United Kingdom, the former colonial power, decided to invest seriously in resolving the crisis. The keys were an international campaign to deal with the blood diamonds fueling the war and a focused military strategy that understood the motivations of the rebel leaders. In addition, the United Nations sent in a large peacekeeping force of 17,000 troops. But in May 2000, 500 of its soldiers were taken hostage, and the RUF began a last-gasp invasion of the capital again.

Great Britain, bolstered by a cacophony of protests and shocking CNN-aired footage from the war zone, responded by sending in troops who secured Freetown in May 2000 and began a massive retraining and restructuring of the Sierra Leone army. With operational and planning support from the British troops, the Sierra Leonean army then launched several campaigns to disarm the RUF, and these campaigns were ultimately successful. Importantly, the United Kingdom and other donors also began a ten-year program to help reconstruct Sierra Leone, committing significant aid to roads, police restructuring, and other efforts to rebuild the country's infrastructure, thereby ensuring that its investment in peace would quickly be put to good use.

The British intervention worked because it was bolstered by three other initiatives:

- *Local activism:* Sierra Leonean civil society played a critical role that has often gone unmentioned. The community leaders, women's groups, and chiefs provided accountability to the warlords.
- *Sanctions:* UN sanctions on blood diamonds as well as

on timber and travel by the RUF's top leaders helped financially squeeze the rebels at a key point in 1999 and 2000. The RUF's demise accelerated when the UN Security Council sanctions were imposed on Charles Taylor. Further, RUF leader Foday Sankoh was captured in 2000 after being ousted because of financial arguments with other RUF leaders, in large part a result of the sanctions.

• *Justice:* The Special Court for Sierra Leone was set up to prosecute those most responsible for the atrocities. It has had a very successful track record and has indicted thirteen of the top militia leaders, including Charles Taylor, who went on trial at the end of 2009.

Overall, Sierra Leone remains at peace today, a remarkable success story in which the transformation from atrocities to reconciliation occurred very rapidly. There is no question that the country is still threatened by continuing corruption, illiteracy, and poverty, and it is the poorest country in the world, according to the United Nations.[4] But thanks to a concerted, coordinated effort by international and local Upstanders, people are no longer under threat of having their villages burned or their children abducted by a rebel group.

For more on how the blood diamonds movement helped end the crisis in Sierra Leone, go to www.enoughmoment.org.

SORIOUS SAMURA, SIERRA LEONEAN UPSTANDER

It's as if the war in Sierra Leone had its own Enough Moment. With the country spiraling out of control after nearly ten years of war, the rebels were about to invade the capital. Governments around the world were debating what to do in early 2000. In the midst of the crisis, one brave Sierra

Leonean thought he could change the debate and catalyze serious peacemaking. Sorious Samura was a documentary filmmaker living in London, but he decided to give up his safe haven from the war and go back to his country.

After seeing footage of individuals filming the war in Kosovo, Samura packed his new video camera and flew to Freetown, Sierra Leone's hot, humid capital city. "If only people could see what is happening in Sierra Leone, then they'd realize they have to do even more than what they did in Kosovo. I thought I should do something, to go back and film." Almost immediately after touching down, the rebels invaded Freetown, and he was trapped in a building. But he couldn't be dissuaded from heading out to find the facts. "I said to myself, 'If I stay in here, I'm possibly a dead man. If I go out there, I'm possibly dead too.' Rather than stay in the house and die here, I decided to go out."

He started to film killings in the street, and then he found himself in the rebel RUF camp and he managed to shoot for three days. Filming in the rebel compounds was unprecedented and extremely dangerous for Samura, but he went on. "These boys in the RUF, they were permanently drunk or on drugs. They were totally unpredictable. I walked into the middle of a humiliating rape, and they told me to clap. If I didn't, they would have killed me. But they allowed me to film many things which had never gotten out in the Western media."

When Samura returned to London, media outlets didn't want to air his tapes. The footage was too shocking for a British or American audience to bear, they said. But in the end, his message was too powerful, and CNN agreed to air his documentary *Cry Freetown* in February 2000. Immediately after the broadcast, Samura was invited to brief the United Nations. The United Kingdom intervened shortly thereafter with a powerful military and political presence that was a catalyst for ending the war. "I know that my footage wasn't the only thing that led to the end of the conflict, but I hope it helped," said Samura humbly.

MOZAMBIQUE

In 1977, just two years after the country's independence from Portugal, Mozambique entered a brutal civil war that ravaged the country for the next sixteen years. The war was largely a struggle between the government of Mozambique, supported by the Soviet Union, and rebels supported by the apartheid regime in South Africa and white-ruled Rhodesia (now Zimbabwe). South Africa and Rhodesia were looking to ensure white minority rule in southern Africa, and they spent large sums of money to destabilize Mozambique by supporting the rebel group Renamo.

Renamo committed horrific atrocities against civilian populations, mutilating victims and leading Mozambique to have one of the highest amputee rates in the world. Renamo set standards in human cruelty later matched by the Lord's Resistance Army, Darfur's Janjaweed, and the genocidal Rwandan militias. By the time the Mozambique war ended in 1992, roughly 1 million people had been killed, and 5 million had been forced to flee from their homes. The economic costs reached $15 billion, an enormous amount of money for one of the poorest places on earth.

In mid-1990 President Joaquim Chissano began negotiations with Renamo, looking to end his country's civil war. Chissano offered major concessions to the Renamo fighters, including space and assurances for Renamo as a political party, the ability to join the country's army, and, perhaps most remarkably, forgiveness for crimes committed. By the end of 1990, Chissano was able to lead the process of enacting of new constitution that enabled a multiparty system and an open market. President Chissano's negotiations led to the 1992 Rome General Peace Accords that officially ended the Mozambican Civil War.

In 1994, President Chissano won Mozambique's first multiparty elections. By mid-1995, more than 1.7 million refugees who had fled famine and war had returned. Another estimated 4 million of the people displaced within Mozambique had returned home. President Chissano was reelected in 1999, and he decided to step down at the end of this term despite the fact that the constitution allowed him a third term. Since leaving office, Chissano has been a negotiator in other peace processes in Africa.

Mozambique had one of the highest growth rates in the world from 1994 to the present, with growth rates consistently averaging between 8 and 11 percent annually. The country has no oil and no mining, but it does have extremely good governance and the rule of law, despite its emerging from a deadly war so recently.

GRAÇA MACHEL, MOZAMBICAN UPSTANDER

For human rights advocate Graça Machel, life has always been about "try[ing] to fight for the dignity and the freedom of my own people."[5] Machel grew up in a poor Mozambican peasant family, and she later studied in Lisbon and trained as a freedom fighter in the Mozambican Liberation Front (Frelimo).[6] After the tragic death in 1986 of her then husband, President Samora Machel, she dedicated her life to the cause of education, especially for women and young girls, and later to solving conflicts around the world.

In 1994 the secretary general of the United Nations asked Machel to undertake a study of the impact of armed conflict on children. The *Machel Report*, released in 1996, concluded that the inability to defend children's rights "represents a fundamental crisis of our civilization." Her report proposed practical ways to stem the involvement of children in armed conflict. Machal is also a member of The Elders, an independent group of global leaders that includes her husband Nelson Mandela, Archbishop Desmond Tutu, former Irish president Mary Robinson, former UN Secretary General Kofi Annan, and Jimmy Carter. In this role she has been involved in a number of peacemaking efforts around the world, including those in Sudan, Zimbabwe, and Burma. Her latest initiative is to sponsor the education of underprivileged women in South Africa with a scholarship program. Humble as ever, she has said, "Of course, what I'm doing is only a drop in the ocean, but I feel I have to do something."[7]

ANGOLA

In Angola, a brutal civil war began in the winter of 1974, and it lasted for almost three decades. In total, fighting killed almost 2 million people and forced almost 4 million to leave their homes. Soldiers planted over 10 million landmines—many of which were manufactured in the United States—throughout Angola's central highlands. The war created armies of child soldiers.[8] Driven by the exploitation of conflict diamonds and oil, Angola's crisis was intimately tied to natural resources. However, the end of the conflict diamonds trade paved the way for lasting peace. Angola remains imperfect, but the story of its journey from war to peace is a testament to those tireless advocates in Angola and around the world who spent decades working for change.

War in Angola came in the wake of the colonial Portuguese authorities' withdrawal in 1974. Fighting was bloody and pitted neighbors against one another. Child soldiers were recruited on all sides and fought on the front lines for decades.[9] Rufino Satumbo was eighteen when he was drafted into the army of the main rebel group, UNITA, about which he narrates a typical day:

> When we went into the villages, sometimes we set fire to them, while the people we knew to sympathize with the MPLA were killed. . . . [T]he women were for the leaders, who picked them out in the villages. They chose girls of 12, 13, 14, and 15 years old; those who didn't come by themselves were tied up. . . . [M]any starved of hunger because the nourishment was not good.[10]

UNITA's leader Jonas Savimbi carefully cultivated an image that appealed to American "Cold Warriors" intent on fighting Soviet power abroad,[11] and the enormous value he placed on his relationship with the United States is well documented. Between 1986 and 1991, the United States provided UNITA with an estimated $250 million dollars.[12]

Angola's natural resource wealth lay at the center of the violence throughout the brutal war. The government controlled the massive oil reserves, and UNITA's trade in conflict diamonds was critical to financing the group's predations. Between 1992 and 1994, UNITA made an estimated $3.7 billion from diamonds.[13] Most diamonds were smuggled into what is now the Congo (then called Zaire) and purchased by the company De Beers.

It took Savimbi's death in a firefight and the end of the Angola's conflict diamonds trade to stop the violence.

Today, Angola is becoming a stable African regional power. It has surpassed Nigeria as the continent's largest oil producer. Angola still has major challenges to overcome, such as endemic corruption and lack of democracy, but the country has hope and more stability than ever. The cycle of violence and chaos, which was intimately tied to the trade in diamonds throughout the conflict, is ending, and Angolans are slowly but surely rebuilding their lives.

SOUTH AFRICA

More than fifteen years after Nelson Mandela was elected president of South Africa, the awe-inspiring end of the apartheid era is beginning to recede into history. Although South Africa never experienced a full-scale civil war, the process leading to the end of apartheid could have led to one.

Beginning in 1948, South Africa's minority white government introduced the racist system known as *apartheid*, decreeing that black and white people should live separately and tearing apart the fabric of South African society to enforce this discriminatory system. Through a series of infamous laws, the government uprooted hundreds of thousands of people. Resistance began with the African National Congress (ANC) party, originally formed to protect the rights of mine workers but which shifted gears to oppose the ruling National Party and promote equality through mass protest. The ANC's Youth League was started by activists like Nelson Mandela and Walter Sisulu. When the government banned the ANC in 1961, its members went underground and adopted violent opposition.

The apartheid regime successfully stifled resistance for much of the 1960s and 1970s, opening fire on peaceful protestors at Sharpeville in 1960, arresting Nelson Mandela in 1962, and gunning down student protestors in Soweto, a township near Johannesburg, in 1976. But the violence and oppression of the apartheid government, which brutally cracked down on domestic resistance and also lashed out at its neighbors, funding violence in Angola, Zimbabwe, and Mozambique, contributed to its growing international isolation, as much of the world recoiled from the regime's racism. Even the United States, which had pursued a policy of "constructive engagement" with the South African government as an ally during the Cold War under the Reagan administration, eventually came around to the objective of economically isolating the regime. In 1986, Congress passed the Comprehensive Anti-Apartheid Act over President Reagan's veto, which imposed comprehensive economic and diplomatic sanctions on the apartheid regime.

Within South Africa, elements from across South African society—including student groups, trade unions, and faith-based communities—developed new means of resistance, including school boycotts and industrial sabotage. These tactics increasingly threatened the economic base of the ruling party. In 1990, F. W. de Klerk became prime minister, and he committed to ending the apartheid system. On February 11 of that year he released Nelson Mandela from prison and opened a series of negotiations culminating in South Africa's first democratically held elections in April 1994.

South Africans developed an unprecedented and influential institution: the Truth and Reconciliation Commission. Chaired by Archbishop Desmond Tutu, the Truth and Reconciliation Commission heard testimony from victims of political violence on all sides, and it allowed perpetrators to admit what they had done and request amnesty from prosecution. The commission is frequently held up as a model for similar reconciliation processes around the world. However, of the similar commissions established elsewhere, few have been perceived to be as inclusive or successful as South Africa's.

Although South Africa continues to struggle against severe social challenges, including an HIV/AIDS epidemic, economic inequalities, and rising crime rates, it has nonetheless managed to institute sound democratic practices and significant economic reforms, as well as carve out a leadership role on the African continent.

DESMOND TUTU, SOUTH AFRICAN UPSTANDER

Archbishop Desmond Tutu has spent most of his life fighting for racial equality, justice, and peace, a fight that began in Johannesburg, where he grew up. When he was about twelve, Tutu and his mother, a housekeeper and cook, passed a white man in the streets of Johannesburg. The man was wearing priest's clothing, and he greeted his mother politely. Tutu expressed his shock at seeing a white man greet a working-class black woman. Tutu formed a relationship with the priest who had greeted his mother, and, from then on, the priest played a significant and formative role in Tutu's life.

Tutu joined the Anglican priesthood in 1960. Congregations at this time were mostly white, but he was determined to speak out against the injustices faced by black Africans. Tutu became increasingly outspoken about apartheid while simultaneously pleading for reconciliation. After the end of apartheid, Tutu went on to chair the Truth and Reconciliation Commission. "The Arch," as his friends affectionately call him, has continued to speak out forcefully against injustice throughout the world and to work for peace both as an individual and as a member of The Elders. His voice is a beacon of truth that lights a path for those working for human rights in zones of conflict and dictatorship around the world.

OTHER AFRICAN UPSTANDERS

The heroic actions of many African Upstanders go unmarked and unnoticed by the rest of the world. But the work of some of these Upstanders who grace the world stage cry out for recognition due to the enormity of their achievements, and their courage.

KOFI ANNAN, GHANAIAN UPSTANDER

Although he couldn't have known it at the time, Kofi Annan's preparation for his position as the seventh secretary general of the United Nations began as a young boy in Ghana, where he grew up observing his grandfathers and his uncle, all of whom served as tribal chiefs, and his father, who was governor of Ghana's Asante province. Annan completed studies in Ghana and the United States, and he worked with the World Health Organization (WHO) and the Economic Commission for Africa in Addis Ababa before returning to Ghana in 1974 to find that the country had become politically unstable and rife with military coups. According to Annan, "I wanted to make a contribution to Ghana but I found [myself] constantly fighting the military, so I went back to the UN." Annan returned to the United Nations, and he was later chosen to be the UN secretary general, a post he took up in 1997.

As UN secretary general, Annan presided over peacekeeping operations around the world, and he advocated for increased assistance for developing countries fighting the HIV/AIDS pandemic. After his term as UN secretary general, Annan continued his peacemaking efforts. He has played an integral role in spearheading peace efforts, especially in Africa. In the aftermath of a disputed presidential election in Kenya that had left more than 1,000 people dead, Annan led successful mediation efforts that prevented the killings and rioting from escalating into an even deadlier war. He continued to stay involved after the deal was brokered in order to monitor its progress and assist with reforming Kenya's constitution and institutions.

International mediators who watched the peace deal unfold agreed that the unexpected resolution was a testament to Annan's diplomatic skills and the respect he commands across the globe. In the summer of 2009, when the Kenyan leaders hadn't lived up to their pledges on accountability, he presented a list of names of war crimes suspects to the chief prosecutor of the International Criminal Court, demonstrating that justice must be a part of any lasting peace.

BETTY BIGOMBE, UGANDAN UPSTANDER

In 2004, Betty Bigombe was a consultant with the World Bank, working on development in African countries, when she started a journey to rejoin the fight for peace in her native Uganda. She remembers having her own Enough Moment after seeing a television broadcast that reported that an LRA massacre in Uganda had left 259 people dead.

It was at that point in time that Bigombe decided, " 'No, it can't go on anymore. I can't stay here anymore. . . . People are dying. Children are not going to school.' So I decided to go right back and take it on."[14]

Bigombe worked tirelessly for the next eighteen months as the chief mediator between the government of Uganda and the LRA, this time as an impartial broker rather than a government minister, a post she had held twenty years before during her first efforts at bringing an end to the LRA insurgency. She arranged the first ever face-to-face meeting between the Ugandan government and LRA. She then helped create a multipronged peace effort that included traditional leaders, women, youth, and the international community in a dramatic push to end the twenty-year-old war. This initiative helped lay the foundation for the peace talks between the government and the LRA held in Juba, southern Sudan, that resulted in a final proposed deal that LRA leader Joseph Kony ultimately decided not to sign. Although no peace was forged, the international community united around the understanding that military operations would have to be undertaken to stop the LRA, since Kony clearly had no interest in peace.

Bigombe has the true craft of a peacemaker, trying to walk in each side's shoes and base negotiations on this thorough, deeper understanding. She continues to work on issues of mediation, peace building, transitional justice, and the empowerment of youth in northern Uganda, and she has provided support to the Juba peace talks. In addition, she works with international donors and local NGOs to equip the people of northern Uganda with tools for achieving sustainable peace.

WANGARI MAATHAI, KENYAN UPSTANDER

Growing up in rural Kenya, Wangari Maathai pursued education in her home country and later the United States, eventually returning to Kenya as a professor of veterinary medicine. Throughout the course of her work, Maathai was profoundly affected by her exposure to her homeland's ills: endemic ethnic patronage, discrimination against women, and shocking changes wrought on the Kenyan landscape by environmental degradation. Rather than viewing the environment, women's rights, and politics as separate problems, Maathai understood the interconnected nature of these issues as they related to everyday life: "I listened to women saying that deforestation was forcing them to walk farther and farther to find firewood for cooking, that they couldn't grow enough on depleted soil to feed their families, that they had no money to buy food."[15]

Maathai soon developed the idea that would later spawn a movement: planting trees. The Green Belt Movement, which began in 1977, was a grassroots effort to reduce poverty and promote environmental conservation by planting trees. The movement would go on to plant more than 20 million trees on farms, schools, and church compounds in Kenya. The movement's supporters built hundreds of tree nurseries and provided more than 100,000 jobs, mostly to women. In 1986, the Pan African Green Belt Network took the movement across the continent, launching similar initiatives in Tanzania, Uganda, Malawi, Lesotho, Ethiopia, and Zimbabwe.

At home, Maathai encountered increasing hostility from the Kenyan government of longtime ruler Daniel Moi:

The former Government was completely against the Green Belt Movement and our work of mobilizing women into groups that could produce seedlings and plant them. The Government was also against the idea of educating and informing women. It didn't want citizens to know that sometimes the enemy of the forests and the environment was the Government itself, which was supposed to be protecting the environment. If citizens saw the linkages, they would put pressure on the Government to improve governance, to create democratic space, to help them protect their environment, and to be responsible managers on citizens' behalf. When we were beaten up, it was because we were telling the Government not to interfere with the forests. We were confronted by armed police and guards who physically removed us from the forests as we sought to protect these green spaces from commercial exploitation. Sometimes in the process we got hurt, arrested or thrown into jail.[16]

Since winning the Nobel Peace Prize in 2004, Maathai has become even more directly involved in peacemaking, following the outbreak of postelection violence in Kenya in 2007, speaking out strongly on behalf of reconciliation and accountability.

LAZARO SUMBEIYWO, KENYAN UPSTANDER

Lazaro Sumbeiywo was the chief of staff of the Kenyan army, not the typical background for a peace mediator. But in 2001, he was named the lead mediator for the north-south war in Sudan. Sumbeiywo immersed himself in Sudan's notoriously intricate peace process, demonstrating the patience and tirelessness crucial to being an effective mediator. It took more than six months just to organize the first meeting between the parties, a meeting that was followed by a series of disagreements and setbacks.

Nonetheless, Sumbeiywo persevered, and his approach laid the groundwork for talks in Machakos, Kenya, which produced a crucial breakthrough: a single negotiating text (this was a point that Sumbeiywo learned from Jimmy Carter, who used the same approach at Camp David). The result was the Machakos Protocol signed on July 20, 2002, which granted the south the right to a referendum on self-determination following a six-year interim period, dictated that sharia law would remain in force only in the north, and provided the framework for the future final peace deal, which was finally struck in January 2005. Sumbeiywo remains modest about his achievements and attributes much to his faith in God and what he learned from his father, a chief in the rural village of Iten in Kenya's Rift Valley: "He used to settle a lot of conflict. I learnt a lot from him, not from formal teaching so much as simply watching him work."[17]

CHAPTER THREE

Saying Enough to Genocide

DON: So we are talking about stopping genocide, a concept against which there isn't any real opposition, and yet strangely there still is a shocking lack of success when it comes to the twenty-first century's first genocide: Darfur. What has been tried so far doesn't seem to be moving the ball very far forward at all. And although the Janjaweed militias aren't burning villages much anymore, because most of the villages they wanted to burn are ashes now, we are still talking about millions of people displaced from their ancestral homes, dying from diseases they shouldn't be, being raped in appalling ways and numbers, and being completely disenfranchised. They've been driven out of their homes, and they have lost family members. They have no feeling of security or safety, and they live under the thumb of a dictator who's been indicted as a war criminal. The Arab nations are really doing nothing, and no one has truly come forward to correct the situation, even though the world collectively is saying this cannot stand.

JOHN: Yes, there are definitely reasons why Darfur has continued to churn. There hasn't yet been an Enough Moment for Darfur because although we had one-half of the equation in place—the people's movement—the other half of the equation—smart policies—were nowhere in evidence. You gotta have both for success. The intention was right. President Bush was personally invested, and I think he was personally affected by the large-scale citizens' movement that was urging him to do something about the suffering. But he was crushingly undermined by a few officials in his administration who pursued the wrong policy track, totally at variance with the issues and history at play in Darfur and with how previous success stories actually worked. Now we have Obama in the same position. When I met with him in the White House in the spring of 2009, he said all the right things and evinced a clarity about what needed to be done that was extraordinary. Then his envoy on Sudan promptly goes out and undermines so much of what Obama had told us. Very frustrating.

DON: The years between 2004 and 2007 were especially re-markable to watch. All these people were asserting that the crisis in Darfur must be brought to an end: President Bush, Secretary Rice, the U.S. Congress, a significant portion of NATO, the European Union, President Sarkozy, Prime Minister Blair, the Arab League, the African Union, the United Nations. All of these leaders were saying that Darfur is a horror, whether they used the "g-word" or not. How could we still be here today?

JOHN: The most remarkable thing was the size of the movement that formed so quickly about a place, Darfur, that no one had ever heard of before. We have seen huge rallies, frankly unprecedented, in New York and Washington. Our first book got to the top five on the bestseller list after a number of publishers had passed on it because they said there was no market for an issue like this. Crazy. And your film *Darfur Now* came out in the theaters, while Clooney's movie *Sand and Sorrow* racked up great ratings on HBO. There is seemingly endless positive celebrity involvement and strident leadership from members of Congress. President Obama then gets elected on a platform that includes pretty aggressive statements from him, Vice President Biden, and Secretary of State Clinton about what they would do about Sudan if elected.

If someone would have told us a couple years ago, as we sat down to write our first book, that all these things were going to happen . . .

DON: We'd have said, "Wow, this is great. There surely won't be a need for a second book."

JOHN: I mean, how could this NOT succeed? How do we even react and respond to that as participants and observers?

DON: Well, it's obviously beyond frustrating. There seemed to be a momentum that was hurtling toward a lasting solution that we were just a small part of. And then there was the International Criminal Court's indictment of Bashir right on the heels of Obama's taking office. If that wasn't the moment of opportunity, I don't know what would be. But the lack of support for that indictment was remarkable. It suddenly felt like there was only one person out there, Ocampo the ICC's chief prosecutor, and he was looking around, and nobody was responding to this call. It's very frustrating. And you find yourself asking, "What is it going to take for the people of Darfur—such as the Fur, Masalit, and Zaghawa—to get some real justice and some protection?"

JOHN: Maybe we need another *Hotel Rwanda*. A "Hotel Darfur" or something. *Blood Diamond* sure put that story on the map.

DON: I carry around ideas for scripts, plays. And when I bring it up, if I have an idea, the reaction is always blah blah blah blah blah. Somehow it kinda went outta fashion.

JOHN: We gotta bring it back into fashion, and we can't quit until there is a lasting solution.

Genocide

As Samantha Power explains in her book *A Problem from Hell: America in the Age of Genocide,* before 1948, the crime of genocide had no name and no definition. In 1948, in the aftermath of World War II, a fledgling and shell-shocked United Nations passed the Genocide Convention, which established the legal definition of genocide as targeting a group of people for total or partial destruction on the basis of their identity, whether racial, national, ethnic, or religious.

But legal documents and international conventions are only one aspect of the tragic story of genocide in our time. There are complex reasons why genocide has happened and continues to occur. And these factors can be ignited by any number of triggers, with horrific consequences—an estimated 1.7 million people dead in Cambodia, more than 800,000 dead in Rwanda, and more than 300,000 dead and 3 million more people displaced in Darfur. But one of the most chilling themes in this disturbing history of genocide is the undeniable failure of the international community to act to *end* them, and to end the suffering of the people who are targeted.

The Genocide in Darfur, Sudan

Sudan is the largest country in Africa, and it has been torn apart by conflict since its independence in 1956. One key dynamic has been at the heart of every one of Sudan's current and past conflicts, and it is a root cause of the widespread suffering that Sudan's people have endured: the hoarding of wealth and power by ruling elites in the capital, Khartoum.

The Sudanese government has been ruled since 1989 with an iron fist by a president who, in March 2009, became the first sitting head of state in the world to be charged with war crimes and crimes against humanity by the International Criminal Court. President Omar al-Bashir's government has at various times during its brutal reign in Sudan targeted particular ethnic groups for attack and starvation, supported militias who use sexual violence and slave raiding as weapons of war in these campaigns, and directed proxy militias to destroy villages and force people from their homes.

And it has evolved from a scorched-earth military campaign to a low-intensity conflict marked by sexual violence, aid cut-offs, and growing levels of displacement. As in other mass death crises, the vast majority of mortality in Darfur has been due to diseases and malnutrition directly resulting from the displacement caused by the village burnings of 2003 to 2005.

To accomplish its task, the Sudanese regime armed and organized the Arab militias collectively known as the Janjaweed. The Janjaweed are Darfur's Ku Klux Klan. The regime knew that the Janjaweed would be far more ruthless and draconian than their own army, and they gave the militias instructions to burn, loot, and kill anything or anyone in their path. Like the KKK today in America, the Janjaweed represent only a very small percentage of the most extreme racial sentiment in Sudan. But they have enormous firepower, courtesy of the Sudan government. And they have gone about their work with deadly efficiency. They have burned over 2,000 villages to the ground. This was not just a divide-and-conquer operation. It was divide-and-destroy.

Maintaining Power by Any Means Necessary

The strategy was to drain the water to catch the fish: the oldest counterinsurgency strategy known to humanity. The regime targeted three ethnic groups: the Fur, Zaghawa, and Masalit. We often hear that the rebels are the main problem in Darfur. There is no question that the multitude of Darfurian rebel factions are some postapocalyptic version of the keystone cops. Some have stolen from humanitarians, raided villages, and stonewalled peace efforts. But understand the context. Since the rebellion erupted in 2003, the Khartoum regime has systematically bought off certain rebel leaders as Benedict Arnolds and used them to attack other rebel groups and rival ethnic communities, spurring cycles of intra-Darfur violence that are usually labeled "anarchy" by diplomats visiting Darfur for the day. Continuing support by the regime for the Janjaweed militias has further stoked inter-communal fires, and it has led many Darfurian armed groups to fight neighbors or rivals rather than the government, playing right into the regime's hands and leading to a phenomenon of warlordism among some of Darfur's rebel leaders.

The officials in power are getting rich from the oil money, and any threat to their absolute authority elicits an overwhelming response. They will maintain power by any means available to them. It is megalomaniacal, murderous behavior, but it is not irrational or random. And now, years later, the sands of the Sahara Desert have swallowed much of the evidence of their horrific crimes.

To this day, millions of Darfuris have yet to return to their homes because insecurity and instability reign in the places they once called home, and many of their lands are occupied by government-supported Arab groups. And at the time of this writing, ominous signs are emerging from southern

Sudan pointing to a return to these same divide-and-destroy tactics that the ruling party in Khartoum used to such deadly effect in the south during the 1990s.

The ruling National Congress Party has been responsible directly or indirectly for the deaths of over two and a half million Sudanese civilians in Darfur and the south. If one actually reads the relevant international conventions, one could conclude that the genocide is not over for those millions of Darfurians still homeless from earlier attacks and facing targeted rapes and aid cut-offs based on their identity.

If you're looking for the root cause of the problem in Sudan, you have to go to the ruling party headquarters in Khartoum to find it. Until there is a willingness to deal firmly with a genocidal regime, then Sudan's cycle of deadly conflict will continue.

The U.S. Response to Darfur

As has been the case in its response to other genocides globally, the United States' involvement has been too little and too late. The Bush administration lurched back and forth between intensifying cooperation with the Sudanese government on counterterrorism, strong engagement in support of negotiating—but not then of implementing—a peace deal in southern Sudan, and feckless diplomatic efforts on Darfur. Without an integrated all-Sudan strategy, the Darfur crisis has continued to burn, with total impunity for its architects.

During the 2008 presidential campaign, Hillary Clinton, John McCain, Joe Biden, Mike Huckabee, Barack Obama, and the other candidates battled each other over many issues, but on the issue of Darfur, the candidates were in lockstep agreement. In May 2008, Clinton, McCain, and Obama declared in a remarkably clear joint statement: "We wish to make clear to the Sudanese government that on this moral issue of tremendous importance, there is no divide between us." On the stump, the three talked tough, pledging to bring real pressure to bear on the Sudanese government and help deploy UN peacekeepers to join the faltering African Union mission.

"We can't say 'never again' and then allow it to happen again," Obama said of Darfur during the campaign. "And as president of the United States, I don't intend to abandon people or turn a blind eye to slaughter."

After Obama's victory, Darfur activists watched the beginnings of a veritable human rights dream team fall into place. Representing Obama at the United Nations would be Susan Rice, a former assistant secretary of state for African affairs under President Clinton. Rice had experienced her own Enough Moment as a midlevel White House staffer during the Rwandan genocide in 1994, when she watched as 800,000 Tutsis and moderate Hutus were exterminated in cold blood—and the Clinton administration stood by and did nothing. Now, from her perch in New York, she swore: "If I ever faced such a crisis again, I would come down on the side of dramatic action, going down in flames if that was required."[18]

Vice President Biden brought a rich legislative résumé to the mix and harsh words on the campaign trail. During the vice presidential debate, he called for a no-fly zone in Darfur to stop the aerial bombing, similar to the no-fly zone in Iraq that protected the Kurds and Shiites after the first Gulf War. Biden's position was more strident than those of the majority of Darfur activists and advocacy organizations. "I don't have the stomach for genocide when it comes to Darfur," he said during the vice presidential debate.

Secretary of State Clinton was also a leading voice on Darfur during her tenure in the Senate. She advocated frequently for a no-fly zone and other measures that would go far beyond current policy.

On Obama's National Security Council staff would be Gayle Smith and Samantha Power, two of the leading voices in the anti-genocide movement. Other human rights champions were spread throughout the administration, including Harold Koh, Eric Schwartz, Melanne Verveer, Tony Blinken, Mike Posner, and David Pressman.

Of course, a few anti-genocide warriors sprinkled around the executive branch doesn't guarantee action. After a lengthy delay, multiple congressional entreaties, and even an urgent visit from George Clooney to the White House, President Obama finally chose his Sudan envoy: Scott Gration. A former Air Force major general, Gration's boosters had a clean and plausible set of talking points. He had grown up in East Africa, the son of missionaries, and he spoke Swahili (though Swahili is not spoken in Sudan). As a military man, he might add a measure of gravitas to negotiations and command the respect of the Khartoum government. And as an advisor to the president, his calls back to Washington from the field were more likely to be answered.

However, a number of high-profile miscues and disputes ensued throughout 2009, as General Gration began articulating positions that directly contradicted the previous words and pledges of Obama, Clinton, and Biden. A slow-burn Sudan policy review had been creeping along within the bureaucracy, so Gration moved into the vacuum with some of his contrarian opinions, damaging the clarity of the president's pledges.

But this wasn't just an internal U.S. policy debate about policy toward one country. President Obama, like President Bush before him, had called Darfur an ongoing genocide. The policy on Sudan would have global ramifications because it was the president's first chance to articulate his policy on responding to genocide.

Twenty years of empirical evidence have demonstrated

that it has been sustained pressure and the credible threat of meaningful sticks that had previously led the Sudanese government to make compromises and change its behavior. For example, a diverse set of meaningful pressures combined with deeper engagement had led directly to the north-south peace deal, the end of government-sponsored slave raiding in the south, and the diminishment of the role of the regime in supporting international terrorist organizations. Now, with Obama, Clinton, Rice, and Biden, we hoped there would be swift and decisive action based on this clear and compelling evidence of cause and effect in the past. Instead, the president's envoy argued the opposite position, and the administration lost its first year and a half in terms of its clear direction on a Sudan policy consistent with Obama's campaign rhetoric.

Why the World Hasn't Stopped the Darfur Crisis—Yet

Sudan is a unique country. We run right smack into three of the great global issues of our time when trying to understand why the response to Darfur has not been appropriately potent: Iraq, counterterrorism, and energy security.

- *Iraq:* Coincidentally, the war in Darfur exploded at the same time as the United States began its invasion of Iraq. Most of the world's energy and attention was riveted on the overthrow of Saddam Hussein and its aftermath. Being so overwhelmed by the difficulties of the Iraqi intervention compromised the ability of the United States and other countries to respond to the genocide in Darfur.
- *Counterterrorism:* Osama bin Laden lived in Sudan from 1990 to 1996 as a guest of the Sudanese government.

He incubated the al Qaeda commercial infrastructure in Khartoum during this period. When the United States invaded Afghanistan after 9/11 and overthrew the Taliban government there, the Sudanese regime became very nervous because the United States was clearly casting around for further targets with links to al Qaeda. Although bin Laden had left five years before in response to coordinated pressure by the UN Security Council, the Sudanese government still retained some ties with terrorist organizations. Concerned about what the United States might do, the Khartoum regime decided to cut most of those ties and begin an active cooperation on counterterrorism issues with the United States. The expanding security relationship made it awkward for the Bush administration to act decisively against its new counterterrorism partner in Khartoum, even as it was committing genocide.

- *Energy security:* China is the biggest investor in the oil sector in Sudan, with perhaps $8 billion committed so far. In return for taking the dominant position in Sudan's energy development, China supports Sudan in all international bodies, most importantly the UN Security Council. This makes it very difficult for significant multinational pressure to be placed on Sudan for human rights or peace issues because China works to block or threatens to veto any action it deems unfavorable to the Sudanese regime.

Furthermore, the peace process itself in Darfur was failing because of specific variables. First, diplomats have consistently displayed a lack of understanding of and patience for the complexity of the Darfur case. Second, key variables of any successful peace process—including leadership by a full-time envoy with gravitas, well-resourced mediation structures involving full-time experts and diplomats, unanimous support from the international community for one process, and having a diplomatic strategy to deal with the spoilers and others who benefit from war and dictatorship—were not being utilized in Darfur. Third, the countries that have influence with the government of Sudan and other combatants have chosen not to use it in support of the compromises necessary for peace, handcuffed by competing priorities and interests. Finally, perhaps the biggest reason why there has been no end to the cycle of war in Sudan is that there have been no consequences for those perpetrating human rights crimes. This has left the warring factions with the clear signal to continue with business as usual.

Rather than walking softly and carrying a big stick, for years the United States has been walking loudly and carrying a toothpick. The Sudanese regime has seen right through this, and it has realized that it can literally get away with mass murder.

What the United States Could Do to End It

As is the case with the other conflicts discussed in this book, Darfur and its related crises in Sudan may seem at first glance to be insoluble. This is simply not true. On the contrary, we have already seen that when the Obama administration devotes real leadership to addressing a complex problem, these high-level efforts can bear fruit. And we have learned from history that smart policies coupled with people's movements are the answer to the world's seemingly most intractable conflicts—the success stories of South Africa's anti-apartheid movement and the campaign to end the trade of "blood diamonds" provide solid proof of the power of activists to influence policy change from the grassroots up.

There is no silver bullet or magic formula to confronting and eradicating the scourges of genocide and mass atrocities. But there is a strategic one. Ending the crisis in Darfur, addressing the root causes of Sudan's conflicts, and preventing these crimes from happening in the future in Sudan should be addressed within a framework we call the three P's: peace, protection, and punishment.

Peace: At the time of writing this, nearly seven years into the Darfur crisis, the most damning indictment of the U.S. and international efforts on Sudan is that there has not yet been an effective peace process for Darfur that addresses the real root causes of continuing conflict. At the time of writing this book, another poorly conceived international mediation effort is playing itself out, and the outcomes do not look encouraging. In the absence of a real international investment in peacemaking marked by more competent and strategic U.S. leadership, in which the interests of the people of Darfur and the south are protected and championed, Sudan's crisis will only deepen.

There is an answer, and the lessons come right from within Sudan. The twenty-year north-south war was resolved not with peacekeeping forces and not by billions in humanitarian aid. It was resolved by a good old-fashioned investment in diplomacy, led by full-time U.S. diplomatic teams working with teams from other countries, and backed by significant incentives and pressures. That is how things get done in response to most crises.

What is needed is a concerted, sustained peace surge for Sudan focused on making and implementing peace deals, both in Darfur and in the south. The objective would be sustainable peace marked by democracy and accountability. This is doable. A handful of U.S. diplomats plus a few regional and issue experts should be deployed to Africa to staff a diplomatic peace cell that would help staff the processes and implementation efforts around the clock in the manner they deserve. The United States should make a more concerted outreach effort to China in order to make the compelling case that

Chinese oil assets are at risk if the north-south peace deal collapses. The United States should also make clear that this is a real opportunity for the United States and China—the two countries with the most influence in Sudan—to work together at a time when other issues are dividing Beijing and Washington.

Protection: The Sudanese government has repeatedly abdicated its responsibility to protect its own people, and in fact, it has become the principal abuser. Pressure from the international community on the Sudanese government is part of the solution, but another essential element is building the capacity of the peacekeeping missions in Darfur (UNAMID) and southern Sudan (UNMIS) to protect people as much as is physically possible.

Punishment: There is total impunity in Sudan. Untold thousands of women have been raped. During both the Darfur genocide and the north-south civil war, millions of people have been forced out of their homes and into exile in neighboring countries such as Chad and Ethiopia. By and large, ordinary people have been unable to seek redress for the crimes they have suffered. Sudan will simply be unable to move forward toward a more inclusive, free, and peaceful future unless the fundamental right to justice is promoted, starting now.

The ICC's arrest warrant for Bashir—the first arrest warrant issued by the court for a sitting president—is a step firmly in the right direction. At present, there is no other legal mechanism powerful enough to enable the Sudanese people to seek the justice they deserve. The United States should provide greater support for the ICC indictments, work with other countries to build a coalition to expand the targeted sanctions, go after the assets of the top officials, deny debt relief, enforce the arms embargo, and plan for targeted military action in the event of a major upsurge in killings or in response to humanitarian aid cut-offs. We need to create a legal, financial, and political cost to committing genocide and other crimes against humanity, just as the international community is building its own protection against terrorism. If there is any hope for protecting people in Sudan, it will be in part through a concerted multilateral effort to impose consequences on those most responsible for the violence, while at the same time ramping up peace efforts.

JOHN: During the eight trips I've taken to Darfur since the genocide began in 2003, I've found that displaced and war-affected Darfuris don't see a tension between justice and peace. They unite the problem in the simplest and purest of ways. How can you have peace, they ask, without justice? We need to understand that respect for human rights is an essential ingredient of sustainable peace, which requires elements of justice. As I was watching Bashir and his cronies mock his ICC arrest warrant, I couldn't help but be reminded of the fates of other indicted leaders with names such as Charles Taylor, Slobodan Milosevic, Radovan Karadzic, Augusto Pinochet, and Saddam Hussein. Hopefully Bashir will be added to this growing list of now imprisoned, exiled, or deceased war criminals, which would give his country a real chance for the peace its long-suffering people deserve.

DON: There is a huge opportunity if the world gets tough with this regime. The north-south peace agreement proves that emphatically.

JOHN: Exactly. There was a credible threat of serious consequences for the regime if it did not resolve the war in the south, and so it did. That is the lesson. But the lesson has been ignored because we don't like imposing real consequences for human rights crimes. Instead, our political system gravitates toward nonconfrontation and noncontroversy. Fighting human rights crimes, it turns out, is messy and inconvenient.

Call to Action

Responding to the lack of political will to do what is necessary to end this genocide and others in the future that may fall off the radar screen of "traditional" U.S. foreign policy concerns. But this is exactly where the growing anti-genocide movement must come in. The movement has proven successful at demonstrating to elected officials in the United States that genocide is occurring on *our* watch and that ending the genocide in Darfur must be a political priority for the United States.

Jim Wallis and John wrote in the *Wall Street Journal* on April 13, 2009:

> *The United States needs to lead the international community in presenting Sudanese regime officials with a choice. If they allow access to aid organizations, sideline their indicted president, and secure peace for Darfur and the south, then they will be offered a clear path toward normal relations with the United States and other coalition partners. But if those officials use starvation as a weapon, allow Mr. Bashir to remain defiant, and make no progress toward peace, then there will be escalating costs in the form of targeted economic sanctions, diplomatic isolation, and potential military action. The crisis is not a new one. The refrain regarding international crises is often, "If only the world had known, we would have done something." The people of Darfur know that we know. What they are waiting to find out is if we care enough to act. When the dust clears and the bodies are buried, burned or left to rot in forsaken camps, the world will mourn for what it did*

not do. What Darfur needs is not a future apology, but steps today that offer hope.

This is the Enough Moment for ending the genocide in Darfur and bringing peace to Sudan.

To take action to help end Sudan's cycles of violence, go to www.enoughmoment.org.

CHAPTER FOUR

Upstanders for Darfur

Darfurians aren't waiting to be saved. They are fighting back against the forces committing human rights crimes and the forces of anarchy in many different ways. Thousands have picked up guns, for better or worse, and joined rebel groups to fight against the Khartoum regime. Thousands of others have joined organizations that help provide sustenance to the survivors of the violence. Still others risk their lives to report on continuing human rights violations, to provide legal aid to victims, or to organize local groups to advocate for their rights. They are redefining the word *hero*, fighting on the front lines in Darfur, being tear-gassed or beaten in the streets in Khartoum, and providing comfort to the survivors in the displaced camps in Darfur and the refugee camps in Chad.

It is these Frontline Upstanders who are risking their lives every day to bring change to their country who are the building blocks of a truly globalized human rights movement. They need our support. They need to know we stand with them and that we find it unacceptable that solutions are not found.

And standing with them in greater and greater numbers, a continent away in the United States, Citizen Upstanders are working tirelessly on behalf of people they've never met and places most will likely never visit. And their numbers are enhanced and their cause magnified by Famous Upstanders who are fighting for peace and human rights as well. Why? Read on and find out when Enough became Enough for these committed human rights and peace advocates, and their courageous Darfurian counterparts.

FRONTLINE UPSTANDERS:
Genocide Survivors Who Are Making a Difference

ABDEL AZIZ ADAM, TEACHER, DJABAL REFUGEE CAMP

The Koranic Call of Duty

"Unto whom wisdom is given, he had indeed been blessed with a great treasure" is a verse found in Al-Baqarah, the eighth chapter of the Koran. This Koranic verse inspires and sustains Abdel Aziz, a Darfur refugee, in his current profession as teacher and headmaster of the Obama School in the Djabal refugee camp on the Chad-Sudan border, where hundreds of thousands of Darfurians fled after the genocide.

Abdel Aziz's journey to headmaster of the Obama School is an unlikely one because he was not always set on a trajectory of becoming a teacher, let alone a headmaster of a school. In fact, when Abdel Aziz completed secondary school in 2004, he returned home to his village in West Darfur unsure about his future but determined to use his newly acquired skills to develop his hometown. However, shortly after he returned to his village of Furbaranga, the Janjaweed attacked his village, killing men, women, and children indiscriminately. Some of Abdel Aziz's family members were killed, and others fled to displaced-persons camps in Sudan. Abdel Aziz and his immediate family walked over fifty miles to the Chadian border, where UNHCR, the UN refugee agency, moved them into a refugee camp further inside Chad.

For the past six years, the Djabal refugee camp has been home to Abdel Aziz and roughly 19,000 Darfuri refugees, most of whom are children. Since they have lived in the refugee camps for years now, with no prospect of returning home until there is peace, the children in the camps desperately need access to quality education or over time they will become severely undereducated relative to their peers in Sudan.

Abdel Aziz saw immediately that there were very few qualified teachers in the refugee camps. The very small number of qualified adults in the camps often fail to respond to the call to teach because of a lack of training and the low wages. Abdel Aziz notes that "most qualified adults in the camps have forgone the teaching profession and have opted to join NGOs or even rebel groups because of the low wages."

For Abdel Aziz, the Koranic verse is significant because he believes he was given the gift of education (wisdom) in Darfur and is responsible for passing this gift on to the next generation. As a result, Abdel Aziz accepted the duty of not only being a teacher but also a headmaster. During each school year, Abdel Aziz is responsible for the welfare of 900 students in Grades 1 through 8 at Obama School.

Obama School is one of six primary schools in the Djabal refugee camp, all of which are being supported by the Darfur Dream Team's sister school's program. According to Abdel Aziz, his primary school is proudly named after President Obama because the "Darfuris feel a direct tie to America's first African American president, and they are sure he will help the people of Darfur to find a solution to the crisis in Darfur."

TEHANI ISMAIL

Keeping Their Memories Alive

Tehani Ismail, a Darfuri woman, was born and raised in Nyala, the capital of South Darfur. Tehani's parents separated when she was young so she was raised by her single mother. The eldest of three sisters, Tehani was studying at the University of Khartoum when the violence in Darfur erupted. As reports of the violence reached Khartoum, Tehani and her Darfurian classmates in Khartoum sat paralyzed listening to the news stories.

With her family and friends still in Nyala, Tehani decided to go home and see with her own eyes what was happening. She traveled to Nyala and volunteered to work with a local organization. On her first field visit with the group, Tehani and her colleagues traveled by car to the countryside just north of Nyala. Tehani recalled that when she had been there before the war, it was the lushest area of South Darfur. "It was a place where any crops grew and all animals grazed." But this time, when they arrived, the area was still smoldering from the fires. They encountered dead bodies of men, women, and children strewn everywhere and homes completely ransacked. There were very few survivors of the attack. They encountered burned village after burned village until they reached Muhajiriya, where they saw signs of life again.

When they reached Muhajiriya, Tehani remembers being overwhelmed by what she had seen. "What happened to the people, animals, and land that she had always admired?" She then realized that "this is not just collateral damage of warfare but rather systematic killing of people and a violation of their human rights. If the people of Darfur aren't aware of their rights," she concluded, "then the government of Sudan could keep violating them."

That was Tehani's Enough Moment. She decided she would forgo getting a four-year university degree and would work with an organization to raise awareness and educate her fellow Darfuris about their human rights.

Tehani joined the Sudan Social Development Organization (SUDO) as a human rights worker in 2004. SUDO is dedicated to the promotion of human rights and international development. While at SUDO, Tehani faced harassment and watched her colleagues disappear to detention centers. Sudanese government security agents had begun targeting SUDO staff and shutting down their operations in 2003. Intimidation tactics used by Sudan security operatives included going to Tehani's mother and sister and advising them that they should tell her that "what she is doing is dangerous and her safety is not guaranteed." Both Tehani and her mother, a public health worker, were prevented from going to work by the security officials.

In spite of this, Tehani continues to be a human rights advocate and is now a correspondent for Radio Dabanga in Nyala. Tehani is currently mobilizing women's groups in South Darfur. The groups have established the Riaheen el-Salam for Maternity and Childhood center, and it is focused on addressing gender-based violence. Tehani notes she has seen the "worst of the worst" cases in her work: women who were raped, who have lost everything, and who must begin picking up the pieces of their lives. Tehani now documents their cases and provides counseling and comfort so they can begin the healing process. Several of Tehani's close friends have died because of the violence in Darfur. Initially, Tehani was always thinking of her lost friends while doing her work and constantly searching of ways to keep their memories alive. Tehani has found the best way is to work with the survivors.

AWATEF ISAAC, JOURNALIST

Telling Darfur's Story

It is said that the sibling bond, particularly among sisters, can be the most significant relationship a person will ever have. Born six years apart in El-Fasher, the capital of North Darfur, Awatef Isaac and her sister Afaf shared a close bond. Afaf, the older sister, was the trail blazer in the family. She attended El-Fasher High School for Girls and dreamed of publishing a newspaper to tell the story of their town. While at El-Fasher High School, Afaf started *Al-Mustakbal* (The Future) newspaper. The newspaper was handwritten on A4 paper and pinned on the tree in front of the high school.

Afaf suddenly died due to complications in her pregnancy in 1998 at the age of twenty-two, and Awatef vowed to carry on her legacy. Awatef continued to publish Afaf's newspaper by hand, but she changed the name to *Al-Rahil* (The Journey) in order both to acknowledge the forced migrations of the Darfurians and to commemorate her sister's eternal journey. She began posting the paper outside her house. The newspaper took on added significance when the genocide engulfed Darfur in 2003. Though somewhat insulated from the violence by virtue of living in the main town, Awatef saw her family and friends directly affected by the violence in Darfur; her grandfather was forced to seek refuge in a displaced-persons camp where he later died. Awatef began writing about and publishing accounts of the violence in Darfur instead of solely focusing on local issues in the town of El-Fasher. The newspaper now focuses on the conflict, including cases of rape. Awatef also includes political jokes and commentary on women in politics and Sudanese society.

Al-Rahil has transformed how people in El-Fasher get information about the government-supported attacks in Darfur.

The tree outside Awatef's house has become a gathering place for the community. As soon as the weekly paper is posted on the tree, residents of El-Fasher crowd around to read it. The newspaper is published locally in Arabic, but Awatef recently began to provide accounts of the humanitarian situation in Darfur geared toward a broader external audience.

Four years after her sister Afaf's death, Awatef began to put together an exhibit of her sister's old newspapers to honor her work. The exhibit also included old editions of Awatef's own newspaper. But before the exhibit opened to the public, the government of Sudan officials shut down the exhibit and confiscated the newspapers.

Although she has continued to receive threats, Awatef has had significant support from her community in El-Fasher and the people of Sudan. Many groups, including the government of southern Sudan, have commended Awatef for her efforts. After the *Washington Post* and *Agence de France Presse* featured articles about Awatef, an anonymous individual opened a bank account in Awatef's name with a modest contribution. She has also received a camera, computer, and printer so she can publish *Al-Rahil* electronically and print free copies. Members of the sudaneseonline.com website have been an instrumental base of support for Awatef and are trying to make *Al-Rahil* available to the world online.

Awatef, now in her mid-twenties, is called the "The Girl-Journal" in reference to a poem by Sudanese poet Mustapha Sayyid entitled "The Garden-Girl." She continues to publish her newspaper despite continuing threats. After a trip to The Hague during which her picture was taken with Luis Moreno-Ocampo, the International Criminal Court's chief prosecutor, her return to Sudan was delayed because of the picture, and her family has been harassed since. Awatef remains undeterred from her mission of telling the truth about what is happening in Darfur and maintaining the legacy of her sister.

ADEEB YOUSEF

"I Will Work for Darfur Even If It Costs Me My Life"

Adeeb Yousef is a human rights advocate from Zallengi, West Darfur. Adeeb comes from a large family with twenty-two children. He remembers his hometown as an island of peace, where the Fur people and their Arab neighbors lived together, and intermarriage and even property exchange between the Fur and Arab ethnic groups was common. Adeeb's family owned a large orchard, with fruits such as mangoes and oranges. He remembers many instances in which his father would turn over his cattle to an Arab friend for safekeeping. Each year, his father's Arab friend would then return to their home for a large feast, and they would discuss the welfare of the cattle. If a cow had died, his father's friend would bring the leather as proof.

This idyllic life is what Adeeb left behind when he completed secondary school and went to Dongole University in North Sudan. While at Dongole, Adeeb, like Tehani, became involved with the Sudan Social Development Organization (SUDO). After he completed his university degree, Adeeb returned to Zallengi to open a regional office for SUDO. Adeeb was charged with managing and coordinating all of SUDO's Darfur activities with the main office in Khartoum, the capital of Sudan.

In 2002, Adeeb heard about attacks in the rural areas of Darfur. Adeeb began documenting the various attacks and providing support to the displaced persons in the area, who were streaming into Zallengi from the rural areas. Most were camping in schools, and some were living on the streets. Since there were no relief agencies providing support to those driven from their homes at that time, Adeeb reached out to the local community, especially the merchants, for support. The merchants agreed to provide food, and SUDO helped set up a local committee to give out the food to the people each morning.

As a result of his work with the displaced people, Adeeb's profile was heightened, and the Sudan security forces began harassing him. Eventually he was arrested. Adeeb vividly remembers the day he was first arrested: Friday, January 2, 2004. Adeeb had gone about his day as usual. He had visited the homeless and had gone to prayers, and he was at his father's pharmacy to check on the business. At around 2 p.m., Sudan national security forces came to his father's pharmacy and arrested him. For four months, government security officers tortured and questioned Adeeb. "I was beaten, tortured, and humiliated daily. I lost over fifteen pounds while I was in jail, and my spirit was nearly broken."

When he was released from jail in April 2004, Adeeb had his own Enough Moment. He realized that nothing had changed while he had been in jail. In fact, the situation had deteriorated, and there were more people rendered homeless, without access to food, shelter, or protection. Adeeb painfully notes, "If you see with your naked eye what I saw, you will never stand by. I saw the stomach of a woman cut, and the child inside was stabbed. I saw people burned in their homes, people whose names I knew. I will work for Darfur even if it costs me my life."

After his release from jail, Adeeb redoubled his efforts to document the human rights abuses in West Darfur for SUDO. The first town he visited after his release was Delge, a town 85 kilometers from the town of Zallengi. In Delge, Adeeb and the SUDO team encountered a horrific massacre. Several children, mostly boys, were tied together and shot in the head.

Adeeb was again arrested when he was visiting Khartoum

for a training workshop. He was taken to a detention center and held for seven months. He was beaten and repeatedly interrogated. Adeeb lost consciousness six times in the detention center. To draw attention to his wrongful arrest, Adeeb went on a hunger strike and had to be taken to Amal hospital. While at the hospital, an individual whom Adeeb believed to be a human rights lawyer convinced him to stop the hunger strike so that he would be released from jail. But as soon as Adeeb broke his hunger strike, he was thrown back in jail and kept in solitary confinement.

Sudanese organizations made noise about Adeeb's wrongful arrest. Prominent international groups such as Human Rights Watch and Amnesty International sent letters to Sudan's vice president, Ali Osman Taha, calling for Adeeb's release. Adeeb was finally released in April 2005, and he continued his work with SUDO, but he still faced harassment from national security forces.

Adeeb has had the opportunity to learn about the reconciliation process communities undergo in the aftermath of crimes against humanity. Adeeb was able to travel to South Sudan to attend the Rift Valley Institute's Sudan course in Rumbek; he also traveled to Rwanda, northern Uganda, and even the United States to learn more about how communities are dealing with reconciliation. Upon his return home from the United States in September 2007, Adeeb was once again harassed by Sudanese government security officers. His family and friends were also being monitored and harassed as well, and they advised him to leave Sudan. With a heavy heart, Adeeb finally left Sudan in August 2008, and he is now in the United States seeking asylum. He is presently getting a master's degree in international relations at the University of San Francisco. Adeeb feels that with an education he can be of better use to the people in Darfur and Africa.

CITIZEN UPSTANDERS:
Darfur's Champions in America

ETHAN BARHYDT

A Choice

In the seventh grade, Ethan took a class at his Jewish congregation on the Holocaust. Rather than focusing on mere dates and facts, Ethan's instructor, Dick Strauss, attempted to explain what might have happened if the United States and neighboring countries had stepped in before the Holocaust took so many lives. What could have happened if people had chosen to say ENOUGH?

Ethan's instructor ended the class with a one-question final exam: "Your final exam is how you conduct the rest of your lives. Can it happen again? The answer is up to YOU and to YOUR CHOICES. Will YOU CHOOSE to get involved, or will you be a bystander?"

It was that exact moment when Ethan decided he would no longer remain a bystander but would instead make a lifelong commitment to help end mass atrocities and crimes against humanity. In 2007, Ethan created the organization Youth United for Darfur in the Chicago area. This organization was a coalition of ten student groups, which until then had not been collaborating very much. Being able to work together, the Youth United for Darfur organized a conference focused not only on educating students about genocide but also on providing effective advocacy techniques.

By January 2009, their efforts had expanded to forty student organizations. It was then that Youth United for Darfur decided to host the Darfur Rally in Chicago. Reaching out to political figures, musical groups, high schools, and colleges, the rally became the biggest rally for Darfur in the United

States outside of Washington, D.C., and New York that year. With thousands of students supporting the rally, they gathered in Chicago to advocate for peace in Sudan and celebrate their month-long fundraising campaign that had raised $17,000 for Illinois' Sudanese Community Center and the Darfur Dream Team's Sister Schools Program.

Ethan graduated from high school in 2009, deferred enrollment to Macalester College, taught English to middle school students in Tibet for a semester, and then headed to Washington, D.C., to join the Darfur Dream Team. Ethan stresses that he has learned the value of fostering relationships to promote awareness and action, and to bring people together for a common purpose.

LEE ANN DE REUS

"I Tapped the Very Core of My Meaning"

"People often ask me why I do this type of work and how I got started. I tell them there's no short answer and that I'm not entirely sure I understand it myself! I have no single childhood trauma to offer as a compelling reason, or great religious conviction—but rather a strong feeling of moral obligation and sense of fairness that years of therapy might eventually connect to any number of personal insecurities or a fear of who knows what. What I do know is there's a drive I can't deny. This took me first to work for years in the Dominican Republic and Tanzania.

"It was a student who came to me about her interest in 'doing something' about the genocide in Darfur. I shared her passion and seized the opportunity to work with a like-minded soul. We organized our first event and managed to get 'the' John Prendergast to make an appearance! Unbelievably, his beloved Aunt Mary, who was a longtime activist herself, was my neighbor. As this issue of genocide became ever more real to me and the gravity began to sink in, so did my need to get involved. But to advocate with any authority, for me, meant having some direct experience and connection with the people and issues. I knew I was returning to Tanzania. Could I possibly get to the Darfur refugee camps in Chad? I was already going to be on the continent, so . . . *why not?* I knew my decision would depend on John's opinion. So I made certain it was I who drove him from the airport to our event venue. Little did he know how significant his words in the car would be. When I asked John if he thought I could pull off the trip, he said unequivocally, 'Yes!' It was the only endorsement I needed! That was April 1, 2007. By June 30, I was in a refugee camp in Chad with a Penn State student and a colleague.

"In other words, this is ALL John's fault.

"Our travel to and from the Gaga refugee camp was actually against all odds. And at times I was worried I'd gotten my companions—Lorraine (a colleague) and Wendy (a returning adult student)—and me in over our heads. Despite our advanced planning, the unpredictability, instability, and chaos we encountered in Chad proved almost impossible to navigate. To travel within the country, we had to 'hitch' rides on eight-seater UN World Food program planes. The unpredictability of when we might fly and whether we'd have to split up added to the vulnerability we already felt. The night before we finally arrived at the camps, a guard for an NGO was shot and killed, raising the local security level and anxieties. Four UN vehicles had been hijacked in the previous weeks, requiring us to travel by convoy. On our ninety-minute drive to Gaga, we passed an unexploded bomb on the side of the road. The temperature was 130 degrees. Water cost $4.50 per bottle and tasted like gasoline as petroleum leached from the plastic. Getting cash was next to impossible and had to be exchanged on the black market. At one point we were banned from UN flights due to a misunderstanding. And while we had an interpreter for part of the trip, we knew little French and no Arabic. We all took a turn at being violently sick, and in the end, we missed our international flight home.

"But as we sat on mats with the women of Gaga, listening to their powerful stories, Lorraine, Wendy, and I knew, through our shared tearful glances, that it had all been worthwhile. Our frustrations and inconveniences were miniscule compared to what the women had experienced. What a privilege it was for us to connect with them emotionally for a brief moment. We all laughed at our absurd attempts to communicate via sign language, felt a shared delight as we bounced their babies on our laps, and enjoyed serving each other sweet tea. I have never been more profoundly humbled or moved.

"This was truly my Enough Moment. Through my connection with these survivors, I had tapped the very core of my meaning and realized a depth of purpose I'd known previously in only small, fleeting glimpses. But now, the self exposed and a mystery revealed, there was no turning back from the gift the women of Gaga gave me. My hope is that in some small way their gift is paid forward and a gift is returned with the telling of their stories."

REVEREND MIKE SLAUGHTER

Darfur in the Middle of an Ohio Corn Field

Ginghamsburg Church is a United Methodist congregation in Tipp City, Ohio, a small city of 9,300 people just north of Dayton, in the heart of the "rust belt." When the Reverend Michael Slaughter arrived at Ginghamsburg thirty years ago, he inherited a 104-year-old small country church on a quarter of an acre, with fewer than a hundred members and an annual budget of $27,000. The population of the Miami Valley region, in which Ginghamsburg is located, has declined by more than 20,000 people since Pastor Mike's arrival because of the region's dependence on, and the national decline of, the automobile industry. In August 2008, *Forbes* magazine named Dayton one of the ten fastest-dying cities in America. Today, however, roughly 4,500 people worship, attend class, serve, or find community each week on the church's campus.

One Sunday afternoon in 1998, Pastor Mike was reading the *Dayton Daily News* when his eye caught an ad featuring a new luxury sedan, a BMW, for lease. Being a car fan, Mike found himself checking out the various features to compare them to his current vehicle. Then, his eye was drawn to a picture on the opposing page of a clearly emaciated child featured in an article about famine in the Sudan and the tragedies of the civil war between north and south Sudan. Mike was stunned by that juxtaposition of the sedan, the heart of our culture, versus the Sudan, the heart of God as he saw it, and the fact that he knew many things about the luxury vehicle and nothing about the conflict in this large African country. Although that afternoon did not yet lead Mike to action, the image and the challenge stayed in his heart.

In the fall of 2004, Pastor Mike was reading one of the very few news stories published in that entire year about the crisis in Darfur. He clearly felt God's urging to engage the Ginghamsburg faith community, "no holds barred" as he says, into serving the needs of the survivors of the Darfur war. That Advent season, he reminded Ginghamsburg attendees, "Christmas is not your birthday. It's Jesus' birthday!" and he challenged everyone to have a simple Christmas that year. All were asked to spend only half as much on their own Christmas as they would normally spend and to give the rest as a "Christmas Miracle Offering" to serve the people of

Darfur. That same challenge has been issued in all subsequent Advent seasons. In an area of the United States badly hurt by the recession and the decline of the auto industry, these appeals have raised a total of nearly $4.5 million for humanitarian relief in Darfur from 2005 through 2009, going for sustainable agriculture, water, sanitation, and education programs.

In addition to Ginghamsburg's humanitarian relief focus, Pastor Mike has encouraged social activism by Ginghamsburg attendees, other churches, college students, and community groups. In April 2006, a bus of Ginghamsburg activists traveled to Washington, D.C., to participate in the rally for Darfur on the National Mall. Ginghamsburg is actively represented in Dayton for Darfur, and it participated in the Dayton-based rally in the spring of 2008. The church has also partnered in educational initiatives about the crisis with Central Ohioans for Peace, based out of Columbus. Congregants are encouraged to participate in Darfur petition drives and to write to congressional representatives, ambassadors, and the U.S. president in support of action on Darfur.

Pastor Mike and other members of the Ginghamsburg team frequently speak on college campuses, United Methodist "schools of mission," and in other venues to advocate on behalf of their sisters and brothers in Darfur. In the spring of 2009, Pastor Mike partnered with the Christian Communications Network (CCN) and the Enough Project to host on Ginghamsburg's campus a live simulcast called "Not On Our Watch" to hundreds of churches around the country.

In his second trip to Darfur in June 2007, Mike took with him his only son, Jonathan, who served as the trip photographer. Mike says that one of his most emotionally and spiritually significant moments as a parent was when he spent Father's Day on the ground in Darfur with Jonathan at his side.

Mike has reminded the people of Ginghamsburg Church, an ordinary church surrounded by corn fields in the rust belt of Ohio, that the true greatness of any local church is measured by how many people are serving the marginalized and, as he says, by how many of us are willing to live more simply and sacrificially so that other people can simply live.

GABRIEL STAURING

Because It's Personal

"During the week of the tenth anniversary of the 1994 Rwanda genocide, I was driving around Orange County, California, visiting homes for my job as a counselor for abused children and their families. National Public Radio had a week-long series on the horrors of Rwanda in which they shared very personal accounts of what happened to victims and survivors. During that week, I went through a series of strong emotions, starting with shock at the numbers, then anger at the world's inaction, sadness at the lives lost, and—finally—guilt at not having lifted a finger ten years before, when I saw the reports of what was happening in that tiny nation that seemed so far away and completely removed from me as a person.

"In the weeks and months that followed, I would have regular conversations with my then nine-year-old daughter, Noemi, about how we had to do more for others. She would ask me where and how, and I did not have an answer. Then I started to hear about Darfur. I knew I had to act. Without knowing where to start, I began with what I know best, my own family and community. I started telling them about Darfur. I then looked around for what others were doing and found that it was difficult for anyone to connect with something as huge and shocking as genocide. It is easier for people to turn the other way and feel, 'There is nothing I can do.' I never could have imaged that a year later I would be walking in a refugee camp in an effort to put a face on the numbers.

"For two years, I continued working full time as a counselor for abused children here in the United States, but I also worked on creating a team that facilitates relationships between children and families that have seen horrors none of us can imagine and people around the world that are in a position to help. I now work full time on this, and my Stop Genocide Now i-ACT (www.stopgenocide.org) team is made up entirely of regular citizens that feel a need to embrace responsibility and do all in our power to make a difference in the lives of the very real human beings that are the victims of mass atrocities and genocide. It is very personal. I do this for all the children I have met on my now eight trips to refugee camps, but I also do it for my own children."

MARV STEINBERG

Never Too Late to Say ENOUGH

Marv is a seventy-eight-year-old retired educator who had open-heart surgery a decade ago and retired soon thereafter from his job as the superintendent-principal of a small one-school district. In May 2005 his thirty-eight-year-old daughter passed away from complications related to multiple sclerosis. For the last eighteen months of her life, Marv spent much of his time caring for her. She was living in the Seattle area, and because of her illness, she was hospitalized for over three months. She then moved home and was finally able to live independently again. She required a great deal of assistance so when she passed away, not only was Marv devastated but there was also a real void in his life.

In March 2006 Marv was once again hospitalized with suspected heart problems. Before going in for a heart scan, he had some time to reflect on his life. "I had a long conversation with God," Marv told us. "I had witnessed a series of reports by Ann Curry on the situation in Darfur, and I thought about my experiences growing up Jewish in San Francisco. I reflected on the many reports by Rabbi Burstein of Temple Beth Israel on what was happening to the Jews in Europe. I knew that family members had been lost in the Holocaust, but I never knew anything about them. As I went in for the test that would determine whether I needed heart surgery, I talked to one of our pastors and told her that if I made it I was going to turn my attention to Darfur."

Luckily, Marv's health was fine, and the next Sunday he spoke to members of his congregation at the First Methodist Church in Redding, California, at all three services, inviting them to join him in praying for the people of Darfur and for peace in Sudan and Chad, to learn more about Darfur, and to participate in a "Day of Conscience for Darfur" in San Francisco later that month. Out of those simple talks was born an initiative called Genocide No More—Save Darfur, a coalition of several churches and other groups in Shasta County. Since then the coalition has raised over $30,000 for humanitarian relief and sponsored many informational events, including speakers, films, and forums.

At his church, Marv has twice led a Bible study class utilizing the *Not On Our Watch Christian Companion.* Emerging from that class came a petition campaign in support of the International Criminal Court and justice for the perpetrators of the genocide in Darfur. The class also helped form an action group within the church.

Marv's local group also worked closely with their representative in Congress after marching on his office twice to get his attention. This member of Congress had been rated a D by the Genocide Intervention Network's Darfur Scores. "He received an A for the year after we 'worked' with him," Marv reported. Marv's group also sponsors Camp Kou-noungo, and it is currently in the process of raising money for a library-classroom for the camp. High school students have made PowerPoint presentations to the Redding City Council, which adopted a resolution of support, and to other agencies in the area. Clubs from two area high schools have raised over $3,000 at benefit concerts in 2008 and 2009. They have also worked with other nonprofits in his area—People of Progress and the Women's Shelter—in fundraising efforts, and they now have a substantial contact list. The last Friday of each month the group has been sponsoring Interfaith Prayer Vigils on the Calatrava-designed Sundial Bridge. They have also been sponsoring monthly Letter Writing Parties, they have been meeting the first Monday of the month for planning meetings, and they have launched a spin-off group called the Darfur Action Group, all at the First Methodist Church.

LESLIE THOMAS

"Humanity Does Not Stop with Borders"

"My son was six months old, and I was holding him in the middle of the night reading an article by Nicholas Kristof about Darfur. The column described a young boy who had been killed because of his ethnicity, and looking down at my child, I realized that this was simply not acceptable, that it was not right that my son should be 'safe' while another boy was not.

"I then found a photo of Mihad Hamid taken by U.S. Marine Brian Steidle. She was a beautiful one-year-old child from Darfur who was shot from a government helicopter and who most likely died some hours after her photo was taken. Looking at the computer screen, I sat and cried for hours—bereft at the idea that we have created a world where this is feasible. I got angry and got started trying to work on the problem.

"To this day I would love to believe that Mihad survived, that somehow she is walking free in this world, though I know that this is likely to be impossible. But her beauty and grace shadow me even now, and she and the little boy will always be my inspiration.

"The photo exhibit we created, DARFUR/DARFUR, started out of my incredible despair at what was happening to a group of people in Sudan and Chad. It was going to be a one-night event in which we would talk about an issue, raise money, and try to help. Three years, multiple human rights projects, forty exhibitions, and three zillion cups of coffee later, we are an organization with plans to work on as many human rights abuses as we can.

"Over 500,000 people have seen the DARFUR/DARFUR exhibition, and more importantly thousands of them have been introduced to the incredible advocacy and humanitarian organizations that have been represented at the installations. It has been used in support of divestment and international diplomacy. Another exhibit, Congo/Women, has been presented on Capitol Hill twice where it was exhibited in support of a successful request for significant funding for women in the Congo. But the most rewarding feeling is getting an e-mail at three o'clock in the morning from a student in a small Texas college town who wants to bring an exhibition to his or her community because he or she feels it will help generate mass support for action.

"When we started DARFUR/DARFUR, I didn't know any photojournalists, film editors, or museums. Or have any money. You need all these things to make such a project work. But somehow it all came together. After things took off, we realized that we had a methodology that we wanted to apply to other issues so we built Art Works Projects backward. First we did a project, then we built an organization. Everyone would tell you to do it the other way around—as someone said today, 'You're trying to build the plane while you are flying.' The other hurdle is that I haven't slept in three years.

"Genocide would be unacceptable here in the United Sates, and it is no less so for being thousands of miles from my home. We are all global neighbors. Humanity does not stop with borders."

We have many other testimonials that we just didn't have room for in the book, so go to www.enoughmoment.org to read more inspiring stories of activism and to find out what you can do. If you have stories of your own or of Upstanders that you know, please send them in, and we'll include them on the site.

FAMOUS UPSTANDERS:
Highlighting Darfur through Celebrity Activism

MADELEINE ALBRIGHT

"We Have a Stake in What's Happening in Other Countries"

JOHN: When was your first Enough Moment?

DR. ALBRIGHT: Well, let me just take a little step back. As you know, I was born in Czechoslovakia. So all through the Cold War period, I watched what the various dissidents were doing, and I wrote my dissertation on the period of relative openness that occurred in 1968 and that became known as Prague Spring. I cared deeply about human rights and democracy in Central and Eastern Europe and in Russia, but I was just a professor and an ordinary citizen, so all I could really do was talk, teach, and write. Then, in 1993, as part of the Clinton administration, I was given the chance to serve as America's permanent representative to the United Nations. It so happens that my Enough Moment really came just before that. I certainly knew about genocide, given what had happened in Europe when major powers like Great Britain, France, and the United States didn't act early enough to prevent it. So I was shocked when, in 1991 and 1992, we began seeing pictures of Bosnians and Croats being put on trains and shipped to concentration camps, and pictures of whole families being driven from homes in which their families had lived for centuries. I thought, I can't believe it. These looked like pictures we had seen in history books of World War II. I remember seeing those pictures and thinking that this was impossible to accept. It also happened that I knew Yugoslavia well because my father had been the Czechoslovakian ambassador there when I was young. So I reacted to the violence there with considerable passion.

When I became U.S. ambassador to the United Nations, Bosnia was at the top of our agenda, along with Iraq. Unfortunately, it was easier to say that what was happening in the Balkans was unacceptable than to actually stop it. We began with a disadvantage because the previous administration had encouraged the Europeans to take the lead on Bosnia. The Clinton administration was divided, with some of us wanting to adopt a firmer line than others. The interagency process within the administration was slow, and we had many meetings where nothing was decided. I was on what I call the "diplomatic front line" because I saw representatives from more countries than any other American diplomat. There were the ambassadors from Bosnia and Croatia at the United Nations, as well as representatives from all the various Muslim countries. Every day someone would come up to me and say, "Aren't you going to do something about this?" During that period one of the UN votes I'm most proud of established the War Crimes Tribunal for former Yugoslavia. But I'm also proud that I was able, along with others, to persuade the administration to eventually stand up to what was happening, persuade NATO to act, and bring the war to an end. I'd had my Enough Moment, and I was fortunate to be in a position to do something about it.

JOHN: What sustains you? What's the cocktail inside that motivates you?

DR. ALBRIGHT: First of all, I saw in Bosnia and later on in the halting of the ethnic cleansing in Kosovo that if you properly marshal your arguments and figure out how to move the process, you can make an enormous difference. People ask me, "What are you proudest of as secretary of state?" It really was ending the terror in Kosovo. I had seen how long Bosnia had taken, and I thought, "Now I'm secretary of state, and I can't let this happen again in Kosovo." Looking back, both Bosnia and Kosovo provide interesting case studies of how to mobilize the U.S. government, NATO, and the world community to implement a humanitarian intervention. Now that I am a professor again, I see value in offering my experience as an example of what works and what might not work in the future. If I can inspire my students to believe in their own ability to achieve change, that is extremely worthwhile.

The other thing that has really made me understand the need to keep a light shining on human rights problems, and on freedom and democracy, has been my conversations with Nobel Peace Prize winner Vaclav Havel. This matters because those of us who are on the outside often wonder whether our criticisms on human rights abuses help or hurt democratic leaders such as Burma's Aung San Suu Kyi or the people of Darfur. If we keep talking about these issues, does that actually make life worse for the people who are at risk? Havel said to me, "The thing that's most important is you have to keep talking about these issues. It helps us if the light is shining on us." That's a very important message. It isn't just that we're helping ourselves. It's that we're giving the victims who are suffering some hope, and it certainly shows the people who are inflicting the pain that outsiders care. That has made a huge difference in how I view my own role.

The other part I feel strongly about is that it took me a very long time to find my voice. I did not have a high-level position in government until I was in my midfifties. Now that I have a platform from which to speak, I'm not going to be quiet. That's true when it comes to promoting democracy, and it's true with respect to upholding human rights. That's why I was so pleased recently to serve as cochair with former Defense Secretary Bill Cohen on the Task Force to Prevent Genocide. The task force made a series of recommendations that I hope the U.S. government and the world community will take steps to fulfill.

JOHN: With all the students you have, how do you get and keep young people interested in genocide and human rights? What are the most effective ways of widening the scope of the population that's willing to get involved?

DR. ALBRIGHT: I have found students these days to be very interested and involved. After 9/11, there was more and more of a sense that we were not an isolated nation that could just sit here and not be involved with what was happening abroad. I have had quite a number of students in my classes who see

Darfur as a clear example of where the "Never Again" philosophy should be applied.

JOHN: The Enough Moment.

DR. ALBRIGHT: Yes. The Darfur movement began with students who really felt that they could make a difference. I think that the more we help students to understand that, there but for the grace of God, this could be happening to them, the more they will identify with the people who are in danger. I was born in Czechoslovakia at the time it was being threatened by the Nazis. When British Prime Minister Chamberlain came back from Munich and said, "Why would we want to help people in a far-away country with an unpronounceable name?" one of the people he was talking about was me. My parents taught me to believe that every individual counts—and my experience has taught me that we have a stake, a national interest, in what's happening in other countries. It's easy to pretend that people in poor circumstances become accustomed to suffering and therefore don't feel the pain, but that's nonsense both morally and biologically. I often think about this when I go somewhere and people are living in abject poverty with flies in their eyes. I think to myself, "I can't stand flies in my own eyes. Why would I think that that person would?" Something I'll never forget was when I was in Ethiopia on International HIV/AIDS day. I was sitting next to a little boy who was an AIDS orphan. I had a ballpoint pen in my pocket that I gave to him, and he said, "No—food, shoes." He was the same age as my grandchildren. I think that personal identification is so important.

JOHN: Thank you for your extraordinary dedication.

DR. ALBRIGHT: Thank *you* for your extraordinary dedication.

ANN CURRY

"An Obligation to Care"

JOHN: What is your motivation for being such a forceful advocate for the rights of people from Sudan, Congo, and other forgotten war zones around the world?

ANN: When I look at people and I decide who is going to be my friend, I don't look at their bank accounts, how famous they are, how beautiful they are, or what they can do for me. I look at, Who are they *really* in the worst of circumstances? What kind of a human being might they be? Would they stand up against evil? Would they stand up to do the right thing? Are they the people who watch someone drown because they are too afraid to call 911? Or are they the people who throw in the life raft? Or the people who jump in to save the person in the water who is drowning? This question I think is a fundamental core question, and it deals with who we are and what makes us who we are.

It can be how we were raised. It can be ideas we let percolate in our brains. For me, it was early on as a young person discovering injustices and discovering that there were people who enlist themselves to make things right. So when as a child I discovered, for example, there was a Holocaust, that was enough to interest me. But then I realized there were people who risked their lives to save people from the Holocaust, and that was mind-blowing. And then what really made my eyes open up was when I realized that people not only risked their lives but they also risked their children's lives, and in some cases their children were killed trying to save Jews. And I thought to myself, "How much love is there when you risk the thing you love the most, your child? What must be within you to do that?"

So that launched an investigation about this question that I have really been conducting my entire life. This idea of who we are and what we're made of, I think, is a key question because it is what will define who we will be. What we pivot into as we evolve, as we continue to evolve into a species that is moving toward greater compassion, greater understanding of each other. That argument I may need to make because most people may not agree with that argument. But if you look back through the scope of history at everything you've learned about history—even if you have to factor in the in-justices of, say, the wars in Sudan, Congo, the genocide in Rwanda, and about what's happened to civilians in Iraq and Afghanistan—you have to acknowledge that the very fact that we are outraged, that we move against these injustices speaks to the rise of empathy. And we can see that even though we once did so, we are not today allowing children at the age of five to run around homeless on the streets of Manhattan. And we no longer consider the killing of civilians to be just a factor of war but rather the crime against humanity that it is. And we can elect a black president given the racist history of this nation. All of these things speak to the rise of empathy.

So that argument now made, I believe that when you have this kind of thinking in your mind, it's not even a question as to whether you should stand against anything that smells like inhumanity. Anything that looks like a crime against our human family. Nothing makes me angrier than when one human being purposefully just puts down, hurts, dimin-ishes, kills, or tries to frighten another human being for no other reason except that one has power and the other does not. One is of one race, the other is of another. One is a man and one is a woman. One is an adult and one is a child. Injus-tice is something we should never tolerate, and I think we are moving toward being a species that will no longer tolerate it.

You never know if you can be that person who, in the midst of the Holocaust, would step forward and have your child walk Jews to a place where they can be safe. You never know who you will be when you are faced with this question. But you can practice, and you can attempt to learn to grow this part in you. And I believe that if you do, you are more likely to step up.

JOHN: What helps sustain you and reinforce your commitment?

ANN: There is a degree of trauma associated with reporting about injustice. There is a degree of trauma that anyone involved with that has to endure, whether you are an aid worker or whether you are someone who is working for the State Department going into Congo, or whether you are a soldier who faces it, or whether you are even a perpetrator. And reporters, any reporters, who tell you they are not to some degree traumatized by some of the kinds of things that we witness when we cover these kinds of stories are liars. I have a tribe of people that I work with—photojournalists, newspaper reporters, television journalists, thinkers. We gather, not very often, sometimes once a month and sometimes once every six months, but we gather and we are all on that same page. They are people that can barely speak to their own families or their best friends about what they have seen because it is unfathomable. It is not describable. I think most anyone who has gone and seen this stuff firsthand can describe it to people who have no connection or experience, and they can't get past the fact that you were in Darfur, that you were in Congo, or you were some other one of these places. So when you are able to be with your sisters and brothers who choose to do this kind of work, there is a kind of comfort, a kind of acceptance, a kind of listening that I think all people need who are in this kind of work.

I think that the most inspiring, most foundational thing in this is my core belief in the future and my core belief that I have an obligation and that each one of us has an obligation to work in some way to make this world better. I'm not saying everybody has to go to a war zone, but I do think every one of us has an obligation to care, that's the first thing. We live in a country where if people care, things change. What Americans care about affects the world.

I think that's the first step. And that to me is enough. If people care enough to be activists, that's gravy, but the fact that they care, that to me is transformative. That's an investment in the future of our world because once you care you have got to acknowledge. You can care only if you acknowledge that no matter whether someone is sitting in a hospital having been brutally raped in Goma, Congo, or suffering third-degree burns in Darfur, or is blinded and will never see again because a Janjaweed put a bayonet in their eyes—that that person matters. And when you say that and acknowledge it, then it's an investment in the future. Then we are all brothers and sisters. That is the way the world is going, and if we don't have that connection then I don't think we've left the world a better place.

We can teach our children this kind of idea. It comes from your own decision making about who you are and what your place is in the world. I think it also comes from your family, and that is where the foundation is laid. When I asked him what should I be when I grow up, my father always said the same thing: "Ann, no matter what you do, do something that is of some service to someone else. Because then, on your last day, on your dying day, you'll know that it mattered that you were here." This idea of living your life so that you can be proud of who you've been, that's a key lesson for our children.

We are not in this life running around and just going from one experience to another. We are going to come to an end some day. Who do we want to see ourselves as having been? I think that is a great wall or an edge to feel and know about as you look to the decisions you make in your life. I frankly do not want to look back and feel that I had not done everything I could to be useful to other people in this world. I do not want to look back and feel ashamed that there was something I might have done to ease suffering and I didn't. I never want someone to accuse me of having been insensitive to a great tragedy in this world or thoughtless to another human being's suffering. I never want that to happen, and so I guard against it looking, feeling for that edge of my dying day.

JOHN: In all of your travels, is there one particular story that stands out that helps sustain you, that helps keep you going when your strength is flagging?

ANN: There is a sea of faces, and they all stay with you, but I think that probably the one in my mind the most right now is Sifa. I found her in a hospital in Congo with her legs in stirrups as she was being repaired for having been so broken up inside. She had been so brutally raped that she was incontinent. She was eighteen, stunning, and in any other world she would have been a model. She's so beautiful. Her hand was shaking, and she stared at me, frightened as the surgery was about to begin. I had been led in there by the doctor, and I held her hand for a bit and then backed out. The next day I came to speak with her. I introduced myself and explained to her that it was her decision as to whether I would continue talking to her. I asked her if she would tell her story, which she did. And what she told me just broke my heart.

She was sixteen or seventeen when she watched Congolese rebel troops slaughter her mother and father. The troops kidnapped her, tied her to a tree, kept her for weeks, and raped her so that she could no longer walk. Then they left her for dead because she didn't mean anything, she didn't matter. She got loose and crawled until someone found her and took her back to the village and nursed her back to health, except that she was broken up inside. She discovered she was pregnant, but of course couldn't keep the baby because of all the damage that had been done. I asked her, "Do you want revenge? Do you want those men who killed your parents and raped you, made you pregnant, and broke you up—do you want them to be punished?" And she said, "No. All I want is to rise from this bed so I can thank the people who took care of me. All I want to do is rise from this bed and work for God and try to be good in this world. All I want is maybe to feel a mother's love. Maybe someone will help me feel that."

That is what is possible in human beings. The ability to rise above suffering into greatness. I have discovered that only with adversity is there greatness.

I have become a great admirer of humankind, even despite seeing some of the worst in human behavior, the worst in humanity. It has never ceased to amaze me that no matter how terrible some of the acts are in our human family, I am still in awe of the greatness of what's possible in that same humanity. That is, more than anything else, what pushes me forward.

JOHN: What is the most effective way that we can communicate that these things are occurring in the world in ways that can grab people and make them want to do something to help change things?

ANN: Empathy. I think what people don't realize is a fundamental truth. The only way out of your own suffering is to take up somebody else's. The only way to stop being self-absorbed and sad and broken by what has happened to you in your life or what you think you didn't get in your life or why you're not satisfied, the only real way out of that I have found is to turn your eyes outside yourself and look into someone else's life and you can feel empathy. What I still don't get is why more people don't understand this very selfish thing. It is so rewarding when you see someone who needs a hug or needs a thought . . . just today I met a twelve-year-old boy in a crowd outside the *Today* show. He for some reason told me that he was living with his parent's divorce. They got divorced when he was six, and he looked at me. There was this whole crowd around him—his parents weren't even with him, they were across the way. And he looked at me, and I either had that opportunity to say something to him or not. You damn bet you I did. I jumped right in there and told him that life was going to become amazing. Every sadness that he has in his life is going to become the fire that is going to propel him like a rocket into life and opportunity. Oftentimes, when we don't have a challenge, we don't have that fire, and he's got it. And everything he wants to make happen he can make happen. You damn bet you grab that opportunity.

ANNIE DUKE

Living the Message

JOHN: What motivated you to get involved?

ANNIE: It is important when you are in a situation where you have so much, that you stand up and recognize it, "I have been very lucky in life, and I have a lot, and I certainly have a voice to protect myself." I just felt that, at that point, if I could, I should do something to help in whatever way to protect people who didn't have a voice to protect themselves.

That's where Don and I came together. I play all these poker tournaments that make so much money, and I thought

"Why don't we try to do something for Darfur?" Obviously I knew he was passionate about Darfur as well. I think that, as I got deeper into it and started working on it, my passion grew.

It was really a slow process. I think that part of it came from the fact that one of the things I'm very vigilant about with my children is the idea that often we have this attitude that when we do well, it's through hard work and we deserve it, which is fine. But then I think people infer the flip side, which is when we are not doing well, and things aren't going well for us, that somehow we don't deserve to succeed and we're not hard-working. That is not true. Not doing well in life is not the reverse.

In looking at what is happening around the world, certainly Darfur is one of the most in-your-face cases of people wanting a better life, but how are they supposed to have one? Certainly one of the key ingredients to having a good life is that you are in a place where you feel protected by the people who are supposed to be protecting you, namely, your government. If your government isn't protecting you, what kind of hope do you have? If you are living in a tent trying to find out how to get firewood and you could be raped or murdered along the way, you tell me how you would improve your life? I don't care how smart you are or how hard-working you are or how diligent you are or any of those things. It's just not going to happen. So I always felt that if I was going to send that message to my children, then I should live that message.

JOHN: Where does this feeling of responsibility come from?

ANNIE: First of all, I credit my parents. When I was younger, my mom was politically active. She worked with the Democratic Committee in New Hampshire. We had McGovern posters on our wall. One of my first memories is in our den with wall-to-ceiling bookshelves, because my dad was an English professor. They were covered one year with posters of McGovern. I think I was six years old.

They were very active, but they were also very diligent about teaching us a sense of social responsibility. They are real flaming liberals. In our political views, my brother, my sister, and I ended up being a lot more fiscally conservative than my parents are, but on the social side we are completely in line with them. We feel that social responsibility and social activism are really important.

JOHN: How do you sustain people's interest over time? How do you keep them in the game?

ANNIE: The interesting dilemma is that the real help comes from the policy side, and the policy side is a harder public relations sell. It is harder to say, "Aren't we excited because we had another hearing or there was another vote?" I think that generally it's just hard for people to get excited about policy and working toward policy change. That's the catch-22 here because it's the change in policy and political pressure that will actually create lasting change in the region. So that's the thing that people really need to be paying attention to, but the good public relations sell is the starving children and aid to the refugees. The key, at least the approach that Ante Up for Africa has taken, is to do both. Clearly the Darfurians need direct aid, and so Ante Up is going to direct quite a bit of our resources toward aid and helping people in Darfur, which I think is the piece that the general population can get really passionate about. Then on the other side we are going to donate a significant portion of our resources to getting policy changed so we can get some kind of lasting solution as well. It's harder to sell the lasting solution and keep people excited about that.

DAVE EGGERS

*"By Feeling and Acting Obligated
to Our Fellow Humans, We Are Freed"*

"I have a strange personal theory about when and why we act on certain issues, on needs and injustices. For me, it's being confronted with the problem through first-person contact, and then having the means of addressing it readily available.

"This is how I got involved in Sudanese issues: One day in 2002 I got a letter in the mail. It was from Mary Williams, who had started an organization, the Lost Boys Foundation, to help the acclimation of Sudanese refugees in the United States. She basically said, there are thousands of young men who need help, so would you like to write a book about the Lost Boys of Sudan—and about Valentino Deng in particular—thus bringing attention to their plight and to the millions who have died and are still dying in the Sudanese civil war? That was all pretty much in the first paragraph.

"It was quite a letter.

"I'm a journalist by training, so my interest was piqued. I thought I had to at least meet Mary and Valentino. So I went to Atlanta, and I met Mary and Valentino at a celebration, a birthday party actually, for all the Lost Boys in the region. When they were processed as refugees in Ethiopia, the UNHCR had given them all, thousands of boys, the same birthday, January 1, and so once a year they celebrated this faux birthday. At the party, there was food and dancing, and even an inspirational lecture from Manute Bol, the famous basketball player who had donated most of his NBA earnings to the plight of the people in his native country, Sudan. Valentino and I talked briefly amid the hubbub, knowing that we had all weekend to get acquainted.

"After the event, I was introduced to Manute Bol. Someone

told him that I was a writer and that I was in Atlanta to learn more about the civil war and the state of Sudan. He got very serious, and he grabbed my arm. 'You have to do this,' he said. 'You have to bring this story to a Western audience!' Now, Manute Bol is a very big guy, almost eight feet tall, and he has very intense eyes. I hadn't decided what exactly I would do with Valentino and Mary, but Manute's directive stuck with me.

"Over the next few days, Valentino and I spent a dozen or so hours talking in his apartment, and I recorded the basic outline of his life story. What he had seen, what his family had endured, and the immeasurable injustices visited upon the southern Sudanese people by its government in Khartoum were beyond comprehension. I was outraged, and I agreed that the story needed to be told, and as soon as possible. 'We need to do this!' I told Valentino. 'We need to tell this story, and now.' I was so full of righteous fury that I promised him we could publish the book within a year.

"So I went back to San Francisco, and in the cold light of day, I wondered what the hell I was doing. All I knew about Sudan I'd learned from a few articles, and from what Valentino himself had told me. I was starting from scratch. And when I really thought about it, I realized that the book wouldn't take a year, it would take many. It would entail trips to Sudan. It would entail hundreds of hours of interviews. And it would entail feeling an obligation to do justice to the story—not just of one man but of the thousands who had shared his journey, who had seen the indescribable things he had seen. So I hesitated. I didn't tell Valentino I was hesitating, but damned straight, I was thinking twice about all this.

"But then again, I thought, what else was I doing with my time? What was more important than this work? I'm no believer in fate or any kind of determinism, but hadn't this man, Valentino, come into my life at a moment when I was actually in a position to help? I had written a few books before, and so while I wasn't confident I would do the story justice, I felt that I could probably bring a new audience to the story of Sudanese immigrants like Valentino. I could help, in some way, to tell a few more people, in a few new ways, about what had happened and what was happening, so the horror and suffering—and also the individuals and their losses and triumphs—would never be forgotten. So what excuse could I possibly have for not doing it?

"I worked on the book for the next four years, mainly because it all conformed to the theory I mentioned at the beginning. I had been apprised of a need through personal contact, and when my help was asked for, I had the tools available to provide that help. I didn't ever again overcomplicate it from there. When you're walking down the street holding a ladder, and someone needs a ladder, you hand over that ladder. It's almost a relief, to have a tool in hand and meet someone who needs that very tool. There is such comfort, life-affirming comfort really, in feeling useful. We go through life, most days, unsure of our usefulness, unsure why we're here and for how long, and so to have a purpose guiding your days, well, there is liberation there. It's strange but true: by feeling and acting obligated to our fellow humans, we are freed."

CONGRESSMAN KEITH ELLISON (D-MINNESOTA)

Keeping the Focus

"Darfur is a tragedy of enormous proportions. I have followed this issue since 2002, and I am committed to preventing an escalation of this crisis. My visit to Darfur was a haunting experience. How can people inflict such pain and suffering on their fellow human beings? I visited the Zam Zam refugee camp in Darfur where tens of thousands of people struggle for their daily survival and fear further attacks from the Janjaweed. Darfur's humanitarian crisis has not passed. The situation could worsen—millions of people remain displaced and scattered in refugee camps, most of which are overcrowded and underresourced.

"We simply cannot let Darfur fall off the world's radar screen as so many other human tragedies have. Continue to write e-mails, make phone calls, and protest the horrific conditions in Sudan. We must be ever vigilant until the last refugee walks safely home."

MIA FARROW

With Knowledge Comes Responsibility

"Who among us is not haunted by the genocide in Rwanda? Its components define us, condemn us, demand better of us, and pose profoundly wrenching questions. My country, my Church, the United Nations, and all the nations of the world did nothing to halt that nine-month rampage in which a million people were slaughtered. Collectively and individually, we must bear the burden of our abysmal failure. We failed to protect our brothers and sisters in their darkest hour, even as we failed our most essential selves.

"In that context, a 2004 *New York Times* op-ed piece by Samantha Power stopped me in my tracks. On the tenth anniversary of the Rwandan genocide, Ms. Power wrote that another genocide was unfolding in a remote region of Sudan. This time it was an Arab government attempting to eliminate the non-Arab populations of the remote Darfur region.

"Now, I have always told my children that 'with knowledge comes responsibility.' This time, I thought, I could not stand by. And so I first went to Darfur in 2004. Sudanese government aircraft and their proxy militia, the Janjaweed, were busy. They were attacking village after village, raping, mutilating and murdering, stealing livestock, torching crops and food stocks, and poisoning wells with butchered corpses of people and animals. Traveling through Darfur I encountered dazed and terrified survivors, sheltering under scrawny trees or walking across the parched terrain in search of food, water, and safety.

"Aid workers were there too, struggling to sustain the massive numbers of people displaced since the killing began in 2003. Hundreds of camps had been hastily assembled throughout Darfur and across the border in neighboring Chad. They were hauling water bladders on the backs of trucks, setting up latrines, drilling bore holes, and distributing grain and plastic sheeting to more than 1 million traumatized desperate people, mostly women and children, and the number was swelling. It would eventually approach 3 million.

"The camps were, as they are today, deplorable places where the inhabitants are barely surviving. Food and water are minimal; medicines minimal; sanitation minimal to nonexistent; education minimal to nonexistent; hope minimal to nonexistent. And they offer little safety. While I was visiting Kalma camp, it was invaded by Janjaweed. When the women leave the camps to gather firewood needed to cook the sorghum donated by the World Food Program, they are often raped. The Janjaweed are never far away.

"In one such camp a woman named Halima told me about the day her village was attacked. It had been an ordinary morning. Halima was preparing breakfast for her family. Without warning, planes and helicopters filled the sky, raining bombs upon homes, upon people as they slept, as they prayed, as they scattered in all directions. Halima tried to gather her children, and holding her infant son, she ran for her life. But then militia swarmed the village. On camels and horseback they came, shouting racial slurs and shooting.

They chased Halima, and before they raped her, they tore her baby from her arms and bayoneted him before her eyes. Three of her five children were similarly killed that day, and her husband too. 'Janjaweed,' she told me. 'They cut them and threw them into the well.' Halima clasped both of my hands saying, 'Tell people what is happening here. Tell them we need help. Tell them we will all be slaughtered.'

"As I traveled from camp to camp, I met many people, and they were eager to talk to me. Their stories of loss and terror, of torture and rape, of beloved homes and carefully tended fields ablaze, of lives destroyed are with me always. Like Halima, they begged me to tell people what was happening there. They hoped that the world would hear their cries and that the United Nations would send forces to protect them.

"Darfur in 2004 was an inferno for which no words seemed adequate. On the plane trip home, I tried to process all I had seen and learned. With knowledge comes responsibility. An inescapable knowledge of Darfur was now mine. As a mother, an actor, and a citizen on this earth, I knew only that I must honor my promise to Halima and the other courageous people of Darfur. I would do my best to 'tell the world what is happening' there.

"I didn't know then what my 'utmost' would mean. I couldn't know that over the next five years I would return to the Darfur region and to refugee camps in eastern Chad eleven times. I would write scores of op-ed pieces that appeared in publications around the world. My photographs too found their way into print in newspapers and magazines. I, who had shirked interviews all my life, would now do at least a thousand. I went on every TV or radio show that would have me. I would speak to students on countless campuses, to U.S. leaders at congressional and senate hearings. I set up my own website, (miafarrow.org) so that people could inform themselves and access the photos and articles as well as the links to the best Darfur-related sites I could find.

"A relentless focus on the crisis revealed that revenues from Chinese oil purchases fund a majority of Khartoum's assaults upon Darfur's civilians and its instruments of destruction: bombers, assault helicopters, and small arms. The vast majority of weapons are of Chinese origin. Beijing has repeatedly used its place on the UN Security Council to obstruct international efforts to curtail the slaughter.

"I found myself at the front of a national movement urging investment firms to divest in companies that have holdings in the Chinese oil companies. Colleges, universities, and dozens of states divested. On a hugely popular women's TV show, my message was that we must all be responsible for our own savings and retirement accounts. I urged people to send a clear message to our investment advisors that we refuse to have our savings used to slaughter innocent people. Every day of that week 45,000 people visited my website.

"On April 27, 2009, I began a fast of water only in solidarity with the people of Darfur and as a personal expression of outrage at a world that is somehow able to stand by and watch innocent men, women, and children needlessly die. My blood sugar dropped to dangerous levels after thirteen days. But my fast was taken up by others; by members of Congress, celebrities, business tycoons, sports figures, and ordinary folks in thirty-three countries. And incredibly, after four months it continued, unbroken.

"I have begun my own project, the Darfur Archives. I am filming the traditional ceremonies, songs, dances, and stories of the tribes of Darfur. Their culture was a rich one. 'But we don't do the ceremonies any more,' the leader—or Oumda—of one tribe told me. 'We are suffering. We are in mourning.' I promised the refugees that when peace comes, I will build a museum in Darfur, and this footage will be there for their children and their children's children. It is for them. I just operate the equipment. And so in the thousands they came each day, and they brought forth their treasures. I filmed in the camps for four weeks. The task isn't finished, but I'm on my way. I have some forty hours of footage and a bonus: the refugees gave me almost 200 artifacts, everyday items they used before their lives were destroyed.

"Until we can have the museum in Darfur, I will be uploading their testimony on the Darfur Archives website. I believe seeing the ceremonies and hearing the stories will bring Darfur's people into focus in a new way. Its primary importance is for the Darfuris in the future, but also, at this point in advocacy, it will serve as an important tool to show the world what extraordinary people we have been talking about and how rich and meaningful their customs and traditional way of life once were.

"I think this is how I will spend the rest of my life. As I write this, violence has torn apart traditional ways of life in the Democratic Republic of Congo; in the Central African Republic; in Somalia. I will continue to archive, to try to preserve the cultures and tell the stories of victims of genocide and mass atrocities.

"Did I actually make a difference for the people of Darfur? Maybe not. But I can help to preserve their culture. In that one sense, perhaps Darfur can be saved. And the old Oumda eventually rewarded me bountifully when he said, 'Thank you for reminding us to remember.'"

SENATOR JOHNNY ISAKSON (R-GEORGIA)

Fulfilling an Obligation

"I first became aware of the atrocities in Darfur in 2004 while serving in the U.S. House of Representatives. Since becoming a U.S. senator, I have cosponsored many pieces of legislation aimed at stopping the violence and achieving peace in Darfur. Most recently, I traveled to Sudan to engage with officials from the government of Sudan on many issues including Darfur, as well as to visit an internally displaced person (IDP) camp in el Fasher, North Darfur.

"I believe that I have an obligation as a husband, father, grandfather, and U.S. senator who is the ranking member on the Senate Foreign Relations Subcommittee to ensure that innocent women and children in Africa are protected from conflict and violence. My official travels have allowed me to see firsthand much of the violence and suffering taking place in Africa, and I do not believe that any person should have to live in such deplorable situations.

"While the issue of Darfur is always on my radar, I do have many constituents who contact me on a regular basis to express their views on the current situation there. Constituents affiliated with groups such as Save Darfur and the Darfur Urgent Action Coalition of Georgia regularly contact my office and meet with me and my staff. While my position on the Senate Foreign Relations Subcommittee on African Affairs keeps me well aware of what is going on in Sudan, in particular Darfur, it is very beneficial to me to hear from my constituents who are working toward ending the violence in Darfur."

BIG KENNY

"I Don't Want a World Like That for My Son to Grow up In"

Kenny Alphin is one-half of the country duo Big and Rich, but he is also a tireless advocate for the people of Sudan. We caught up with him right before he was going on stage in Big Flat, New York. There was a bit of a storm, so the concert manager delayed his act. Perfect time for Big Kenny to tell his story . . .

"Let me first say that having a child myself, I couldn't stand the thought that something like what is happening to the kids in Sudan could happen to my boy. I would hope that if something like that happened to him, someone somewhere would reach out and help him. Secondly, it seems to me that we can always break barriers with music. We can develop a common understanding between people. We are all the same, even if there might be some cultural differences.

"For some reason, I've always watched what is happening in Sudan, even when I was a kid reading *National Geographic*. I've always considered myself a common man. I was raised on a cattle farm in Virginia. My father taught us the lesson of stewardship. We don't own what we are given here on earth. We keep it and improve it for future generations.

"Living down in Nashville, I was asked by a local anti-genocide group to bring a guy down to speak to the people there. That was Brian Steidle [the U.S. Marine captain who worked for the United Nations in Darfur and blew the whistle on the unfolding genocide], who is deeply committed to educating people about what is happening there. Brian came to my house and showed me his pictures. I saw schoolgirls shackled and burned alive. Horrible things. Children should not be allowed to live through that. I don't want a world like that for my son to grow up in.

"So I started reading everything I could get my hands on to try to understand what was going on in Sudan. Then Gloria White-Hammond, the dynamic founder of My Sister's Keeper and former board chair of the Save Darfur Coalition, came to Nashville, and after I heard her speak I was on a mission. My band had a fifty-foot banner up on our stage for a year after that at every one of our shows.

"I decided to buy a bunch of supplies and take them to

Sudan. We brought twenty military-sized crates of educational and medical supplies from Nashville, plus 300 refugee survival kits. A doctor came with us to help treat the kids. We also dedicated a school that My Sister's Keeper had funded. There are 550 girls in that school. They have a school now! My first check from my first number 1 song went straight to My Sister's Keeper. I learned so much at that school from those kids. I can be an instigator to get more education for kids in Sudan, and to raise awareness of what is happening there over here in America.

"We went back to Sudan again and I brought eighteen people with me this time, including doctors and filmographers. I remember one day we saw a little two and a half year old kid. The doctor in the clinic thought he was gonna die. But we had brought rehydration fluids. They hooked the kid up to an IV, and within a day he was playing with the other kids. We can do so much with so little. I want to see the way paved with flowers for these children."

NICHOLAS KRISTOF

Addiction and Inspiration

"When I first went to Darfur in early 2004, I never imagined I'd become a frequent visitor or a regular commenter on genocide. Frankly, genocide is a lousy issue for a newspaper columnist: you want to be stimulating, surprising, and counterintuitive in a column, and criticizing genocide in a remote part of Africa that no one cares about isn't surprising at all. Indeed, it's essentially a recipe for the reader to turn the page.

"The problem was that the story just grabbed hold of me and wouldn't let go. On my first visit, I reached the Chad-Sudan border and was blown away by what I found.

Darfuris had been driven from their villages and were in hiding, but they were in desperate need of drinking water to stay alive. The only sources of water were wells scattered across the landscape, and members of the Janjaweed militia were camped at the wells. When men showed up to get water, the Janjaweed would shoot them. When women showed up, the Janjaweed would rape them.

"So I watched these Darfuri families sending their little children, ten-year-olds, with donkeys across the desert toward the wells to fetch water, because the Janjaweed often didn't bother the children. The parents were terrified when they sent their children, and I couldn't imagine sending my children into danger that way. But there was no alternative. Unless the little children went, the entire families would die of thirst.

"I returned from Darfur to the comfort of America, but those scenes haunted me. I went on to writing about other topics—Iraq, domestic policy, and so on—but I knew that those Darfuri families were still in hiding, still sending their children on these crazy missions to get water.

"Frankly, those Darfuris seemed to need my help more than other people I might write about.

"People often think that newspaper columns are powerful, but in fact that influence is often overstated. If I write about topics that people already have thought about and have a view on—health care, capital punishment, abortion—I change very few minds. People who start out agreeing with me think that I'm brilliant, and those who start out disagreeing think that I've completely missed the point. Yet where we as journalists truly do have power is when we shine our spotlight on an uncomfortable truth and force the public and policy makers to take account of it. In other words, our power doesn't lie in shaping the issues that are already on the agenda but in helping place certain issues on the agenda.

"So as the months passed, and I grew increasingly

frustrated that nothing was happening about Darfur, that others in the news media weren't covering the story. I began to think that maybe I should make a return trip. Darfur nagged at me. So I returned three months later, and then again three months after that—and then I couldn't shake the addiction.

"People often ask if it isn't incredibly depressing to go again and again to Darfur and talk to survivors. Yes, at times it is. You go to Darfur, or Congo, or similar spots, and you encounter the worst atrocities imaginable. But the worst of humanity also tends to bring out the best, in other people. In places like Darfur, I'm truly humbled and awed when I see local people, aid workers, and elders risking their lives on behalf of other people.

"In New York, some people don't want to comment on an issue because they can't be bothered. In Darfur, I interview rape victims who allow me to use their names and show videos of them, despite enormous stigma and risk, because they say it is the only way they can fight back against the rapists. They express their humanity by risking their own safety and honor to protect other women—and that's inspiring, not depressing. In contrast, I come back to the United States and see young people who can find no higher way to express their humanity than to have the hottest cell phone or coolest car.

"And that's what's truly depressing."

TRACY McGRADY

"How Can We Stand By?"

Every summer off from his grueling basketball season, Tracy McGrady would take a vacation overseas. Something moved him in 2007 to talk with his manager, Elissa Grabow, about doing something different than the usual recreational vacation to Cancun or wherever. So they literally called Amnesty International's main number and eventually got to Bonnie Abaunza, who at the time was coordinating Amnesty's work with artists and athletes. Bonnie called John, and they conspired with Tracy and Elissa for a trip to the Darfur refugee camps in Chad.

Dorothy, we're not in Cancun any more.

Tracy and Elissa went with John, Darfurian activist Omer Ismail, and a film crew led by documentarian Josh Rothstein. The stories Tracy heard were like nothing he had ever encountered, and they moved him to tears, and to life-changing action.

We met Isaac, a young man whom we met sitting on a mat in a humble community center in one of the refugee camps we visited. We listened closely to his story to understand why a government would try to wipe out entire groups of its own people such as Isaac.

Before late 2003, Isaac was a student in a high school in West Darfur. His village wasn't wealthy, but his family lived well, growing all kinds of crops, nurturing large orchards of fruit trees, and raising goats and a few cows. He had heard about a few battles between the Sudan government and some rebel groups based in Darfur, but he was concentrating on his schooling and hoped it wouldn't disrupt that.

But on December 1, 2003, everything changed.

Isaac had just left a wake at his mosque when his village came under attack. The Sudanese government and their main militia allies, the Janjaweed, came into town on horseback and trucks, hunting all the males in the village, whether children, adults, or elderly. At least 150 males were killed that morning, including 42 children. The village was looted, and most of the houses were burned to the ground. Isaac lost two uncles, two aunts, and two brothers.

Dazed and devastated, the survivors hid in the orchards

outside the village. For the next two months, the Janjaweed scouted out their locations and warned them, "If you don't want to turn to ashes, you better leave this place." But for Isaac and the others, "this place" was their home, and they didn't want to leave.

But on February 13, 2004, the Janjaweed and government forces attacked again. Many more were killed, and this time many of the women who were trying to hide were raped.

It took Isaac and some of his neighbors three months to find their way to the safety of the refugee camp in Chad. There we found him, three years later, trying to make sense of his ordeal.

He told us that the government of Sudan had decided to destroy the communities like Isaac's from which rebels were being recruited, even though no rebels lived in his village. And he said the Janjaweed want their land, so they have to get rid of the people on it. This is why there is an alliance between the government and the Janjaweed to destroy the non-Arab communities of Darfur.

We met dozens of people from both Sudan and Chad with stories like Isaac's. All of them told us that they just want to go home. They said that to get there, three things were necessary: a fair peace deal, a UN force to protect them, and punishment for those who had driven them from their homes."

These "three Ps" inspired Tracy to change the number on his Rockets uniform to 3, and it is the name of the documentary that resulted from the trip.

But something bigger emerged from this visit as well. On their last night in the refugee camps, the team came up with the idea for a sister schools program that could connect students in U.S. schools with students from Darfur in the refugee camp schools. The Darfur Dream Team's Sister Schools Program (www.darfurdreamteam.org) resulted, and it now has hundreds of schools in the United States actively involved in raising funds and awareness for the refugee camp schools. A number of basketball stars have joined in as supporters, including Derek Fisher, Baron Davis, Luol Deng, Etan Thomas, and Jermaine O'Neal. And most importantly, just as Tracy did, the students are connecting directly with the students in the camps, thus putting a human face on war and investing young Americans personally in helping to find a solution to the Darfur crisis.

Tracy concluded about his trip and the aftermath:

> *As I was hearing more about Darfur, something inside me needed to learn more about the conflict. I was filled with questions and was compelled to get answers. But as my journey brought me to the refugee camps, I realized that there are no easy answers, just more questions. How can we stand by and allow this to happen to these innocent people? How can the world be aware and do nothing? After looking into the eyes of my brothers and sisters who sit in those camps, I made a promise to tell their stories, to share what I saw, and to help in any way that I can. If I put a hand out in aid, then maybe, just maybe, it will inspire another to do the same.*

CONGRESSMAN FRANK WOLF (R-VIRGINIA)

"To Whom Much Is Given, Much Is Required"

"I have long been interested in Sudan—having traveled there five times since 1989. My most recent visit to Darfur was in July 2004 when I led the first congressional delegation with Senator Sam Brownback. I witnessed the unfolding nightmare with my own eyes. I spoke to women who had been raped and brutalized by the Janjaweed. I saw burned out villages, decimated by war. I visited with families living in makeshift camps. The misery that we saw demanded action—the status quo was simply unacceptable.

"Defending human rights, thereby giving a voice to the voiceless, has long been a priority during my service in Congress. I believe that in order for America to truly be the 'shining city on a hill' envisioned by our founders, we must continually affirm that we stand for the defenseless, champion liberty, and confront injustice the world over. Further, my faith teaches that to whom much is given, much is required. America has faced its share of difficulties, but as a nation, we have been richly blessed. This reality leads me to seek to draw attention and prompt action to confront human rights abuses in places like Darfur.

"In my experience, members of Congress get involved in these types of issues for a variety of reasons. Sometimes they have a large diaspora community in their district from a particular country that takes an active interest in events of their home country. Sometimes they've traveled to these regions and personally witnessed something that stirred them to action. My own travels to places like Sudan, Sierra Leone, and Ethiopia have served to inspire policy recommendations and other congressional action upon my return.

"With advances in mass communication, I have seen a dramatic uptick in the amount of constituent mail, specifically e-mail, in my nearly thirty years in Congress. E-mail makes it easier for constituents to share their views with me. But often times we receive huge numbers of form letters, with identical text, simply cut and pasted into an e-mail. This is obviously one way for constituents to share their opinions, but when someone has taken the time to write a personalized letter in his or her own words detailing their thoughts about any given issue, that certainly stands out."

CHAPTER FIVE

Saying Enough to Child Soldier Recruitment

DON: One of the most harrowing experiences I've ever had, outside of visiting Darfur, is when you and I visited that rehabilitation camp of former child soldiers in northern Uganda, run by World Vision. It was particularly overwhelming, especially sitting there with my daughter, who was not much younger than the child I was talking to, who was telling us the story of how he had to kill his best friend so that he would not be killed by the Lord's Resistance Army commander. What a horrifying choice to have to make.

JOHN: For anyone. But especially for a kid.

DON: This isn't the first time something like this has happened in history. You think of the Khmer Rouge in Cambodia and how they press-ganged kids into military service. You think of the Hitler Youth. You think of the exploitation of completely undeveloped human beings and the most horrific way they could be employed and how that changes the individuals forever. How are you rehabilitated out of that? How do you ever find peace if you have been made to do some of the things these kids have been made to do to survive?

JOHN: Just as incredible as the LRA problem is, equally extraordinary is the fact that a solution has been within reach for a long time, but the world has barely lifted a finger to implement it. There are many precedents, many successful models. Sierra Leone was one of the most violent wars in the world for a decade. A murderous rebel leader named Foday Sankoh kidnapped thousands of kids and forced them to commit terrible atrocities. Finally, the world woke up. An international strategy was developed thanks to the blood diamonds campaign and the willingness of the British and Nigerians to intervene, and Foday Sankoh was captured. His rebel group collapsed. Today, Sierra Leone is a democracy, completely at peace.

DON: And Idi Amin, the Ugandan dictator back in the 1970s, was taken out by a military intervention by neighboring countries, right?

JOHN: Yep, Tanzania led it. And for decades the wars in Angola were some of the most violent in the world. A rebel leader named Jonas Savimbi terrorized the country and forcibly recruited kids to be his foot soldiers. Finally, after the blood diamond campaign undermined rebel diamond revenues and led to some serious internal rifts among its leadership, a bullet ended Savimbi's life, and his rebel group ceased fighting almost immediately. Angola today is a country at peace.

DON: This is often how these situations seem to get "resolved."

JOHN: It's time for something like this for Joseph Kony and the LRA. Two million rendered homeless in four countries.

Tens of thousands of innocents kidnapped to be child soldiers and sex slaves. Enough Is Enough.

DON: Are you saying that killing him is the solution?

JOHN: I think a credible military strategy that focuses on apprehending Kony and the other LRA leaders is where our efforts should be focused. Attack the roots of the problem. And
yes, war can be messy, and it is possible in an operation like
this Kony could be killed.

DON: When we were there, there were sporadic peace efforts.

JOHN: Each time Joseph Kony has shot down any chance of a
peace deal.

DON: So one guy says no, and thousands more kids get
abducted?

JOHN: It doesn't have to be that way. As always, there is a
solution. And frankly, I'm a tree-hugging peace advocate. I
belong in sandals, a Grateful Dead t-shirt, and a pony tail.
So when someone like me advocates for a military solution,
you can rest assured all other peaceful means have been ex-
hausted, and I was personally involved with some of those
ill-fated peace efforts. As with so many of these armed groups
that abduct kids to fight for them, the LRA is not fighting for
a cause. Kony is not a rebel leader in the classic sense. His
methods and tactics end up terrorizing the people he claims
to represent rather than liberating or protecting them.

DON: The LRA is like a mafia.

JOHN: And Kony is like the worst mafia don imaginable, with
his dozens of "wives" and child soldier home guards. The
LRA's sole rationale is to sustain itself through looting and

abducting more children as soldiers and sex slaves. The answer is to arrest Kony, to execute the ICC warrants, and end this mafia insurgency once and for all.

Child Soldiers

History is full of examples of the use of child soldiers. The term *infantry* is derived from the Italian phrase *enfanteria*, which described boys who followed knights into battle during the Renaissance. However, the modern era has seen an unprecedented increase in the use of children in war. At any given time, more than 300,000 children, some as young as eight, are exploited in armed conflicts around the world. That's a staggering number; more than three times the number of people that the biggest football stadium could accommodate. Children living in almost any conflict zone around the world are vulnerable to recruitment into war.

In his book *Innocents Lost,* investigative journalist Jimmie Briggs—who has spent more than a decade reporting and writing about children in war—notes that child soldiering is the result of "a breakdown in society, making the youngsters vulnerable to war's abuses with daunting odds of escape."[19] Child soldiers have served in significant numbers on almost every continent in the world. From Sri Lanka, to Colombia, to Sudan and Sierra Leone, children have been exploited and have suffered unimaginable trauma.

One of the primary methods of recruiting children is through abduction from their homes, schools, or communities. In countries mired in conflict, children are often kidnapped or abducted during village raids. Groups that rely on children to carry out the gruesome realities of war often go about recruitment systematically and intentionally. Some groups set quotas for the minimum number of children who must be recruited into war. The LRA, for instance, sets numeric goals for child recruits and raids villages with the intent of capturing a specific number of children.[20] In Sri Lanka, the Tamil Tigers reportedly maintained computer databases that guided their recruitment efforts.[21] The kidnapped children who meet physical size requirements, usually determined by their ability to carry a weapon, are deemed ready to fight in combat. Those who are unable to fight are forced to serve as scouts, porters, sex slaves, cooks, or spies. Some child soldiers claim to have joined combat "voluntarily," but, most likely, these children have been driven to join out of desperation and the need to flee extreme poverty, abuse, or discrimination. Once they are under the control of armed groups, child soldiers are subject to brainwashing, abuse, and sexual exploitation. These children see things no one should ever see, and experience things no one should ever experience. They are deprived of their innocence and their freedom, and the world has an obligation to stand up and fight as hard as they can to end their suffering.

Child Soldier Recruitment by the Lord's Resistance Army

The Grimm Brothers could not have concocted a fairy tale as surreal as that of northern Uganda. For many years, each night before the sun set, tens of thousands of Ugandan children would march in grim procession along dusty roads that would take them from their rural villages to larger towns. The children were afraid to sleep in their beds, terrified that they would be abducted by a madman who would force them into a marauding guerrilla army that would hunt down their friends, families, and loved ones. The fleeing children would sleep in churches, empty schools, makeshift shelters, and alleyways. And every morning at sunrise, the children would walk home, free for another day.

This was no make-believe fairy tale though. It was not the creation of some imaginative writer intending to scare his or her audience and then create a hero to rescue the children. No, this was the reality of northern Uganda's two-decade conflict, where nearly everyone at some point has been rendered homeless and where there existed for years the highest rate of child abductions in the world.

The rebels, in what may be the most ironically titled insurgency in the history of war, call themselves the Lord's Resistance Army. They are led by a self-proclaimed messiah named Joseph Kony, a man rooted in a grotesquely distorted view of the Old Testament. He likens himself to Moses bringing the Ten Commandments to a people who are largely deaf to his message. He believes—or says he believes—he is instructed by God to punish anyone who collaborates with the Ugandan government, and he accuses everyone from northern Uganda of collaboration, so everyone is therefore, conveniently, a potential target.

Kony, his few disciples, and an army comprised largely of kidnapped, tortured, and brainwashed child soldiers fight not for a cause but rather to maintain their warlord existence and to embarrass the Ugandan government by undertaking spectacular attacks that usually involve sadistic mutilations. Driven out of northern Uganda by the Ugandan government army, the LRA has spread to three neighboring countries, bringing along its continued reliance on child abductions for recruits and sadistic mutilation for terror. For lack of better term, the LRA is a mafia that has run amok.

Stealing Children by Any Means Necessary

Rarely in human history has such a small group of people caused so much suffering for so many. The LRA is a militia of 1,000 to 1,500 mostly child soldiers headed by the indicted war criminal Kony. The organization has no clear political agenda. Its support comes from what it plunders, and at times from its patrons in the government of Sudan in Khartoum. This small but ruthless force has caused havoc in northern Uganda, southern Sudan, eastern Democratic Republic of Congo, and the Central African Republic.

The LRA's toolbox of war tactics includes murder, torture, mutilations, rape, sexual slavery, and widespread child abductions. Since 1986, the LRA has abducted as many as 40,000 children in northern Uganda and thousands more in neighboring countries. In an effort to prevent looting and abductions, the Ugandan government created "protected villages." Sadly, these were often overcrowded, unsanitary, dangerous camps for the internally displaced, and most of the camps' inhabitants were forced by the government to enter these camps against their will. In 2002, Uganda launched Operation Iron Fist in an attempt to definitively defeat the insurgency, but the operation sparked more intense and violent attacks by the LRA—and instigated the LRA's return from southern Sudan to northern Uganda. The military operation dramatically increased the number of internally displaced people, and it failed to end the war. At the height of the conflict, nearly 2 million northern Ugandans were living in displaced-person camps.

Throughout late 2005 and early 2006, the LRA shifted its base of operations into northeastern Congo, where no state existed and the jungle terrain offered a perfect sanctuary for Kony. Around the same time, the International Criminal Court (ICC) unsealed arrest warrants for five senior LRA leaders, including Kony. The ICC's actions, coupled with increasing pressure on the battlefield, pushed the LRA to agree to peace talks with the Ugandan government, and these negotiations began in July 2006 in Juba, southern Sudan. While many Ugandans, activists, and diplomats were hopeful that a deal might be struck, talks fell apart late in 2008, with Kony repeatedly refusing to sign a deal that his delegation had helped draft.

The U.S. Response to the LRA

> *The word* terrorism *is used loosely by governments around the globe. In northern Uganda, touring through displaced camps and centers for war-affected children, we hear story after story of spectacular violence, the aim of which can only be to terrorize. "We are awaiting death," one young man in a displaced-person camp told us. "Will it be the LRA or hunger that takes us?"*
> —RYAN GOSLING AND JOHN PRENDERGAST FOR *ABC NEWS*

In late 2008, after nearly four months of renewed LRA attacks, the armies of Uganda, Congo, and southern Sudan—with the support of the United States—launched Operation Lightning Thunder, a joint military operation in Kony's Congo hideout. Though the offensive weakened the LRA by cutting off food stores and other supplies, it also forced the LRA back into its familiar and highly advantageous position as a highly mobile insurgent force that knows the terrain and lives off the backs of the people it loots and pillages. The LRA also retaliated with brutal attacks against Congolese villages.

Why the World Hasn't Succeeded in Stopping the LRA—Yet

Operation Lightning Thunder was seriously flawed and was unable to end the LRA insurgency. The aerial bombardment of LRA hideouts in northeastern Congo and subsequent ground operation did not achieve their initial goal of surprise, and ensuing military incursions have been indiscriminate—endangering children previously abducted by the LRA and creating significant risks for civilians in the region. Scattered LRA units were dispersed and stretched across hundreds of kilometers, able to conduct hit-and-run attacks against their pursuers. It is likely that many of the children who were forcibly abducted to become soldiers are too traumatized and sometimes drugged to envision a life beyond the LRA.

After the failure to capture any of the top LRA commanders, most of the Ugandan soldiers returned home to Uganda, and military operations against the LRA were reduced, with disastrous consequences for civilians throughout central Africa. An angry, hungry, and violent LRA remained on the loose, preying on civilians with frightening efficiency. As a result of the LRA's predations in the first half of 2009 alone, over 1,000 people were killed and 200,000 people were forced out of their homes and into squalor, mostly in southern Sudan and northeastern Congo, with millions of dollars spent on humanitarian operations to help clean up the mess. The LRA began abducting en masse again at the beginning of 2010, and it also started to train children again. Children abducted in the Central African Republic fight in Congo, and vice versa. As of the time of this writing, LRA units had been spotted in Darfur, receiving sanctuary from the government of Sudan. The longer that the regional and international powers wait to figure out what to do next, the more time the LRA will gain to regroup and rebuild, particularly if the Sudanese regime resumes large-scale support.

The United States had a major role in encouraging and supporting regional military operations against the LRA, and the U.S. military was directly involved in planning Operation Lightning Thunder. For years, the U.S. Army has been training Ugandan Special Forces for operations such as this. The United States provided the Ugandans with the equipment to listen in on the LRA's satellite phones and triangulate the group's positions. U.S. military advisors provided the

Ugandans with satellite imagery and maps to plan out the operation.

What the United States Could Do to End It

This is the Enough Moment for redoubling and reinvigorating international and regional efforts to finally bring an end to the LRA's devastating reign of death and destruction. Closing the book on this nightmare requires a more comprehensive approach than just occasional military operations, as called for in the congressional bill signed into law by President Obama in May 2010. Once again, the effective common three P's strategy can lead to success by promoting peace, providing civilian protection, and ensuring punishment of the perpetrators.

Peace: A peace process in Juba unraveled in April 2008, despite intense and lengthy negotiations, when Kony failed to come to the table to sign the final deal. The LRA exploited a year of negotiations to stave off international pressure, collect food and money from donors, and buy time to abduct, train, and equip new combatants. This failed peace effort, however, was not entirely without reward. Many Ugandans as well as governments around the world had long called for peace talks rather than justice initiatives or military strikes to end the LRA insurgency. But now it has been proven beyond a shadow of a doubt that this particular militia leader, Joseph Kony, has no interest in a peace deal. Consequently, Ugandans throughout their country and governments around the world are increasingly supportive of bringing Kony to justice, even if his apprehension requires targeted military operations.

However, there is still much room for peacemaking. A great deal of investment must be made in long-term reconciliation in and rehabilitation of northern Uganda to address the conditions that might lead potentially to a future Lord's Resistance Army II. Furthermore, support for the reintegration of former child soldiers—both economic and psychosocial—is imperative for long-term peace. Putting together a credible reintegration program that supports the children as well as their home communities will create a further incentive for the LRA child soldiers to try to escape and go home.

Ryan Gosling and John, on their trip to northern Uganda together, heard the story of Bosco, a former abducted child soldier, who stood up one day in primary school and in a frightening moment announced, "I have killed eighty-two people." He lunged for the boy next to him, proclaiming, "You will be the eighty-third!" He was physically restrained, and the school sent him for psychosocial counseling through a local NGO. Bosco is now successfully attending secondary school and planning for his future.

Ryan and John also met Sarah, who was abducted by the LRA in 1996 at the age of eight. She was trained to fight, and she was part of a group that killed thirty people. She told us that if she had not participated in those killings, she would have been killed by her commander, the infamous Okot Odhiambo, one of the ICC indictees. She became a rebel's "wife" at the age of thirteen in a forced arrangement, and the next year had a child. "If I said no, I would have been killed," she told us. She escaped during a Ugandan army raid. After going through counseling, Sarah is now attending school full time, studying and deciding what she would like to do for a career. Uganda's children are full of hope. They just need a helping hand. Supporting the former child soldiers is a crucial element to a broader peace building agenda in northern Uganda.

Protection: While northern Uganda is finally experiencing relative peace, civilians throughout the broader central African region are at risk and have increasingly fallen victim to LRA attacks. As one international official told us, "If the people resist, as they did in Uganda, you can be sure the LRA will massacre them, as they did in Uganda."[22] And if increasing numbers of civilians resist, the numbers of casualties will grow. It is thus critical that efforts are made now to ensure the protection of civilians from this increasingly dangerous regional threat posed by the LRA. Additional protection should come from the government armies and peacekeeping forces in the region, bolstered by logistical and training support from the United States and other capable countries, as well as military justice when those forces commit human rights abuses of their own.

But frankly, the best defense is a good offense, and the answer to protecting civilians is ultimately to neutralize the source of their problems, the LRA. More effective and better internationally resourced military operations focused on ending the threat of the LRA are still at the core of the answer. But such operations require a shift from a battle with the LRA generally to a much more targeted and focused mission that isolates and takes the LRA leadership off the battlefield, which will crater the organization.

Punishment: Most of the LRA's leaders have never been held accountable for their crimes, though efforts are ongoing to bring them to justice. Kony and two of his key commanders are wanted by the International Criminal Court, for war crimes and crimes against humanity. (Two other commanders that were originally indicted are now dead.) In July 2005, the ICC issued arrest warrants for Kony and four other key LRA commanders: Raska Lukwiya, Okot Odhiambo, Dominic Ongwen, and Vincent Otti. Formerly Kony's second-in-command, Otti was killed on Kony's orders in late 2007, and Lukwiya was shot during a battle with the Ugandan army. Kony, Odhiambo, and Ongwen remain at large. Bringing them to justice or otherwise removing them from the battlefield will end this nightmare. Also investigating the sources of support for the LRA from the Sudanese government and a small segment of the Ugandan diaspora around the world would diminish Kony's prospects.

A structural problem that exists today in the quest for improved global justice is the lack of an international strategy and force to apprehend those that are indicted for war crimes. After Kony and his main henchmen were indicted on multiple counts of crimes against humanity, the ICC's global backers—most notably a number of European governments—did nothing to enhance the prospects that the warrants would have any chance of execution. No plan was developed concurrent with the issuance of the warrants that would set forth the strategy for apprehending the suspects. And of course there is no world police force that would automatically be tasked with tracking and arresting Kony and his cohorts. The legislation in the U.S. Congress that the Enough Project, Resolve, and Invisible Children successfully promoted requires President Obama to create such an apprehension strategy for Kony and his henchmen.

Call to Action

Despite the fact that the LRA has survived by feasting on children, women, and defenseless villages for over twenty years in northern Uganda and the surrounding region, this is one of the easiest wars in the world to resolve. Dependent solely on its charismatic leader Joseph Kony for strategy and survival, if he were somehow neutralized, the LRA would collapse.

Here's the challenge, and why success is likely: in Congo, there may be upwards of 150,000 men and boys under arms. In Sudan, the number is only slightly less. By contrast, the LRA has perhaps 1,000 troops at any given time. That is the entire scope of the threat. The fact that the world has not yet dealt with this mafia militia full of abducted children is a legacy of failure that may well be unmatched anywhere globally.

When Ryan Gosling and John were visiting northern Uganda together with author Jimmie Briggs, they met a young Acholi woman named Margaret. She asked with fire in her eyes, "What level of suffering do we have to experience here before you come to help us?" This is the question we have to ask President Obama and our members of Congress: "What level of human suffering do the people of Central Africa have to endure before you act?"

The brutal nature of the violations against the "invisible children" of northern Uganda and the surrounding region has put this issue on the global map. We can help these children become visible to the entire world, and with the right effort we can make sure these beautiful, precious, very visible children can soon all go home in peace.

**To help end the scourge of child soldiers,
go to www.enoughmoment.org.**

CHAPTER SIX

Upstanders for Northern Uganda

Just as in Darfur, there are Frontline Upstanders in northern Uganda, survivors of the LRA's worst atrocities, who have had their own Enough Moments and have been working on behalf of their communities and other former child soldiers to help make things better. They are joined by ordinary citizens and celebrities who have taken up the cause and are doing what they can to help make a difference.

FRONTLINE UPSTANDERS:
Former LRA Child Soldiers Who Are Making a Difference

JACOB

"Please Help Us Make Sure the Rebels Do Not Return"

If you meet Jacob today, he seems like the most jovial, hopeful person in northern Uganda. He greets you with a wide smile, introduces you to his family of five, and tells you about how a community farming group that he manages expanded to farm thirty new acres this year. Excited about his successes, he even offers to take you to the farm on the new bicycle he just bought with his portion of the proceeds from the project. And yet behind this façade lies a deeper story that makes you wonder how anyone could live through such an experience, let alone flourish the way Jacob has.

"I was eleven. The rebels came to Olwal, our village. They burned many huts, and they found me. I spent the next one and a half years with them." Jacob was abducted by the LRA in northern Uganda.

"I fought in five major battles and had to kill many people. They thought I was strong, even though I was young. I lost three brothers to the rebels. My family had lost hope."

Then one day the rebels camped near the Paico River, and Jacob was sent to collect materials to build a shelter for the night. As he walked out into the woods, he saw a window of opportunity when no one was looking, and he took it. Jacob was finally free, and his family was ecstatic to lay eyes on him one more time.

But just a few months later, the rebels came again. This time, Jacob tried to employ skill to avoid being seen by the LRA fighters. But the troops were too many, and they re-abducted him. At this point, Jacob felt as though he would never live a normal life again. But thankfully, just two days later an opening came, and Jacob managed to get out, never to return to rebel life again.

Since coming back home, Jacob has faced many challenges. His home community in Olwal turned into an enormous camp for people displaced because of the war. At the height of the war, over 25,000 people lived in the overcrowded camp, with the entire camp population sharing only three boreholes as toilets.[23] He also got married, and taking care of his four children has been a challenge.

But Jacob wasn't going to give up the fight. Under tutelage from Tom Okello, Olwal's inspirational camp leader, and a partnership with the NGO Grassroots Reconciliation Group,[24] Jacob helped set up a group of twenty-five former child soldiers and community members to aid reconciliation in the community. "We faced a lot of stigmatization when we got back from the bush [captivity with the LRA]. It wasn't good; people called you a mad person, and you felt bad. We wanted to do something about this, so we formed this group," explained Jacob. He called it "Pok ki Lawoti," or "Share with a Colleague" in the local Acholi language.

Jacob and Tom started the group out with a brick-making project, aimed at both providing income and helping the other former child soldiers better integrate with the community. "We work together every week, and the differences [between ex-combatants and local community members] become much less," he explained. On its own initiative, the group established a microlending program with profits from their projects. Along with several other group members, Jacob was able to take out a loan and set up a small retail shop that sells groceries in the community. The revenues from the shop now help him feed his family. Jacob's group also has a contingency fund to take care of community problems. In 2008, when one of its members' children got sick with tuberculosis, Pok ki Lawoti paid for the child's medical treatment out of this fund. Because of the treatment, the child's life was saved.

In 2009, Jacob talked to other fellow group members, and they decided to start a farming project. The success has been rapid. "We started with five acres with a startup from the Grassroots Group, but we then expanded the land to thirty acres and hired workers to farm it." The group earned over $400, a substantial amount in local terms, and they reinvested it by buying goats, which they plan will in turn yield even more income for the group.

ROBERT

A Long Walk Home

Three weeks. Twenty-one days. Five hundred and four hours. That is how long Robert spent walking back home as a child after escaping from captivity in the Lord's Resistance Army in northern Uganda. In his seemingly endless two years with the rebels, he was forced to kill, abduct young children, and walk over 300 miles, usually in dense jungle without shoes. And yet now just three short years later, he is leading a successful community project to help his fellow former child soldiers to generate income and reintegrate back into society.

"The LRA is terrible. They make you do terrible things, and then these memories stay with you," Robert explains. Making a bad situation worse, abductees often carry a stigma when they return home, despite the fact that they were forced by the rebels to carry out crimes against their will. The home community is often angry at the former child soldiers, since some of those who were killed or maimed by the LRA often have come from the local community.

Even after his incredible journey back home, Robert also faced this stigma upon his return. It nearly broke his strength. "When I came back home, people said I had evil spirits. I felt as if I was being chased away, and people would bring back those horrible memories from the bush [from the time I spent with the LRA]. Anyone who was angry would vent his or her anger on me, because of what I was forced to do in the bush." Approximately 66,000 youth have been abducted by the LRA over the years, and many thousands of them have expressed similar sentiments.[25]

But these bad experiences didn't stop him. The situation in northern Uganda was changing at the time in 2006: the rebels were moving out of northern Uganda into the surrounding region, leaving Robert's home area more stable than it had been in two decades. The peace process seemed to be moving forward, and people were starting to rebuild. Robert knew that he had to pick up the pieces and move on. He had a family to take care of—he now had three children of his own.

Not only did Robert move on, he led. "I wanted to take my bad experiences and turn them into good," he explained. He wanted to help his family, his community in Alokolum, and the people who were abducted with him. "They don't deserve those bad things. We need to rebuild together."

Last year, Robert became chairman of the group "Can Bwone" (pronounced Chan Bwon-ay, meaning "Poverty requires humility"), a community group formed two years ago with the support of the Grassroots Reconciliation Group. Robert explained "Can Bwone" to us in his own words: "We have twenty-five people, and half of them are returnees [former LRA child soldiers and concubines], and we work together three times per week on a farming project. When we are working hard like that on our project, we are transforming ourselves. We sensitize the community to not stigmatize other returnees, so that they won't call them names or bring back the bad memories."

The new opportunity has not only changed his life but it has also transformed the community's perception of him. "Being in this group has helped erase the bad memories from the bush, because we interact very well and socialize often. Now people don't say that I have those evil spirits any more. They say I have a humble, good character. That is why they chose me to become a group leader."

Robert then took initiative and went even further. "Last year I also organized our group to form a cultural drumming and dancing group, and I entered us into a regional dancing competition. The music and dancing helps our community heal, especially the returnees. We are like a family."

Not stopping there, Robert is already making plans to help his fellow former child soldiers and his community rebuild in additional ways. "I also now started a small fish-selling business from the profits we made from the farming project. This helps me support my family and pay school fees for my children. This year I want to help Can Bwone start a microfinance project from the profits of the farming project, so I can supplement my business and help other returnees and others in the community with small businesses. We need that boost. I want to help give it."

NELSON OCHAYA

Making Life Better for Others

Nelson lived in a village near Gulu, the main town of northern Uganda. He was twelve years old at the time of his abduction by the LRA. He had heard the LRA was in his village, so he ran away and hid with his father. When they were on their way home, they ran into the rebels. He and his father were tied up. But he knew that if he admitted that he was with his father, he would be forced to kill him so he wouldn't run away and return to his village. So he denied that his father was beside him.

They took Nelson away and told him that he must be caned so that "civilian behaviors" would be beaten out of him. The rebels brought heaps of sticks and he lay down on the ground. Five rebels caned him ferociously; his hand was so swollen that if he pressed it, it would crack. If he survived they said it meant he was very strong.

Nelson was anointed with oil to show he was now part of the LRA. He recovered from his caning and began his military training in southern Sudan. He was trained to use a gun, lay an ambush, and loot for food. Nelson was taken to a Sudanese government barracks in Juba to receive artillery training. He trained for six months and was given the rank of sergeant. He was then ordered to attack an outpost of southern Sudanese rebel soldiers and cut a male organ to prove his talent. He succeeded and this got the attention of the rebel high command. Nelson was then sent to Uganda to abduct a group of girls from a boarding school.

Nelson finally escaped from the LRA after a battle. He was too traumatized to be taken to his father, who was still alive. But a generous Frenchman provided counseling for him and helped him get treatment for a gun wound he had sustained. Nelson's parents were very poor and could not afford an education for him. He stayed at a World Vision rehabilitation compound for nine months, and he was still wearing army combat uniforms.

One day he went to see where his mom lived, and he told her that he wanted to go to school. But he still had "rebel hair" (dreadlocks) that distinguished him from the other students. Most of the students kept away from him when he started attending the local school. The teacher at the school was so scared that she couldn't teach—she kept repeating herself—and everyone in the classroom was looking at him, so he left the school.

After these experiences, Nelson wanted to do something to change perceptions and to support his fellow abductees. He joined with a few other former child soldiers to create the War Affected Children's Association (WACA) to help his friends who were in captivity like him. WACA provides former child soldiers with formal and vocational education to help them reintegrate back into their home communities in northern Uganda. He hopes to help other people and his colleagues who are still there in the bush. He wants to be a good example to them.

Nelson is happy working with WACA, although he is "still traumatized" by what he experienced in the LRA. He is gradually feeling better about himself and working with WACA has helped. He is helping other former child soldiers, and he wants to be a good mentor and example to them, to assist in any way that he can. He hopes that life will get better in northern Uganda, and he wants to do what he can to help his fellow former child soldiers so that a better life can be possible for all of them.

VICTOR OCHEN

Justice and Reconciliation, One Person at a Time

"I was born and raised in northern Uganda, in the village of Abia, which is the location of one of northern Uganda's camps for displaced people. It is also near a former command post of the LRA. On February 4, 2004, the LRA attacked Abia. Under the command of Vincent Otti and Okot Odhiambo, the LRA massacred hundreds of people.

"My childhood was very painful. I witnessed all sorts of human rights abuses. Together with my family, I often survived on just one meal a day and sometimes had to go without food. Education in the displaced-persons camps in which I lived was a nightmare. My brother and I burned charcoal and sold it in order to pay for our school fees. Because we chose not to pick up guns or join the army, we became targets for abduction by the LRA. Some of my classmates felt such desperation and helplessness that they deliberately allowed themselves to be abducted by the LRA.

"We suffered immeasurable burdens, miseries, and inequalities. Sometimes I have trouble believing that I made it through all these challenges. But we remained with our loving parents and hoped that one day, the war would end and we would all be fine.

"In 2003, the LRA abducted my elder brother and my cousin. I blamed myself for not learning how to shoot a gun so that I could protect them, and I contemplated picking up a gun to try to get them back. To this day, no one knows what happened to them. I have a feeling that if my brother were alive, he would have escaped and come back by now, but I still hope to see him some day.

"What has happened in northern Uganda over the last twenty years is shocking and unbelievable, but it has happened. Nothing can cool down the burning feelings of the people pained and hurt by this war. One young girl described her parents and others being killed and cooked, and other abductees were forced to eat their bodies. She told me, 'Every time I try cooking using the pot, I see my parents inside the pot.' She has wept too bitterly and suffered too much, and it's sad to witness many people like her whose situation only worsens without assistance. It haunts me that I have been unable to help people like this young girl escape circumstances that leave them vulnerable.

"Today I work with the communities affected by the war. I meet and hold in-depth discussions with victims, and these help me to help them help themselves. I am the director of an organization called the African Youth Initiative Network, or AYINET. We work with the victims of the war; we deliver lifesaving health assistance and help to promote tolerance, reconciliation, forgiveness, and development. AYINET strongly believes that justice for the victims is necessary to prevent new atrocities in the future.

"A year ago, I had a trying moment during an interview with a formerly abducted child. I discovered that this person was one of the ex-combatants who was ordered to tie up my brother during his abduction. To date, he doesn't know that it was my brother whom he was talking about to me. I felt tortured, but I never told him and never will, and not even any one from my family will get to know him. It was very hard for me to concede this, but I feel that this ex-combatant is innocent since he was forced to do that.

"Given my experience working with victims from northern Uganda and at a time of crisis, I am confident that rehabilitating northern Uganda is not possible without rendering justice for those who have suffered the grave crimes committed by the LRA."

MORRIS OKWERA

Becoming a Role Model

In February 2004, the LRA launched one its most gruesome massacres of the entire war in the northern Ugandan displaced camp called Barlonyo. Out of the camp's population of nearly 12,000 people, the LRA killed and abducted around 700 people in one night, according to local sources. The people in the camp had expected the government to provide sufficient forces to protect them in this confined area, but the Ugandan army didn't deploy and instead recruited local children to serve as "local defense forces." Some were as young as fourteen years old. On the day of the attack, fewer than forty of these local defense forces were in the barracks. The camp was burned to the ground. LRA commander Okot Odhiambo, one of the three living LRA commanders indicted by the International Criminal Court in 2005, led this attack.

On the day of the attack, Morris Okwera was on his way back to Barlonyo when he heard gunshots and ran into his house. A bomb landed in the compound, and Morris started feeling faint, but he didn't know exactly where he was wounded. He ran to another camp nearby to get some medicine. He came back to Barlonyo in the morning to find his mother had been killed and his father had been shot in the leg and was in bad condition. His sister had a bayonet wound through the temple of her head, and she died in the hospital. When he found his mother dead, it seemed as though she may have been tortured but he was not certain. "Even now," Morris said, "I sometimes feel like somebody who doesn't have life again."

Morris had been in captivity for one and a half years, and he had finally escaped from the LRA and come home one week before this massacre happened.

The LRA had abducted Morris from Barlonyo camp in 2003, while he was in "senior 3," at the age of fourteen. He was on his way back from secondary school because he didn't have the money to pay for his school fees. He went home and heard the rebels were coming. He hid, but then he heard it was actually government soldiers, not rebels, so he returned. He went into his house, and he didn't know the LRA had laid an ambush. His brothers started yelling that the rebels had come—Morris found them at his door with a gun. His brothers took off, but he was unable to escape. They tied up Morris along with three or four other abductees and made them carry the food, and they kept looting as they moved. As he was leaving Barlonyo camp with the LRA rebels and the new abductees, three newly abducted elders from his community were killed because they were too slow and old. This was meant as a lesson to Morris and the other child soldiers that they must behave well and be strong. In the group of LRA rebels he was with, the new abductees were each attached to a rebel, and during ambushes this made it very difficult to move when shots were fired, and the abductees had to struggle to keep up.

There were many rebels, and they started dividing the abductees. They wanted more abductions, and they asked their new abductees where the government soldiers were. Morris thought he knew and told them. Shortly after moving, they ran into a government ambush—and it was clearly his fault for misdirecting them. A killing spree began, and Morris was beaten and punished because the LRA was angry with him for misguiding them.

Morris and the other boys were trained as soldiers all day and were beaten frequently. The new abductees were told, "If anyone tries to escape, they'll be shot." When one young abductee tried to escape, he was caught and brought back to the camp and the other kids all had to join in beating him up, and then they slit his throat. All of the children had to beat him and then jump over his body. "This was part of the process of making it as a soldier—beating the dead body and then jumping over it to the 'next level.' "

Morris was supposed to loot every day so he could eat during his life in captivity. He took what he could each day to survive, and he carried as much food as he could steal with him because he never knew how long a fight would last and when he would be able to eat again. "Life was full of looting." The biggest problem was the lack of water. There was no water, just muddy, stagnant water that he would try to strain through his clothes.

On many occasions he had to kill a number of people. The young soldiers were given guns and put on the front lines, and they would shield the commanders, who stood just behind them with guns pointing at their backs. The commanders would say, "If you don't shoot we will shoot you." He was forced to beat and kill people his own age. But in most cases he killed elders. When any of the child soldiers tried to run away, they were all forced by the commanders to kill the escapee.

Finally he had a chance to escape. When Morris made it

back to Barlonyo, he realized the attitude of the community toward former child soldier abductees: "Formerly abducted people are useless and aggressive." That was the stigma he felt. He wanted to be a part of his community again, and he wanted to learn about peace and development. He wanted to show that formerly abducted people like him "could do something."

He became a community counselor with AYINET, the African Youth Initiative Network, which aims to improve relations and build trust between the community and former child soldiers. Initially, he was not trusted, but over time, as he continued to work hard, he showed them that "I am from here, and I am part of this suffering also." As a former child soldier, he can support fellow soldiers as they also attempt to reintegrate into his community.

CITIZEN UPSTANDERS:
Anti-LRA Champions in the United States

LAREN, JASON, AND BOBBY

Invisible Children's Founding Fathers

In 2003, nineteen-year-old engineering student Laren Poole and his good friend Bobby Bailey followed their friend Jason Russell, a recent University of Southern California film school graduate, to Africa. They found themselves in northern Uganda in 2003, and their lives were changed when they saw the car in front of them on the road near Gulu attacked by the LRA.

Ending up in Gulu town, the guys then met Jacob, a Ugandan student who had been abducted by the LRA. The friendship between Jacob, Laren, Bobby, and Jason grew, and the group stayed with Jacob for over a month. While with Jacob, the guys saw firsthand how children walked to towns nightly to escape the predations of the LRA.

Jacob and their experiences in Gulu inspired the friends to return to the United States in order to do whatever they could to end a conflict that very few people seemed to know about or were working to stop. The result of their interest and activism was the creation of the organization Invisible Children, which has helped develop a grassroots constituency of activists in the United States intent on ridding Central Africa of the LRA. Their movement has succeeded in dramatically raising the profile of an issue that had previously been swept under the rug.

From its humble beginnings as a rough documentary, Invisible Children quickly grew to a movement of hundreds of thousands of young people. Captivated by the compelling stories of night commuting and child soldiers, a generation has rallied behind Invisible Children, attending major events each year to highlight the LRA crisis. Volunteers tour across North America with the documentary and other films produced by the team, bringing the story to classrooms and churches with educated representatives. In only four years, over 250,000 young people had taken part in Invisible Children rallies and events. Even Oprah spoke with the Invisible Children guys on her show after they gathered thousands of activists in front of the Chicago studio where she films.

In the summer of 2009, Laren and the rest of the Invisible Children team joined with the Enough Project and Resolve Uganda to host a series of lobby days in Washington, D.C. The team called the event and ensuing campaign "How It Ends." The three groups then launched a political campaign primarily directed at President Obama. Invisible Children developed a nationwide, awareness-raising tour ultimately converging on Washington, D.C. To make as much noise as possible, they held call-in days and delivered a citizens' arrest warrant for Kony, aimed at bringing him to justice. This "Hometown Shakedown" aimed at having activists meet with their elected officials back in their home district offices ended up doubling to fifty-one the number of senators cosponsoring legislation aimed at apprehending Joseph Kony from mid-November to the end of 2009. On one day in November, thirty-two meetings were held in different Senate offices throughout the country. This represented the most cosponsors for any stand-alone Africa-related bill in the U.S. Senate since 1973.

The three founders of Invisible Children each came to the issue in different ways:

Bobby Bailey: He had no idea that their first trip would lead to the formation of their own nonprofit focused on children in northern Uganda. When they got back, they started small, with a bracelet campaign and their first film. Now, their programs employ hundreds of Ugandans, and their grassroots movement involves hundreds of thousands of American youth. As Bobby says, "Media shapes the way we view our lives." He worked on the first film because he saw the impact it could have on young people across the country. He is driven by a desire to give the children of northern Uganda the same opportunities he and his friends have had. The chance to inspire the youth of America to take a stand, Bobby says, has shown him that life is more meaningful when you're giving your time and talent to something bigger than yourself.

Laren Poole: He was an engineering student at the University of California at San Diego when he first learned about Joseph Kony and the LRA. Since his trip to Uganda, Laren has used his interest in filmmaking and activism to highlight the LRA in documentary films that are seen by thousands of students and activists across the country. He also funnels his interest in new media into working on the Invisible Children's website and other multimedia products.

Jason Russell: He credits a church group trip to Kenya in 2000 for transforming his mindset and fomenting his interest in Africa. His ultimate goal is "to raise enough money to build a refuge for the children of northern Uganda so they may grow up in peace." Until he traveled to Uganda in 2003, Jason had planned to make Hollywood musicals once back in the United States. Instead, he has devoted himself to telling the stories of the children he met on that trip. The first step was producing the documentary *Invisible Children: Rough Cut.* Since his first trips to Africa, Jason has married and had a child. Fatherhood has only strengthened his resolve to do all that he can to help end the scourge of the LRA.

BRITTANY DEYAN

Finding Her Voice

"I am from Orange County, California, a place overly stereotyped for its focus on materialism, wealth, and the quest to obtain the unnecessary. This had been all I had known for most of my childhood. I was very much naïve to the world around me. I credit this upbringing to my initial shock in hearing about the travesties taking place in northern Uganda.

"The fall semester of my senior year of high school was a defining moment for me. A teacher with whom I was very close handed me a documentary entitled *Invisible Children,* telling me she thought I would like this film. I sat there and watched it with her in her classroom. I didn't understand. I was watching a film about three young guys from San Diego, not much older than me, traveling to Uganda, a country I had hardly heard of. In the film, I saw children holding guns, being brainwashed and destroying land—all for the desires of a crazy warlord. It didn't make sense to me. I was living a very comfortable life, and these children woke up each day fearing what the day entailed. At the end of the film, the three young filmmakers said they needed help: they wanted to see an end to the war in Uganda, and they wanted me, a seventeen-year-old girl from Orange County, to help them.

"Much about what we know of what is going on in the world, especially in Africa, is communicated through starving children and feelings of extreme desperation. And sadly, oftentimes that is a reality. However, *Invisible Children* tells the story of a crisis taking place a world away from a different angle. They expose the tragedy of war and poverty, but additionally, they expose joy; and most importantly, they give you a specific call to action in how you can help.

"The fact that *Invisible Children* has not only engaged but has also relied on a very young demographic might seem crazy. Perhaps even more crazy is that they are relying on us as young people to end a war, to stop a warlord, to put kids in schools, to facilitate an end to displacement, to pressure the U.S. government to make this a political priority, to help the rehabilitation of brainwashed child soldiers, and ultimately, to raise the profile of this issue. It seems crazy, and it is crazy, but putting the onus on us to make a difference is also empowering.

"At the end of the film they asked for my time, talent, and money. Three boys with a goal of ending (at that time) a twenty-one-year-long war, and I immediately knew that I was going to try and help them. At that time, however, I just didn't realize how much impact I could really make.

"My journey from the day almost three years ago when I saw that film has been a whirlwind. I became an Upstander because at seventeen I felt, for the first time, that I, as a young person, was empowered to have a profound impact on this world. I was standing up for something I believed in, and still believe in: pursuing peace in northern Uganda.

"Since 2007, I have realized that if you are committed and work hard, anything is possible: I started two clubs at my high school and university campuses, raising a total of about $90,000. I traveled to northern Uganda to meet the people and understand the situation firsthand. I traveled to Washington, D.C., on two separate occasions to participate in Ugandan Lobby Days and lobby my congressman to make ending the scourge of the LRA a priority. I taught a class at UC Berkeley for fifty students on the power of social activism and the rise of social movements toward international issues with a focus on specifically what is taking place in Uganda through Invisible Children. I helped in founding a women's university-level scholarship that has currently put over 100 women in universities in northern Uganda through Invisible Children. The first recipient was the friend I made on my trip to Uganda who, more than anything, wanted to pursue a higher education in order to emerge as a female leader of some kind in Gulu.

"Perhaps most importantly, I have found my voice and have begun to understand the impact that I as a seventeen-year-old—well, now a twenty-year-old—can truly make in helping to end Africa's longest-running war."

JOSHUA DYSART

Telling the Story in Different Ways

For many comic book artists and aficionados, comics are a form of escapism, but comic book writer Joshua Dysart is interested in how comics might interact with the real world. This interest in bringing together his creativity and his keen sense of social justice are what eventually led to the creation of a comic book teaching readers about the predations of the LRA.

After first learning about the LRA, Dysart spent years reading whatever he could get his hands on, trying to understand how exactly it was possible that such a small group could be responsible for so much bloodshed and violence. Learning and understanding the crisis was an important part of his life, and an opportunity from DC Comics (best known as the home of Superman and Batman) opened the door for a revolutionary new project. When DC Comics approached him with the concept of re-creating the character from the World War II comic called the Unknown Soldier, Dysart immediately saw the opportunity to use his art to raise awareness about the LRA by setting his book in northern Uganda. Dysart created a series of comic books about Dr. Lwanga, a fictional doctor who as the Unknown Soldier returns home to Uganda and does all he can to ameliorate the suffering of those victims of LRA atrocities.

When talking to Dysart about his work and its juxtaposition with efforts to end the conflict, the first thing he does is offer a caveat. "It's violent," he says, "very violent." But that is Dysart's medium, and he conceded that it very consciously uses some "pulp, mainstream action beats" to accidentally educate. In fact, Dysart stays awake some nights in fear that he is exploiting those who have endured atrocities committed by the LRA. In order to learn for himself, he spent more than a month in Uganda talking with anyone and everyone willing to speak with him. He spent nights in IDP camps and visited AIDS hospices and found himself inside the lives of people who persevere despite unimaginable hardship.

While Dysart continues to worry and work tirelessly to ensure that he is doing his best not to exploit the situation, he has begun to see the fruits of his labor. "When a sixteen-year-old wealthy white kid comes up to me and knows who the president of Uganda is," he says, "I feel good."

FAMOUS UPSTANDERS:
Highlighting the LRA Crisis through Celebrity Activism

SENATOR RUSS FEINGOLD (D-WISCONSIN)

Letters Matter

"I have been a member of the Africa Subcommittee since I came to the Senate in 1993, and I have been chairman of that subcommittee for five of those years. It is my job in that capacity to follow human rights crises very closely, and I take that job very seriously. I also learn more about these crises from constituents—and even my daughters, in the case of the LRA—who care about these issues and raise them in letters, phone calls, or the listening sessions I hold throughout Wisconsin each year.

"Through my work as chairman of the Africa Subcommittee, I have come to believe strongly in the strategic importance and vast potential for the United States to partner with Africans so as to advance both our security and shared prosperity. At the same time, we have a proud tradition of social justice in Wisconsin, and I believe the United States has a responsibility to do what we can to prevent and respond to genocide and mass killings wherever they take place. My trips to eastern Congo, northern Uganda, and many other areas affected by conflict have only strengthened that conviction.

"It makes a big difference when my constituents raise issues at the listening sessions I hold throughout Wisconsin—seventy-two of them a year. Personal letters and phone calls also let me know that people care about these issues and want to see specific actions."

RYAN GOSLING

"If You Make a Big Enough Noise, They Will Listen"

JOHN: I know you're self-critical about how much you are actually doing, but you've done a lot, going to Africa twice, and lobbying on Capitol Hill and at the United Nations. What made you initially get involved?

RYAN: It was around the time that I met Don Cheadle. I had worked with him on a movie. So I went to see the *Hotel Rwanda* premiere. And Paul Rusesabagina, the gentleman that the film was based on, was there.

First of all, I was really impressed with the film, and with Don, not only for his performance but also because he had become so involved with the issue afterward. And he just seemed to have such a sense of purpose. Not that he didn't have one before, but he had come alive after that experience. Angelina Jolie gave a really powerful speech at the premiere about what was going on in Darfur. I ended up talking to her about the film she was making, and she asked me if I would go to Chad to film something for her movie. I don't think that was actually my Enough Moment, but I think I was going more out of curiosity, just to see what all of this was about.

I had a moment when I went to the first camp, which had thousands of kids, and I had been briefed on what they had probably been through, a list of things. I tried to prepare myself for that. I wanted to be respectful, and I didn't want to be too prying. I wanted to try to figure out how to be in the situation. I ended up being surrounded by something like a hundred kids, who were all looking at me with this look in their eyes, as if they were thinking that if I just flew away at that moment, it wouldn't surprise them.

It was really quiet. They were all just following me and watching me. And there was this one little girl who was kind of getting crushed, squeezed, by the group that was trying to be close. And I said, "It's okay, it's okay." And in that exact tone, they tried to mimic me and say, "It's okay, it's okay." A hundred kids at the exact same time. And then, I kind of laughed, and I said something else, and they mimicked it. And I realized the potential of this. So I kinda taught them that part to "Sweet Caroline, Bah, bah, bah." And I started singing the song. So when I pointed to them, and they would sing the "Bah, bah, bah!" We ended up having a really fun day after that. We made little films together. I gave them the camera, and they filmed each other. They were just really cool. One kid made sunglasses out of a piece of unexposed negative film, and so when he looked through the glasses, he could see pictures. Another kid made a hat out of vodka bottle labels. They were just really creative, and cool. And I liked them. And so, when I left, they weren't just these faceless kids anymore. There was a small group of them that I felt I got to know. And so I felt invested in them after that experience.

When I got back, I began to try and figure out more of what they had been through. And I found this book, *Innocents Lost,* written by Jimmie Briggs, and it was all about child soldiers. I was really impacted by those stories. I didn't even know that that was going on, and so I started doing a lot of research on it. I found their perspective on what they had been through compelling. Most of the kids from Uganda didn't seem to have any bitterness about what had been done to them. There were no revenge fantasies. The fight had been taken out of them. Not in the sense that they weren't willing to fight for their freedom, or they weren't fighting to keep their spirits hopeful, but they weren't interested anymore in physical fighting.

They were able to forgive each other in a really amazing way. Or at least it was amazing to me that I had heard stories about kids sharing the same bunks in rehabilitation camps after they had been in the jungle together, and you know the kid on the top bunk had been forced to rape and kill the mother of the kid on the bottom bunk. And beaten him to an inch of his life. Yet they were able to be best friends as soon as they got out. Because they both had the understanding that this was something they had to do, and had they not, they wouldn't have survived. There isn't a lot or resentment there, although it's not completely idealistic. These kids are very traumatized, and so sometimes they act up. And it's not always that way, but it seemed to be the major theme of most of the interviews I was reading. It was so different from how I think I would experience that, so much more evolved. Just so different from us. We are so revenge-fantasy driven. I was compelled by them.

I really wanted to go back. During that process, I met you. So when you and I started plotting, I was very inspired by you. And it's difficult to do this because you asked me what keeps me inspired, what keeps me going, and the truth is that it's you. Haha. I'm truly grateful for that. You are that kick in the ass for me, and for a lot of people. And you should be proud of that.

JOHN: Thanks, bro. Let's go back to this whole issue of why you said yes to Angelina, not that anyone would say no to Angelina. You said it was curiosity that made you decide to go to Africa. What was piquing your interest?

RYAN: I just felt compelled to do it. It's not because I felt as though I would be of any service. But it's just not that often that people are given an opportunity like that. Most people hear about these things, but they don't have someone saying, "I'll fly you there, and I'll connect you with all these aid agencies and workers, and they'll give you a tour and access." It was a once-in-a-lifetime opportunity that would be stupid to turn down. But I had no idea how to be effective, if I could be effective, or any of that. I wasn't really educated on the situation. I didn't know what I was getting into. And when I got there, I was kind of struck with the reality of it. We landed kind of in the middle of the desert, and we had to take a two-hour detour because two days before, the UN vehicles had been shot at by Janjaweed militia. We couldn't take the main road. We realized how immediate the danger was when we got there. It was not relatable to home. We were right in it, and there was a real sense of fear among the aid workers because these vehicles had been shot at. And they were wondering if they should be there, let alone us, and so we hit the ground running when we got there.

A lot of the stories that you hear, although they are incredible, they aren't real to you. You don't have a personal connection to those people. But now that I have gone there, and I've been able to hang out with these kids, getting to know them, I can plainly put into perspective what they have been through. Suddenly it all became possible. It seemed impossible before I went. It seemed like a fairy tale. You and I have used this analogy before, but the child soldiers and the night commuters in Uganda were kind of like something out of a Grimm Brothers fairy tale. It was hard to understand how this could be real.

JOHN: In the Darfur refugee camps, were there people you connected with? Was there any particular story that impacted you in any way?

RYAN: There were two sisters, twins. Zena was the girl I got to know. We were set up to interview them. And when we came into the tent to interview them, they were afraid of us. This was the last thing we wanted to do, to add any stress to them, so we left. We didn't want to impose on them. But one of the girls told an aid worker that she was protecting her sister because her sister was afraid of us, but that she would be willing to talk to us. But I didn't want to interview her, and have her relive her experiences, even if she has been asked to do so a thousand times.

So we just kind of gave her a camera, and I asked Zena if she would be my camera person. She could film her friends, and it would give viewers more of a sense of what their lives are like if they were to just film each other. So I got to spend the day just with her. Not talking very much, just shooting. Asking her to shoot something, her pointing, asking to shoot something. She started wearing my sunglasses, wearing my buddy's hat. Over the course of the day, her personality totally came out. You could tell she was a real character, you know? She was just really dynamic, completely aware, so fast and smart, just a really impressive young lady. And I didn't really know what had happened to her until the day was over. I asked the refugee camp worker about Zena as we were leaving, after we had spent the day together: "So what's the story? How did they get here?" And the camp worker told me that the girl and her sister had been raped by a bunch of the Janjaweed militia and left for dead. But they had found a way to escape this village. And they walked by night, in the direction of Chad, hoping to find the refugee camp because everyone in their village had been killed. They were traveling by night so that they wouldn't be seen in the day by the Janjaweed. And it was a miracle. They picked the right direction and landed into this camp.

JOHN: How old was Zena?

RYAN: Maybe twelve or thirteen.

JOHN: Whom do you remember from northern Uganda?

RYAN: Patrick was this guy from northern Uganda. He was a young guy, really cool and funny. And he was showing us around. And it wasn't until a few days into it that I found out his story. And it was a really crazy story. He was one of Joseph Kony's bodyguards in the LRA. The first time Betty Bigombe, the Ugandan mediator whom we were with, met Patrick, he was pointing a machine gun in her face, and now she was employing him. She basically hired him to show us around. I was asking her, "So how did you and Patrick meet?" And she said, "Well, he had a machine gun in my face.'"

Patrick had heard about some fellow rebels in the LRA setting a little girl on fire, where they killed a family in a car and set the car on fire, and this little girl Joyce, I think she was two or three, crawled out of the car when it was on fire, and she was on fire. And they threw her back in the car, but somehow she got out again. So the rebels wrapped her in a carpet and set the carpet on fire. Somehow she was able to hold out long enough for the government army to arrive, and they fought off the rebels and rescued her. She had 80 percent of her body covered in burns.

Patrick heard this story, and he decided that this was his Enough Moment, which is probably the one we should really be talking about, because he did this really amazing thing where he escaped from the LRA, which is punishable by a pretty brutal death. And I'm sure Patrick had been a part of doling out some of those punishments, so he knew what he was risking, but he escaped and found her. And he decided he was going to spend his life taking care of her. Because her father was an army soldier for the government, he decided he would be her substitute dad.

So when we met him, he kept telling us, "I want you to meet Joyce, I want you to meet Joyce," and we were so busy and overwhelmed, that we kept saying, "Yeah, yeah, yeah," though we didn't really make a plan to do it. And then we finally showed up to see Joyce, and we saw this beautiful little girl, just covered in burns, and he told us her story. So that became our focus. She was very sick, and we tried to take her to the hospital. It was an interesting but very frustrating process because you could see why it's difficult for people living in a displaced-person camp in Africa to stay healthy. Thousands of people all just stacked up on top of each other. There is literally no room. They are just packed into this place. And they are not starving to death, but they are certainty malnourished. And disease spreads so rapidly.

Joyce was just so sick. So we took her to the hospital. I think we waited for like a whole day, and we couldn't find a doctor to look at her. It was just so unorganized, so we took her to another place the next day and found out she had bronchitis. We had to take her to another doctor, and I just can't convey how frustrating it is, how many lines we waited in. You get there, and it's like they are selling tickets to some show. . . . It's not even a line for the doctor. And, you know, it ended up taking weeks to get her blood tests to figure out the diagnosis. And we were on our second to last day when we got the blood tests back and found out she had HIV, which was a total shock obviously to us. But it was even more of a shock to Patrick, who now just really didn't know what to do. It was because she had received so many blood transfusions for her burns. She had received contaminated blood. The next day we went to see her, and she had a bloody nose. And she was playing with a bunch of kids, and they were all wiping the blood off her nose. You can see how difficult it is to stay healthy there.

We tried to put her in a hospital. And we got her a room, and all these things. And at night, she and her family would sneak out and go back to the displaced-persons camp, because for them, from what I understood, community and family were everything. Isolating her from her family and community to keep her healthy was our intention, but for her and her family, there was no point in living if she could not be with her community. They are a unit; they aren't individuals. I'm not trying to speak for the whole culture, but that is the experience we had with this particular family. And there was a certain point we reached when we said to ourselves, "What do we do? It's not our place." Joyce should have had a doctor looking over her. And at the same time, for the other kids, they can contract either bronchitis, or potentially HIV, and a ripple effect comes from that.

JOHN: With all the communication tools that the new information age provides, what are the most promising things out there that can help make it easier to teach people about what's happening and connect them to these communities, to these people?

RYAN: I think that the Internet is going to play a huge part. Not just in this but in everything. In the future. Haha.

JOHN: Very profound insight.

RYAN: And from what I understand, there are kids who have pen pals, iChat pals, kids from the United States who can iChat with kids in the camps. So I think people in these kinds of situations are now so much more accessible, and that's definitely something that you can build on. It's going to keep growing. There are ways to build personal relationships without having to travel all the way to Africa. It seems to me that there is a shift and that people are becoming more globally minded—because we must be and because we are so accessible to one another now. The borders have sort of all come crashing down because we have access to everyone and everything, to all information, whenever we want it. So I hope that this will help.

JOHN: It would be a grotesque failure, through the media that exist now—through the pictures, and stories, and videos, and everything that exists—if we could not resolve these crises. Does anything stick out in your mind from all those experiences that might have wider relevance to people and give them hope that our voices can actually make a difference?

RYAN: Yeah, that experience when we lobbied Congress was really great because we got a crew together and we walked around Capitol Hill and knocked on doors, and we talked to quite a few representatives and senators. We explained the issues of northern Uganda and what we had seen. The reaction from the representatives was fascinating. Voters think that these officials don't get their calls or letters, but they do get them. It was interesting to actually see that they do have an office. And if you have sent a letter to that office, they have received it. And if they get 100 letters in that office, they pay attention to that. A few of the representatives said, "Look, it would be embarrassing for me if I got 100 letters in my office and I didn't deal with the issue." So it was nice to go and put perspective on this place that seemed so inaccessible to me before and to realize it is just a building with a bunch of people in it, and yeah, if you make a big enough noise, they will listen.

CONGRESSMAN DONALD PAYNE (D-NEW JERSEY)

Hold Your Representatives Accountable

"Regarding the LRA, it was around the time that I came to Congress in 1989 that Kony began wreaking havoc in northern Uganda. I knew Uganda well, having traveled there in 1973 to meet with Idi Amin to protest the expulsion of the

Asians. In the late 1990s and early 2000s, the media's spotlight was shown on the recruitment of children by Kony and the LRA, and it was really then that the world began to learn about the phenomenon of the night commuters—hundreds, maybe thousands, of children who had to leave their homes in rural parts of northern Uganda for the town centers to take shelter and sleep for the night.

"I decided to take this issue up personally because I had been involved in the civil rights movement in the United States during my high school and college days, and I have been a fierce fighter against injustice. As an extension of my work internationally, when I became involved in the worldwide YMCA movement and became chair of the World Council of the YMCA in 1973, I started to focus attention internationally the way that I had domestically.

"People often think lobbyists hold so much power because they can influence lawmakers. It is true that lobbyists have a great deal of influence, but at the end of the day, it is the people—the constituents—who are the most effective and have the greatest potential to influence lawmakers. Members listen to constituents and will side with them over lobbyists if they assert themselves and hold their representatives accountable. Church groups and advocacy organizations can be particularly effective."

CONGRESSMAN ED ROYCE (R-CALIFORNIA)

"Bringing One Man to Justice Can Lead to Peace"

"I have served on the Foreign Affairs Committee since I came to Congress in 1993. I chaired the Africa Subcommittee for eight years, starting in 1997. I traveled to Uganda with President Clinton. Uganda is a bit deceptive, in that many sections, including the capital of Kampala, are free of violence and enjoy relative prosperity. Because the violence occurs in rural areas, and because Uganda has been celebrated as an 'African success,' the spotlight on LRA atrocities and its recruitment of child soldiers hasn't been so bright. Frankly, without advocacy NGOs, this would be a forgotten conflict.

"I fought very hard to bring to justice the president of Liberia, Charles Taylor, who threw his region into war. My efforts included a well-timed *New York Times* op-ed that I wrote pressuring the president of Nigeria, Obasanjo, to turn over Taylor, then exiled in Nigeria. Many opposed me, arguing that the apprehension of Taylor would destabilize the region, or alternatively, would be inconsequential. Today Taylor is being tried for war crimes, and the two countries are at peace. Bringing one man to justice can lead to peace, whether it's Charles Taylor, Joseph Kony, Omar Bashir, or an indicted Congolese warlord. Indeed, imposing accountability can work wonders, while unaccountability guarantees conflict. I'm committed to resolving these conflicts because they're not irresolvable. There is hope.

"I meet with many constituents interested in these issues, both in Washington and in my Orange County district. They also write my office. I always learn from them. Step 1 is simply calling or writing your local member of Congress, requesting a meeting in his or her district office. In July 2009, Resolve Uganda, the Enough Project, and Invisible Children organized a lobbying day on Capitol Hill, encouraging members of Congress to support my bill on northern Uganda. Having a physical presence in Washington is very effective. I think it's great that there are so many activists, including young people, concerned about human suffering in Africa."

CAST FROM NBC'S *THE WEST WING*

"Art Can Be a Bridge to Understanding"

A group of actors, led by Melissa Fitzgerald, from the television series *The West Wing* have committed themselves to telling the stories of people affected by LRA attacks and abductions.

Martin Sheen: "It was when I saw the film *Hotel Rwanda* that I was able to witness from afar what had happened there. I learned more about what was happening in Uganda when Melissa Fitzgerald went there to volunteer. When she returned and shared her experiences with me, I offered to help and support her work there. As artists, we can make choices that speak to the great issues of our time, and if we don't, what we do is a waste of time. We can shine light on the horrible human rights abuses and the increasingly terrible situations we witness going on today. George Clooney, Don Cheadle, Mia Farrow: I am proud to be in the same profession."

Allison Janney: "About ten years ago, my dear friend Melissa recruited me for Voices in Harmony, a Los Angeles theater program for at-risk teenagers. Over the past decade, I've witnessed firsthand the life-changing impact this program has had on these teens—giving them confidence and empowering them to take on the challenges they face. It's been a privilege to be a part of this effort. So when Melissa asked me to help her adapt Voices for teenagers in the displacement camps of northern Uganda, it was a no-brainer. Of course I wanted to be involved. Voices in Harmony has had such a powerful impact on American teenagers that it was my personal hope that we could replicate that experience with the teens in northern Uganda.

"And we have. I've watched some of the video footage from the Voices program in Uganda. Watching these teenagers flourish and shine has been amazing. I was particularly moved by one of these teens, an orphan who had been abducted by the rebels and forced to be a child soldier. He had escaped and returned to the camps, but he still clearly struggled with the nightmare his life had been. While Voices is certainly not a cure-all, watching this teenager participate in the theater program, watching him gain confidence, I could see the hope bubble up in him, and it was both heartbreaking and inspiring.

"I think art can be used to enlighten, to be a bridge to understanding. So I was thrilled when Melissa asked me to perform a monologue based on interviews of women who have suffered tremendously because of the war. I was asked to do what I know how to do: share stories. And it has been an honor to travel around the country and try to give voice to these beautiful, heartfelt, and, ultimately, hopeful stories.

"There is so much injustice, pain, and suffering in the world. At times it feels overwhelming. But by making a small contribution to help even one person, it no longer feels overwhelming and I feel hopeful. My mother has always been an inspiration in this regard—throughout her life, she has given so much to so many people. She has worked often behind the scenes for everyone from Planned Parenthood to the Dayton Ballet to Muse Machine, an organization that educates teachers about the arts. I am thankful for all that I have in my life, and with that comes an obligation. I believe if you can make a difference, you should. I hope I have made some small difference for the teenagers Voices has worked with here in Los Angeles and in Uganda."

Janel Moloney: "I remember looking at pictures from Melissa's trip after she returned from Uganda. There was this one, a picture of her holding a small, sick child from northern Uganda. I found it so moving. There was my friend Melissa, the same friend that drove me to the hospital when I was sick, that hugged me when I was happy, that listened when I was sad—that same friend was a world away, holding this child in her arms. When I saw that picture, my eyes stung and I got a lump in my throat . . . and I couldn't look away.

"I hadn't known much about northern Uganda, but I knew it was ravaged by war and that the United States and most of rest of the world were doing nothing. I was guilty too. I did nothing. It was thousands of miles away. How could I do anything? But then I saw that photo of Melissa holding that child, a child who's known more brutality and loss in his young life than all of my friends and family are ever likely to know. And I realized that I don't have to save the whole country or stop the war, but I could do something, right? After all, there was Melissa, helping that child.

"Sometimes, we can't see beyond what's familiar to us. Beyond our immediate family and friends. But seeing that child in my friend's arms, I could feel the weight of his little body through her arms and hear his voice through her ears, and just like that, I knew him. He was my nephew, my neighbor, my child. And then, it was obvious. You know what to do. You reach out, and you do your best to help. So that's what I've tried to do in whatever little way I can."

Dulé Hill: "My grandparents left a legacy of helping those in need. They came from Jamaica, so this meant being there for family in good times and bad. For me, this goes beyond my immediate or blood family. We are all one big family. We are all brothers and sisters.

"I am grateful for this legacy and saddened that so many children in northern Uganda have lost their grandparents and parents to war. I have been blessed to be raised by a wonderful family, but I can't receive this blessing without trying to bless others. I can't just take in and never give out. I've got to keep it moving.

"Melissa asked me to participate in Voices of Uganda by performing a monologue about what was happening there. She wasn't dropping me off in the middle of northern Uganda and saying, 'Hey Dulé solve all the problems here!' She asked very little of me. But I think, if we all do a little, we can achieve great things.

"One of our *West Wing* writers, Josh Singer, wrote the monologue I perform. It is based on one of the boys in the Voices of Uganda theater program. Through the monologue, this boy drew me in. He's a kind, thoughtful boy, wise beyond his years, living in poverty, his father killed by rebel soldiers. Being an African American young man, I feel a kinship with him. Knowing that he is out there in the world, the least I can do is give voice to his story.

"There is an immovable mountain made of a billion little stones. I can't move the mountain, but I can lift a stone. If you join me, we can move twice as many stones. And if we get more people to help, one by one, we will move those billion little stones. Together we can move that immovable mountain."

Melissa Fitzgerald: "I am an actor and an activist. I like to call myself an 'actorvist.' The common thread? Act. To act is to do. It is not to sit around and wait for the spirit to move you to do something or to hope someone else does it. It is not to wait for the perfect time to do it. It is not to wait until you have enough money to do it. It is not to say you don't have enough to offer to do it. It is simply to do it. I think this is as true about life as it is about acting.

"So in 2006, after I learned about the brutal rebel war in northern Uganda from International Medical Corps (IMC), I knew I had to do something—to act. So a few weeks after we wrapped the final episode of the *West Wing*, I was on a plane to northern Uganda to volunteer with IMC.

"That summer, I was allowed to join a field team working with malnourished children and their mothers in camps for internally displaced persons. The mostly Ugandan field team welcomed me with open arms, especially a wonderful woman, let's call her Josephine. She was kind and patient despite what fate had dealt her. Her father died of malaria; her sister and brother-in-law were killed by the LRA, leaving three sons who Josephine now cares for. Her brother was abducted twice by the LRA. Both times they captured him for over a year before he was able to escape. The second time he escaped, Josephine told me he was so abused and malnourished when he got home that he almost died. He is unable to work or do anything, so in addition to caring for her sister's three sons, she has also cared for her brother.

"Josephine and I worked closely together every day for several weeks. We were the same age, and although the circumstances of our lives were completely different, the things we hoped for, the love we had for our friends and families, seemed much bigger, deeper, and more significant. I couldn't help feeling that the only difference between Josephine and me was that I had the good fortune to have been born in the United States to a family that was able to care for me, educate me, and support me, whereas Josephine was born in northern Uganda and her life was torn apart by war.

"I had done nothing to earn this; it was luck, the luck of birth. I won the lottery, and I didn't even have to buy a ticket. I have been given so much, and with that comes an obligation to share some of that with others.

"In 2007, I went back to northern Uganda with my friend and producing partner, Katy Fox, and a small group of actors, writers, and filmmakers. We went to work with fourteen teenagers living in a displaced-persons camp on a theater program and documentary film. We collaborated with the teens to turn their personal stories into dramatic plays about HIV/AIDS, peace building, and reconciliation. These plays gave the teens the opportunity to share their voices and stories with over a thousand of their friends and neighbors in their camp. We returned home with documentary film footage from the program, dramatic monologues based on interviews with war-affected northern Ugandans, and a strong commitment to help resolve the desperate situation facing its people.

"Recently, I received a letter from one of the young men who participated in Voices of Uganda, and in it he wrote, 'The USA is the signal for freedom and equality of all humanity. I can't imagine anything more noble than that.' Please join us in making sure he is right."

Conflict Minerals Supply Chain

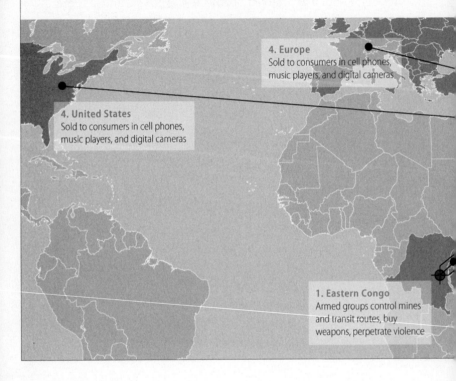

4. Europe
Sold to consumers in cell phones, music players, and digital cameras

4. United States
Sold to consumers in cell phones, music players, and digital cameras

1. Eastern Congo
Armed groups control mines and transit routes, buy weapons, perpetrate violence

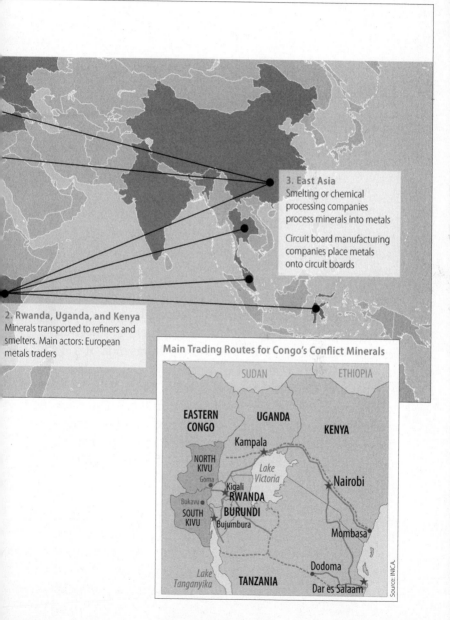

3. **East Asia**
Smelting or chemical processing companies process minerals into metals

Circuit board manufacturing companies place metals onto circuit boards

2. **Rwanda, Uganda, and Kenya**
Minerals transported to refiners and smelters. Main actors: European metals traders

Main Trading Routes for Congo's Conflict Minerals

SUDAN
ETHIOPIA
EASTERN CONGO
UGANDA
KENYA
Kampala
NORTH KIVU
Lake Victoria
Goma
Nairobi
Kigali
RWANDA
Bukavu
BURUNDI
SOUTH KIVU
Bujumbura
Mombasa
Lake Tanganyika
Dodoma
TANZANIA
Dar es Salaam

Source: INICA.

CHAPTER SEVEN

Saying Enough to
Rape as a War Weapon

JOHN: We as an "international community" have failed so far to address three of the great human rights challenges of our time. We've failed to check a genocide in process in Darfur. We've failed to stop a little insurgent group from Uganda that has been able to kidnap thousands of kids and force them to become child soldiers and sex slaves. And perhaps worst of all, we've failed to counter the highest rate of sexual violence in the world in the Congo. This is all the more amazing given all this goodwill out there. Do you get the feeling, as an informed observer, that it's more a lack of attention or more a lack of the right policies that has caused this?

DON: I think it's both, and I think that one feeds the other. They're difficult, complicated, convoluted problems. I think very few people at any level, whether they are government officials or normal everyday human beings, get involved in trying to address something as devastating as the issue of violence against women. For politicians, it helps if there is some kind of political payoff on the other side for them somehow. For others, it is the humanitarian or altruistic impulse that keeps them in these issues. And the really committed have to wonder what they are going to get out of this. If I go risk life and limb and commit all this time and energy, and even maybe contract malaria, and have to run away from a militia in a Jeep while people are shooting at me, . . . it's like, what, why would I do this? And it's sad, such as when the police used to harass me and my friends over nothing. I would complain, and some people would say, you know, the police are just human beings too, and they get frustrated and overworked. But I say you shouldn't pick up the badge at the police academy when you promise to serve and protect because when you put the uniform on, the badge on, you are saying, "I'm not just a person anymore. I'm the guy that comes in when people are just being people, and I need to be a little more than just people. I've sworn to protect and help and serve." So I don't give you that out. And I feel the same way with these government officials who have stood up to be de facto leaders on the ideals of their nations or communities. They are standing up and saying, "I am the focal point of what we should be doing, and what is right, and what is correct, and what is just." And yet there is an insufficient response to some of the greatest injustices in the world, like what is happening in the Congo.

What is the altruism that produces the commitment, the desire to say, "Okay, I'm going to get my hands messy. I'm going to get involved in a situation that I may not be able to fix in five minutes. That I am going to really commit and throw some resources into the mix, and I'm really going to get some of the brightest minds on this, and not just force something down a community's throat but also to try and get from them their brightest minds and resources, and work together to find a solution." I think if you look at that and say, "I don't have a lot of hope for success," then it becomes a fait accompli—and why even go into it? If I may walk out of this without a success, then all I have is all that work and frustration and it led to nothing. And everyone points to me and says, "That's what you did with our time, our resources? THAT?" So I think that it's regrettable, but it seems like leaders are incentivized to go after objectives for which they can get a quick solution.

JOHN: Yeah, that's the essence of politics. And that's why I think that even though we can draw cynical conclusions, we can also derive a great deal of hope from this because it means that doing the right thing politically can be incentivized somehow, that doing good in this space can actually be rewarded politically. And that's why, ultimately, if we can succeed in really creating a constituency of conscience, a genuine mini-movement of people, not just some grandiose aspiration, but if we can marshal just a few hundred people per congressional district all across the United States, then we can move mountains politically. At the end of the day, if a president or other elected officials believe that there will be some kind of a political reward, that they will be perceived to be Upstanders, that they'll be credited to have solved a problem and will be rewarded by a small but important and dedicated constituency in favor of that issue, then they're going to look at the best way of getting that done. And one of the best things about our political system is that when that kind of incentive exists, then the elected officials will bring the best minds together. There is a real commitment to try and fix things, to solve problems.

I think this juncture in history might be an embryonic Enough Moment for Africa in the sense that we have a growing political constituency, partially because of what Bono and his organization ONE, as well as (Product) RED, have achieved. We saw faith-based groups help fuel a dramatic increase during the Bush administration for aid to Africa, particularly in how they moved President Bush from opposition to AIDS funding to having one of the largest increases in foreign assistance outside of the Marshall Plan in the history of the United States focused on fighting AIDS in Africa. I mean, it was a politically driven thing that was incentivized. If you do good, there will be this constituency of folks that will reward you, and it's the right things to do, so let's find the policies and resources to do it.

DON: Then again, with HIV/AIDS, you are talking about something that everyone realizes can touch them. It can be in your family, and it can happen to you. I think that, again, people are more incentivized to move on to things that have a more direct impact on their lives. I think that people don't really have a spiritual, visceral, or sort of kinesthetic understanding of what some genocide 15,000 miles away might have to do with them, sitting on their couches. I think people understand it on an idealistic level, but I think that people are understandably consumed—and it's not their fault—with their everyday lives. "I have a mortgage that went into default." "I'm trying to pay my rent." "I can't afford my car payments." "I have terrible health care, and my mother is sick. What do I do?"

JOHN: Especially now, in how the American economy broke badly for so many folks out there.

DON: In so many ways. So the challenge is to get people to think beyond their own particular circumstances and to think in a much bigger way about something that is the right thing to do because if mass rape goes unchallenged in Congo, then how long does it take before you start seeing it spread and get closer to home? There are no barriers around it, no walls. Things of this nature do not stand still. I think that if people feel that an issue is too far away geographically, and if they don't have some kind of a visceral connection to it, and they don't know anyone from there, anyone who has been killed, then it is easier to turn away.

JOHN: That is exactly why we launched the Congo "conflict minerals" campaign, to highlight the connection between our consumer demand for cell phones and laptops and the mineral exports from Congo that are fueling the worst sexual violence in the entire world.

DON: So you were just down there in Congo with *60 Minutes*. I know you ran into some real trouble.

JOHN: Being held at gunpoint by thirty drunk and angry militia-men in the middle of the night on a deserted road in one of the most dangerous war zones in the world was not our plan when we started out that day. But we were digging into the links between the mines and the militias, so we didn't expect a walk in the park. We had visited a gold mine contested by some of the most vengeful armed groups on the planet earlier that day, and the militia that had lost the mine wasn't happy about the result. So when we limped by on the road on a slowly deflating tire, they saw their chance to strike. After hours of negotiations, guns poked into ribs, and death threats, and being taken to a remote militia barracks lit only by the full moon, we emerged relatively unscathed and a few hundred dollars poorer. Congo-lese civilians, however, are usually not so fortunate.

Rape as a War Weapon

Rape has long been used in wartime because of its ultimate power to demoralize the enemy. Literature and historical doc-uments from the Old Testament to the *Iliad*[26] suggest that rape has been viewed as a common spoil of war or even an impetus for going to battle. Research indicates that the opposite can be true as well—that wartime rape is not driven by sexual desire but rather is employed systematically by commanders as a weapon to control populations[27] and as a tool of retribution. More recent examples of the vicious practice indicate that rape is also used as a method for achieving the ultimate end goal of some of today's most sinister conflicts: the genetic obliteration of a group of people.

In recent decades the use of rape as a weapon of war has increased in scale, organization, and brutality around the world, according the UN Development Fund for Women, leading a former UN force commander to declare, "It has probably become more dangerous to be a woman than a soldier in armed conflict."[28]

Systematic rape was used to carry out ethnic cleansing and genocidal campaigns in the former Yugoslavia, Rwanda, Sierra Leone, Sri Lanka, and Darfur, prompting renewed attention to the use of rape as a weapon of war. Sexual violence in the former Yugoslavia set the stage for how modern rape is deliberately utilized as a weapon, often with the most heinous tactics. As the region descended into war, a group of senior Serbian officers adopted a military strategy proposed by psychological experts that concluded that Muslim communities "can be undermined only if we aim our action at the point where religious and social structure is most fragile. We refer to the women, especially adolescents, and to the children."[29] The judgment continued that raping women and girls would evoke panic among the Muslim populations, forcing them to flee, thus creating *ethnically cleansed* regions. A similar strategy was employed in Sierra Leone after the rebel Revolutionary United Front (RUF) was on the brink of losing a conventional civil war against the government. In 1993, the RUF transformed into a guerrilla insurgency using rape as a means of removing populations from the diamond mines that would come to finance the brutal war.[30]

Rape as a Tool of War in Congo

Over the past decade, waves of violence have continuously crashed over eastern Congo, the world's deadliest war since World War II, with nearly 6 million new graves dug as a result of the conflict. The human wreckage that washes ashore in Congolese camps for displaced people has few parallels globally in terms of pure human suffering. Eastern Congo is Africa's Ground Zero. Over a thousand people die every day there due to the legacy of war. Continuing attacks on villages, the highest rate of sexual violence in the world, child soldier recruitment, village attacks, looting, and forced labor all lead to cycles of displacement, frequent health epidemics, lack of health care, persistent malnutrition, and spiraling impoverishment. As in Darfur, it isn't violence itself that causes the majority of Congo's war-related fatalities. It is the disease and malnourishment that result from the displacement caused by the violence.

The stories that survivors from Congo tell defy comprehension. How does one even begin to fathom the experience of one teenage girl who was brutally gang raped when she was thirteen years old and now has a baby boy whom she cares for alone—because her parents were killed in a massacre in her village—even though the child reminds her every day of the horror she endured?[31] Or the fifty-three-year-old woman whose husband and children were killed in front of her eyes before members of a local militia took turns ramming guns into her vagina and raping her, who wakes up at night thinking of her family and wishing she too had died that night?[32]

Rape is often used as a tool of war in Congo, but its motivations vary. Systematic rape has evolved over the last dozen years of war in the Congo as a tool of vengeance, social control, and collective punishment against civilian populations deemed supportive of opposing armed groups. As one Congolese woman activist named Solange told us, "When they rape the women, they send a message to the men and the community that they have the power and the control. It is designed to humiliate and to spread HIV/AIDS. And if they capture an area that was under the control of a competing group, they rape and say they are punishing the women because they were spies."[33]

Congo analyst Jason Stearns further points out, "Rape is also used by commanders to indoctrinate and socialize new recruits and also occurs opportunistically [i.e., without orders] amongst soldiers who have developed a highly chauvinist and sexist military culture."

There's no way of knowing how many women in Congo have been raped. Societal taboos dissuade women from discussing their experiences and often lead to the rejection of rape survivors by their own husbands, family members, and villages. But by any account, we're talking about numbers in the hundreds of thousands of rape survivors, many of whom lack the basic support network that would enable them to treat the wounds they sustained during the rape, cope with resulting pregnancies, and overcome the accompanying emotional trauma.

Making Money by Any Means Necessary

We are blessed with all kinds of technical advances and creature comforts that we often take for granted. But the lives we have inherited or created are often based—unbeknownst to us—on a great deal of misery and suffering by others a half a world away. Nowhere is this truth more searing than in Congo. Once you burrow down to the cause of the suffering, suddenly there is a simple clarity that emerges, something we all understand: greed.

To understand why conflict in eastern Congo continues to boil with devastating consequences for civilian populations, we have to follow the money trail. Greed ensures that these conflicts remain violent and unsettled.

Mass rape in Congo is a direct result of the war, perpetrated by a number of armed groups over the years, including the Rwandan FDLR militias, the Congolese Army, the Rwandan army, and an assortment of Congolese militias and rebel groups. This surge in sexual violence began when the perpetrators of the genocide in Rwanda sought refuge over the border into Congo. While the conflict has numerous roots, the primary fuel for the violence is greed: over $180 million a year from trading in minerals, according to estimates by Enough Project researchers David Sullivan and Sasha Lezhnev. The various armed groups compete violently for control of the mines, mineral transport, taxation of the minerals, and smuggling of the minerals across the border. At times, bizarrely, some of the armed groups that compete on the battlefield will collude for the profits of war.

Deep underneath the picturesque landscape of Congo sleep the very minerals upon which modern circuitry relies: in particular, gold and the three T's: tin, tungsten, and tantalum (known as *coltan*). All of these minerals are conductive, meaning that they are the veins through which information on a circuit board flows. It is unlikely that you are reading this book in a room void of circuit boards: they are in your computer, your cell phone, your landline, your appliances, your televisions, and your MP3 devices. A good portion of these minerals are smuggled out of the country through mafia networks linked to the armed groups, which use the money to buy more arms and keep the war on a slow, agonizing burn.

The mines themselves are an ongoing human calamity: men and boys work endless hours in mine shafts that go sometimes thirty feet or more into the ground. Many of these laborers are forced by the armed groups to work in these mines and to pass pans of dirt from hand to hand out of the scorched earth. Then the soil is panned for trace elements that are eventually melted into tiny pieces and collected for sale. A worker normally makes $1 to $5 a day for his labor, which is not enough to feed, clothe, and house himself or a family.

The reason why we are focusing on the conflict minerals is that they provide the fuel for the war. Take the fuel away, and the original causes of the conflict—involving land, ethnic identity, and power—are much easier to resolve. In the current context of illegal mining, it serves the interest of all the armed groups, including the government army, to maintain an unstable, violent status quo because profits become privatized and the guys with the biggest guns enrich themselves. If that is taken away, the current logic of war will be replaced by a more normalized incentive for stability, investment, and properly compensated labor force. The way to get there is to cut off the fuel for the current illegal system.

The government army is one of the worst abusers of all the armed groups, given that the army possesses the biggest guns, and it is a major culprit committing rape in eastern Congo.[34] Through a series of peace deals, the army has absorbed thousands of fighters from numerous predatory militia factions, thus reducing further any discipline or respect for the rule of law within the ranks of the armed forces. In fact, the deputy commander of the army's military operation in 2009 was Jean-Bosco "The Terminator" Ntaganda, a former rebel commander and a wanted war criminal by the International Criminal Court for recruiting child soldiers, including using thirteen-year-old girls as his personal bodyguards. Many army officers are enriching themselves off corruption and the minerals trade.

The vampires are in charge in eastern Congo and up through the supply chain.[35] It is a Vampire's Ball, a feeding frenzy designed to suck the lifeblood out of the Congo for the enrichment of the leaders of armed groups and companies in Africa, Asia, Europe, and North America.

Vampires take many forms in Congo. They are the armed group leaders who control or tax the mines and who often use mass rape as a means of intimidating local populations, punishing civilians for perceived support of competing militias, and driving people away from areas they want to control. Vampires also include some of the middlemen based in neighboring countries or Europe, Asia, and the United States who arrange for the purchase and resale of Congo's resources to international business interests, run by people who are often accomplices. They need to acquire minerals like tin and gold to be able to satisfy the insatiable demand for these products in North America, Europe, and Asia. It leads them to ask no questions about how the minerals end up in their hands. Then there are consumers like us—completely unaware that our purchases of cell phones, computers, and other products are helping fuel a shockingly deadly war halfway around the world, not comprehending that our standard of living is in some ways based on the suffering of others.

The U.S. Response to the Congolese Crisis

Actions to address the conflict in eastern Congo have largely been reactive and incommensurate to the scale of the problem. The international community has spent billions on elections and peacekeeping, but despite the extensive documentation of the Congolese war economy by an ongoing UN group of experts, existing peacemaking efforts have failed to address the economic drivers of the conflict. There hasn't been a coherent approach to alter the incentive structures of the Congo's conflict mineral trade and its devastating impact in helping to keep the Congo's institutions weak and dysfunctional.

Efforts to date have focused either exclusively on sanctioning individual malfeasance or on piecemeal capacity building for institutions. Some of these initiatives have the potential to contribute to developing much-needed legitimate economic opportunities in eastern Congo, but they have thus far sorely lacked the coherence and diplomatic momentum necessary to alter the status quo.

In 1999, the United States and other UN Security Council members authorized the UN peacekeeping mission known by its French acronym MONUC (later renamed MONUSCO) to help implement a peace agreement. Since 2000, MONUSCO has had a mandate that enables it to use force if necessary to protect civilians, though it is erratically utilized. Despite being the largest and most expensive UN peacekeeping mission in the world and despite its having overseen the country's first national elections in forty years in 2006, violent conflict never actually ceased in the eastern part of the Congo. Congolese people most commonly cite rape as the war tactic that they feel is most unacceptable.[36] Yet despite MONUSCO's presence, sexual violence is still on the rise.[37] To truly end the use of rape as a weapon of war requires a shift from managing the conflict's symptoms to ending the war itself.

Sadly, MONUSCO's attempts to move in that direction have been a complete disaster. MONUSCO supported a blood-bath of a Congolese military operation in 2009 against the Rwandan FDLR militia with logistics and firepower, which resulted in nearly 1 million people being forced to flee their homes, at least 1,100 civilians killed, and over 7,000 girls and women raped.[38] The United Nations' own Group of Experts on Congo reported that the operation was a failure and actually resulted in the FDLR's regrouping and recruiting new fighters.[39] In one horrific case during the MONUSCO-supported operation in the village of Shalio, the Congolese army massacred at least ninety-six civilians, raped dozens of women, and cut off women's breasts.[40]

During its first year in office, the Obama administration

talked about Congo, but it took no game-changing initiative that activists hoped the new team would bring. Deeds have yet to match words. President Obama invoked Congo and rape as a weapon of war in his address to the Ghanaian parliament on his first trip to the continent in June 2009: "It is the ultimate mark of criminality and cowardice to condemn women to relentless and systematic rape."[41] He also referred to Congo in his acceptance speech for the Nobel Peace Prize. As with Sudan, activists want to see his rhetoric backed by more significant action to end these scourges about which he talks so eloquently.

In May 2009, the U.S. ambassador to the United Nations, Susan Rice, visited the Congo with a UN Security Council delegation, and while there, she visited a hospital that cares for victims of sexual violence. She later recalled a story of one victim who pulled her aside: "She asked me, with tears in her eyes, to do everything that I could do, and that we could do, to end this horrible systematic violence that she and so many others had experienced. And I gave her my word that I would."[42]

In August 2009, Secretary of State Hillary Clinton visited Goma, a provincial capital in eastern Congo. In a meeting with Congolese President Joseph Kabila, Secretary Clinton raised the issue of the use of rape as a weapon of war. Recalling the discussion, Secretary Clinton stated: "We believe there should be no impunity for the sexual and gender-based violence, and there must be arrests and punishment because that runs counter to peace." Secretary Clinton made some of the strongest remarks to date of any official worldwide when she spoke out about the fuel for the war—conflict minerals—and the need to prevent profits from the mineral trade from continuing to fuel the violence. Long-time women's rights advocate Melanne Verveer, in her newly created post as U.S. ambassador at large for global women's issues, led efforts following up on Secretary Clinton's pledges on the issue of sexual violence, and Under-Secretary of State Robert Hormats is leading the policy process on conflict minerals.

The U.S. government will need to do much more to back up its rhetoric. It all starts with meaningful action on conflict minerals. There is a huge role for the United States to play. The growing activist movement will help focus the administration's attention on the need to do more.

What the United States Could Do to End Rape as a War Strategy

The United States—pressed by the growing people's movement in support of women in the Congo—can decisively alter these dynamics by focusing attention on the international dimension of the trade in conflict minerals and by ensuring that peacemaking efforts address the long-neglected political economy of the conflict.

A comprehensive approach to ending mass atrocities must be put in place. The three P's—peace, protection, and punishment—are the essential ingredients, and they should be the rallying call for activists and policy makers. Ending the conflict is the most direct way to end the conscience-shocking sexual violence in Congo.

Peace: Although an internationally backed peace process led to the official end of a near decade long war and the Congolese elections in 2006, relations between Congo and its neighbors—particularly Rwanda—have until recently remained severely strained. Early 2009 saw a thawing in this frigid rapport when the two countries did some horse trading and agreed to work together to arrest or fight each other's enemies. What is needed now is deeper diplomatic engagement by the United States and the European Union aimed at the further improvement of the relationship between Rwanda, Congo, Uganda, and Burundi.

Shining daylight on the illicit mineral trade that crosses the borders between this quartet of countries will be a key component of this regional engagement, as Congo's conflict minerals are currently smuggled through Rwanda, Uganda, and Burundi. Creating a mechanism to certify that the minerals that go into our electronics products are conflict free will help lay the groundwork for peace efforts in Congo. A campaign like the one waged against blood diamonds is underway and is necessary to stop the trade in conflict minerals from the Congo.

Protection: The violence in Congo is deliberately targeted at civilians, and therefore it is vital that UN peacekeepers take the lead on providing civilian protection. Of course, this role should, by definition, fall to Congo's own army, but in light of the army's collusion in the conflict minerals trade, which requires instability and violence to continue enriching the armed groups, the UN mission should play the temporary lead role in protection efforts. Civilian protection must be one of the essential building blocks of a comprehensive peace in Congo. Efforts to establish a lasting peace will be consistently stymied as long as armed groups—including the Congolese army—target civilians.

At the same time, donors and governments with military expertise should work with the Congolese government to forge a major multilateral, diplomatically supported, decade-long commitment conditioned on human rights to help reform the Congolese army so that it evolves from being a predator on civilians to being a protector of civilians. One Congolese civil society leader told us, "If our government and army were stronger and more responsible, then neighbors and corporations couldn't take advantage of Congo. If we paid our soldiers and fought impunity, no neighboring country would invade or try to take our mineral resources."

Punishment: The Congolese justice system is sorely in need of a sweeping overhaul to reverse what is now an accountability-free zone. Donors should increase investment in the long-term reform of the Congolese justice system so that it prosecutes the warlords who use rape, village burning, and other attacks on civilians as tools of war. This should include both civilian and military justice.

The United States and European Union should make ending violence against women and girls a central part of their diplomatic engagement and aid conditionality with the governments in Congo and Rwanda, instead of confining the issue into a gender-programming category. The Congolese government should be held accountable by donors and diplomats for its army's abuses of women and girls, and Rwanda should be held accountable as well for its abuses of civilians—particularly women and girls—in the context of its incursions into Congo and its support for any future Congolese rebel groups.

In 2004 Congolese President Joseph Kabila referred the crisis in eastern Congo to the ICC. In September 2009, the first case that included the charge for wartime rape went to trial. Two alleged Congolese rebel commanders, Germain Katanga and Mathieu Ngudjolo Chui, have been charged with rape as a war crime and a crime against humanity. This case and other high-profile ICC prosecutions have the potential to send a powerful message to current or would-be perpetrators of rape, tackling head on the impunity that fuels rape in the Congo.

The International Criminal Court should further target its investigatory efforts on sexual violence in eastern Congo, focusing on the command structure within the various armed combatants who encourage rape as a weapon of war. The UN Security Council and countries with influence such as the United States should focus on countering the incentives for violence as the means of achieving wealth and power in the Congo through the application of sanctions, asset freezes, ICC prosecutions, targeted military operations, diplomatic isolation, focused arms embargo enforcement, and resource export control mechanisms. This should apply to the leadership of nonstate armed groups as well as key officials in the Congolese and neighboring governments that, for their own economic enrichment, continue to undermine peace and protection objectives in the mineral-rich east.

The People's Movement in Defense of Congo's Women and Girls

Over a century ago, thousands of people across the globe joined together in what became the twentieth century's first great international human rights movement. That movement focused on protesting the bloody reign of Belgium's King Leopold II over the Congo. In a murderous effort to exploit the vast natural resources of the country, half of the Congo's population was decimated by King Leopold's predatory rule—an estimated 10 million people. When the atrocities were revealed by a public investigation by British diplomats in 1903, it set off an activist movement from Britain to Belgium to the United States called the Congo Reform Association, led by former shipping clerk E. D. More. Two years later, the Belgian parliament forced Leopold to set up an independent commission to investigate the abuses, and in 1908 Leopold was stripped of his personal power over Congo.

A century ago, this public outcry helped curb the worst abuses of that period. This was before the Internet. Before television. Before the widespread use of telephones. A century later, the people of the Congo are hearing about the beginnings of a new popular movement to end the atrocities once and for all, atrocities that continue to be fueled by our demand for the Congo's natural resources. It is up to us.

Since women and girls have become the primary targets in the economic war of attrition between the Congolese armed groups, the Congo's transformation must begin with them.

We have the power to demand an end to the horrible crimes in the very place where the term "crimes against humanity" was invented a century ago. We have the power to decide when enough is really enough. That power is our voice.

There are two primary campaigns focused on ending the violence against women and girls in Congo, and they cooperate closely, aiming at different audiences with different modes of outreach.

The first campaign was conceived by Eve Ensler and her organization V-Day. In 2007, V-Day, in partnership with UNICEF, launched the global campaign Stop Raping Our Greatest Resource: Power to the Women and Girls of the Congo (www.vday.org). The campaign has been raising awareness about the level of sexual violence in Congo, and it is building the City of Joy in the eastern Congolese city of Bukavu. The City of Joy is a place where V-Day "will turn pain to power, healing and supporting survivors of violence to become the next leaders of the Congo." And personally, Eve Ensler has partnered with Dr. Denis Mukwege from Panzi Hospital and other Congolese activists to educate and activate thousands of people around the world about the atrocities being committed in eastern Congo.

The other campaign is RAISE Hope for Congo, and it is being coordinated by the Enough Project. RAISE Hope for Congo (www.raisehopeforcongo.org) is also raising awareness, but it is focusing its primary work on ending the scourge of Congo's conflict minerals trade. By calling for conflict-free phones and other electronic products, the hope is that consumer demand will influence corporate ethics and change the way minerals used in these products are obtained.

There needs to be action by both governments and corporations. The Enough Project and other nongovernmental organizations have worked with leading members of Congress to introduce legislation that requires companies to trace, audit, and declare whether conflict minerals are entering their supply chains. We are campaigning for Congress to stand up and pass a legal framework within which to audit minerals supply chains. Corporations need to take the lead in demonstrating that they will produce conflict-free products. So the RAISE Hope for Congo campaign is pressing companies to make verifiably conflict-free electronics by tracing, auditing, and certifying their chains. Since gold is the trickiest of the conflict minerals, we are, in addition, calling for jewelry companies and Central African governments to lead a regional certification process for gold that would help cut out conflict gold from the world market.

Call to Action

There is no silver bullet solution to Congo's conflict. The United States and other countries have largely avoided responsibility for addressing the economics that perpetuate the conflict. A new strategy must tackle the political economy of the conflict head on.[43] If the Congolese and regional governments, the international community, and the private sector can align their efforts on the common goal of a legal and peaceful mineral trade in eastern Congo, it would have a major impact in resolving the conflict now and preventing future outbreaks of violence.

There are many Congolese community leaders, churches, politicians, human rights activists, women's organizations, and others who are struggling to create a future Congo that is defined by peace and security. We can play an important role in supporting these Congolese heroes and institutions that will be the vanguard of change.

And let's not forget our direct complicity in the cause and our direct capacity to influence the solution. If we deal with the fuel for the violence, we have a good chance of ending the war. Consider the evidence:

- In Liberia, when the UN Security Council imposed sanctions on the illegal sale of timber out of Liberia, and it began moving on the illegal diamonds being smuggled out of Liberia. That economic pressure made it much easier to end the war there.
- In Sierra Leone, the long blood diamonds campaign began to make it more difficult for the RUF rebels to trade diamonds that were mined there for arms. That helped put a financial squeeze on the rebels. That helped contribute to the eventual defeat of the rebels and an end to the war.
- In Angola, a UN commission focused attention on the illicit trade in diamonds that was funding the rebels there. The commission's actions helped to divide and weaken the rebellion, which eventually catalyzed an end to the war after the main rebel leader was killed.

Literally millions of precious human lives are at stake in the Congo. When you log onto your laptops, remember they might not work as easily or cheaply without minerals from the Congo. When you answer your cell phone, remember the women of the Congo who have survived sexual attacks. We must tell our politicians that we cannot allow such crimes against humanity to continue. We need to tell these phone and computer companies that we demand conflict-free products, and that we'll reward the ones that give them to us with our business. Conflict-free products, in which Congo's conflict minerals no longer fuel violence there, is the game changer the women and girls of Congo need.

To take action, go to www.enoughmoment.org and find out how you can help advocate for conflict-free phones and rape-free computers.

CHAPTER EIGHT

Upstanders for Congo

As the violence continues and even intensifies, Congo's survivors themselves are saying "Enough Is Enough." For the Congolese people living in the midst of a war—in which they have lost family members, dealt with the trauma of having people they are close to raped or killed—it's an impressive feat to rise above the human-driven destruction and reach out to others around them in need. Some of these remarkable heroes are survivors of sexual violence themselves, and they have had their own version of an Enough Moment, when despite what they have endured, they decide they need to go back and help those left behind in the war's wreckage. These exceptional individuals are working miracles in Congo today, and with the help of citizens and celebrities who can amplify their stories and an international community that listens to their recommendations, we're convinced these unsung heroes will be the driving force behind a lasting peace in eastern Congo.

FRONTLINE UPSTANDERS:
Congolese Rape and Violence Survivors
Who Are Making a Difference

FRANCINE'S STORY

The Puppet Maker

Francine (not her real name) is a beautiful young lady, with a soft spoken voice and a shy smile, and she is from the Walungu territory in eastern Congo. When we first met her, the only indication that something might be wrong was her noticeable limp as she walked up the stairs. She was wearing a bright colored scarf, and a yellow band in her hair.

Francine began her story by saying, "Sometimes when I think of these things, it makes me sad in my heart." One night in 2005, Francine's husband went to bed while she stayed up to bathe her sick baby girl—the youngest of four—when she heard a knock on the door.

She told her husband to answer the door, saying, "Your friends are here to see you." He was tired so he told her to tell them to come back tomorrow. Without thinking, she opened the door to tell the friends to return the next day. Instead of familiar faces, there were numerous men outside. Francine screamed and tried to close the door, but she was holding the baby, and they easily forced the door open. Eight men entered with blinding flashlights, and they asked where her husband was. She claimed he was traveling, but they quickly found him under the bed. They lined them up against the wall and had them remove their clothes. Then they asked her husband why he married her, and he said because he loved her. They then asked Francine why she married him, and she also said because she loved him. The invaders told the two of them to look at each other, and they said this is the last time you will ever consider her your wife because she will now become our wife.

Francine's husband begged for mercy and asked what they could give as an offering or bribe. The men said, "Give us two picks, a radio, and clothes," and then they went through the house looting, ultimately demanding a further $100.

"We don't have $100, only $5," Francine told them. They told her it was not enough and asked her to lay down. She refused and her husband said he wouldn't abandon her even if she were raped. But one of the men forced her down and raped her.

The men were speaking Kinyarwanda, the language of Rwanda, and they took turns. Her husband protested, and they shot him, the blood spurting on her and the rapist. She cried out and they told her to be quiet. She kept crying so they shot her through both legs, multiple times.

At some point the attackers left and the children came out of hiding to get help from their neighbors, who brought Francine to a local hospital. She was later transported to Panzi Hospital in Bukavu. When she finally regained consciousness, she learned that one of her legs had to be amputated and that due to the trauma to her uterus, the doctor had to abort an early-term pregnancy of which she had been unaware. Her husband had not survived. Worse still, she didn't know where her children were. The nurse took the names, and word was put out on the radio. They found the children being protected by a Congolese priest.

When she finally left the hospital with her children, she didn't know where to go. Panzi Hospital staff gave her money to get an apartment. The family faced difficult circumstances, and they just had enough money for the house. She became a street beggar, and her children became street beggars. (She wept at this point but insisted she could go on.) It was very hard for her, and she wondered how her children would survive. She only had one leg, and she didn't know what would happen. She started begging on the corner. She couldn't believe that she would have to sit on the side of the road and ask people she didn't know for help. Eventually they were kicked out of their apartment and had no money.

They went to a bad neighborhood to try to see if there was anywhere they could live. A woman had mercy on her and let the family sleep on her living room floor at night. Francine's children were selling water. A staff person from the international organization Women for Women would regularly pass her on the road and give her small things. The staff person told her about Women for Women, and she made an appointment.

Francine enrolled, started training, and got sponsored with $20. She didn't know what to do with the money. "Should I rent an apartment, buy clothes, food?" In Panzi, she learned small things there, like how to make dolls and puppets. So she made eight puppets with the $20. A man she met took two of the puppets to his boss, and he bought them for $40. She rented a house, and she invested the rest of the money in more material, with which Francine made more puppets. She received training from Women for Women in culinary arts and how a woman can survive and transform her life, as well as in running a small business. She learned how to budget.

Francine now makes puppets and cooks pastries. Now she has money, and she is looking for a place to live that is more permanent. She makes forty puppets per month, and the pastries sell quickly. Her children are going to school. She goes around and sells the puppets.

When asked about her dreams for her family, Francine replied, "My hope is that God will provide assistance in helping me be strong and sending me people to buy my goods so I'll be able to send my four daughters to school and that they will be able to take care of me when I get old. And I also dream of my own house because they are always changing the rent."

When asked about her dream for her country, she said, "We need a good president. The government is not good; Congo hasn't changed. My dream is to find the right leader to bring change to Congo. President Obama should talk to President Kabila and ask him to change his mind so that killing and raping will end. I want the opportunity to meet Kabila and tell him my story if it can help. I'm a widow, and I don't have a leg, which is only because of war. We need peace, and to stop shooting and stop raping. Please talk to Kabila and to America, and tell them there are so many children living in the streets. Tell them we need peace."

HONORATA'S STORY

From Teacher to Human Food and Back

Honorata (her real name, which she insists on using because she wants her story told) looks at us with faraway eyes, and a hard smile. She has a very expressive face and wears a beautiful leopard-print dress. She is a fifty-seven-year-old woman from Shabunda province who is married with seven children.

Honorata was a teacher who was paid so little that she would go to the mines in Shabunda to sell salt on the weekends to make extra money. On one fateful day in 2001, she reached the mine at around 4 p.m. There was a Rwandan FDLR militia unit there looting and shooting. The soldiers abducted her and other women and took them into the forest and made them wander for hours. The soldiers wanted the women to be confused as to where they were so they wouldn't try to escape. The women were eventually taken to an FDLR camp in the forest. The FDLR soldiers in the camp said, "We are happy, the food has arrived."

The food they were referring to was the women.

The soldiers said they would kiss and hug, but for them they really meant that they were going to beat the women. They beat Honorata, knocking her bottom front teeth out. After this, four men spread her out, holding her arms and legs down while a fifth man raped her. When he was done, he took a gun and put material on the barrel, putting it in her vagina to "clean" it. This process was repeated by the other four soldiers as well. One of the soldiers noticed her wedding ring and cut it off, damaging her finger. He said, "Now you are not married, you are the wife of everyone, you are the food of everyone."

She was held captive from October 2001 until January 2003 when she escaped. During captivity, Honorata and the other women would go to a new location every three months to meet new FDLR soldiers. She was raped the same way in each of these locations. She could not count the total number.

She got so angry—she was a wife, a teacher, and now she was "food."

She felt that she could not do anything because they had guns and could do anything they wanted. Some FDLR groups were fighting each other over mines, which is why Honorata and the other women moved around so much. One day during heavy fighting, they decided to escape. There were women held captive for sexual slavery, but there were also men who were captured to cut firewood and perform other chores. They all fled, but villagers were afraid to help them because they feared reprisals from the FDLR.

A male nurse decided to protect them. He had a small residence in the forest with a farm. He hid the twenty escapees, mostly women. During the time Honorata spent in the forest, they learned the passwords that allowed people to go safely from one area to another. If they didn't know the passwords, they were killed. The nurse always had them go with people who knew the passwords. Sometimes they had to wait a week until they could move safely. They walked 350 kilometers in the forest to get to Bukavu, battling heat, rain, and wind. When Honorata reached Bukavu, her family refused to welcome her, rejecting her because she had had sex "with those who cannot be called human."

Fortunately, she met a sailor who had a house in Bukavu but was traveling. She and four other women were able to stay in the house, another in a long list of kindnesses from strangers that helped keep Honorata going. In order to survive, Honorata would serve as a porter for merchants. Two of the other four women were pregnant so she had to assist them. She continued on this way until June 2004. Rwandan soldiers came to the house and broke the door in. Two of the soldiers stayed outside and five entered the house. They asked the women where their husbands were. Though the women said they had no husbands, the soldiers accused them of being the wives of mai-mai militias. They told the women that they would have many husbands. They had to take their clothes off and lay down. They said there are no old women in Congo. All seven men raped all five women. Honorata didn't know how they had the stamina for that. She and the other women begged them not to rape the two small women who were pregnant, but they were ignored. As a result, one of the two ladies aborted her baby and the other had surgery after the rape. Because of the rape, her baby died.

Honorata spent two weeks bleeding after the rapes. A nun took her to a health center to be treated, and then she was transferred to Panzi Hospital in Bukavu. She had five infectious diseases and spent three months in treatment. After her treatment, Honorata was enrolled in a small crafts course. She was physically present, but was not really there. She was utterly traumatized.

When the owner of the house returned, he kicked them out saying they brought bad luck. But Honorata had taught a man back in Shabunda who had a brother in Bukavu who gave her a room. With her first money of sponsorship through the American nonprofit organization Women for Women, she started selling bananas and avocados. Her life began changing. Her son went to school as a result of the money she made, while her other children remained in Shabunda with their father.

Honorata began teaching other women in the program. She taught twenty-six topics for an entire year, two classes per month. She taught health, rights, education, and nutrition, and many others. Her son entered university and was studying agronomics and environmental science. She never returned to Shabunda, as she was too traumatized to cross the forest after what she had experienced. "They are still in the forest," she whispered, referring to the FDLR militia.

Honorata has never spoken to her husband since the first attack. If she went back, she is sure she would be rejected. Her husband never asked if she was alive. Now a telephone service has been connected to Shabunda, so she is going to try to talk to him. She doesn't think that he is remarried. She is very excited by the prospect of speaking with her children. Two of her children are now in Bukavu. When she is in Bukavu, Honorata lives with her children. Otherwise, she lives in Fizi territory, working as a teacher and counselor in the Women for Women office there. She believes she should help other survivors because they experienced the same problems as she did and she can use the training that changed her life to change others' lives. She wants their lives to change as hers did.

When asked what gives her hope, she replied, "The work I do gives me hope, and the exchange of ideas with women gives me hope." When asked about her dreams for Congo, she demanded, "Rape should end in Congo. It is a big disease that is devastating Congo, a calamity. I dream of peace and the development of Congo."

The following is a poem written by a Congolese poet in honor of Honorata, titled, "Honorata's Story: From Teacher to Human Food and Back."

HONORATA
BY OMEKONGO DIBINGA

5 million screams falling on deaf ears
Fatherless children fathered by foreign soldiers
Homes with no husbands
Husbands with no honor
Rape as a tool for much more than power
Pregnant women's legs spread
Aborted by their own community
Thus another rape committed
Another violation unforgiven
Another lifeless life lived by abandoned women
But on behalf of men worldwide
I ask you to stand with pride
Because your screams were never silent
We were never compliant in these acts so violent
Across oceans we cried for you when you ran out of tears
Incapable of international intervention to assuage your fears
Your stories became our poems
Your horrors inhabited our homes
But now you must hear that we are here for you
I implore you to forgive the world for having ignored you
As they raped you they said "today you will have husbands . . ."
But as we embrace you I say "today you will have brothers"
For all of my Congolese sisters, daughters, and mothers
Your perseverance is appreciated
Your persistence respected
Though human interest has depreciated
I'll ensure you're no longer neglected

Let the world be your pillow to comfort your despair
And let the love of this one man show you that men do care

IMMACULÉE BIRHAHEKA

Advocating for Rights in the War Zone

Immaculée Birhaheka is a pioneering voice for women's rights in the Congo. For many years, Immaculée has shown remarkable courage in her efforts to challenge authorities and expose human rights abuses, particularly wartime rape. She began advocating for women's rights two decades ago, a nascent concept at the time. In 1992 she founded the organization PAIF, which stands for "promotion and support of women's initiatives," in Goma, the provincial capital of North Kivu.

In the early 1990s, Immaculée became acutely aware that the perspective of women was completely absent in both the public square and in family matters. Girls were not being raised to dream big and excel. Instead, they were being raised to eventually return to the kitchen to care for the husband. Through PAIF, Immaculée organized women to start advocating for political space for women in the public sphere. They focused on educating women about the law and enabling them to confront political authorities and discuss issues. They also began sensitizing the authorities about international law and human rights.

It wasn't long before Immaculée started to see positive results from her work empowering women. After canvassing many women, Immaculée learned that the main problems women faced at the time had more to do with social rights than political rights. In particular, they complained of limited to nonexistent access to water in Goma, which meant that girls had to venture out to the lake to get water. So PAIF set out to educate and organize local women on the issue. They met with the governor, the companies that provided the utilities, as well as international NGOs, and eventually they succeeded in getting water pipes installed and local markets built for women.

Despite the increasingly insecure environment in which Immaculée was working, she continued to fight relentlessly for women. Following the 1994 genocide in Rwanda, Goma endured two violent armed invasions and became inundated with waves of displaced civilians who had been forced to flee their homes. It was around this time that Immaculée started to realize just how many women had been raped in the crossfire of the conflict. And then, through the course of her work, she met a family in which the grandmother, mother, and daughter had all been raped, independently, on three separate occasions. It was this family's story, which she still remembers to this day, that drove Immaculée to start focusing her efforts on rehabilitating rape survivors and publicly denouncing rape as a weapon of war.

Because of her outspokenness, Immaculée continues to receive death threats and has been arrested numerous times. Yet despite the risks, she is tireless in her efforts—she has held peace rallies, she has met with Congolese authorities, and she has consulted with international NGOs. She has even taken her cause to the African Union to denounce the epidemic of sexual violence. Believing that the Congolese authorities must act where the international court does not, Immaculée led a successful campaign to secure passage by the parliament of a stringent law on rape in 2006. This law not only specifically criminalized, for the first time, acts of sexual violence, such as sexual mutilation and slavery, and introduced stiff penalties for these crimes, it also demarcated the rights of the victim. Finally, the law began to recognize that rape is a crime and that survivors are not themselves criminals or condemnable.

More recently, PAIF built a safe house for women in Goma, which provides programs specifically for severely traumatized women, many of whom have been rejected by their families, to help them get medical and psychosocial support. At the center, women also learn how to build new livelihoods, whether through sewing, cooking, or selling other goods, and they receive microcredit to help them get started.

Despite the challenges and risks that she faces on a daily basis, Immaculée still has hope for her country and its women. It's this hope that drives her to keep pushing for peace and the empowerment of Congolese women. Even more importantly, the thousands of women who dream for a better future for themselves and their children, and whose lives she has touched, find hope in Immaculée.

CHOUCHOU NAMEGABE, JOURNALIST

"What If It Were Me?"

When war broke out in eastern Congo in 1996, fueled by the influx of fighters who had crossed into Congo after carrying out the Rwandan genocide, Chouchou Namegabe was a journalist-in-training at Radio Maendeleo, a popular local community radio station in South Kivu. As violence engulfed her hometown and horrific accounts of sexual violence—shared in hushed tones—became more and more frequent, Chouchou found that her microphone and skills as a fearless journalist gave her the unique ability to speak out for women silenced by the unspeakable crimes committed against them.

Chouchou earned a reputation as a journalist with expertise in women, health, and human rights, and she was offered a full-time reporting position at Radio Maendeleo in 2002. A year later, she founded the South Kivu Association of Women Journalists, known by its French acronym AFEM. The same conviction that had led her to radio broadcasting—that the airwaves are the most effective way to reach the masses in Congo—also provided a compelling reason for her to do outreach through the radio to women affected by sexual violence. Her words could reach them in their homes where they coped with the vivid memories and often physical scars of the violence they had endured.

Chouchou's broadcasts have spotlighted sexual violence in Congo and empowered women to share their stories, breaking the curtain of silence that cultural norms and the interests of the perpetrators have imposed over the gruesome practice.

To further spread the message to Congolese women that "you are not alone," AFEM now distributes handheld radios in rural areas so that women can tune in to the programs and catch news updates, connecting Congolese women to the world beyond their remote villages.

Chouchou attributes the shocking prevalence of sexual violence in Congo to the fight by rebel groups and the Congolese army to exploit Congo's mineral riches. "The rebels want to control the mines definitively," Chouchou explains. "Why do they fight on women's bodies? Because they know that women are the heart of the community. Through these women they send a message, a strong message: Leave!" A million people in eastern Congo are currently displaced from their homes, many of whom now live in barebones camps where they are dependent on international aid to meet their basic needs.

Beyond giving voice to survivors of sexual violence, AFEM works to cultivate an active network of women journalists in Congo with the goal of increasing women's representation in the media and mentoring female journalists who will then be able to draw attention to issues important to women through their reporting. AFEM pairs this work with outreach to men in the same communities, raising awareness about sexual violence and combating the societal belief that a woman who has been raped is somehow culpable. AFEM counters society's damaging viewpoint about sexual violence by encouraging men to take a firm stance against the abuse of women in their communities and to provide support to women in their families who fall victim to sexual violence. AFEM's outreach to men also focuses on challenging gender roles in Congo, emphasizing that empowering women does not destroy the household.

"I always say that change will come from women," Chouchou asserts. "When Congolese women have the power to make decisions in our country, we'll see the Congo change."

Certainly, powerful forces in Congo have an interest in silencing Chouchou and the women with whom she works. When we met with Chouchou in Congo in mid-2009, she reported that two journalists had recently been shot and that nearly all journalists who seek to expose the crime of sexual violence live with harassment and the fear that they might be abducted. Chouchou frequently receives threats from people who say they will come for her in the night, but she feels the work is too important for her to be deterred.

"What if it were me? That is a question I ask myself sometimes," Chouchou said. "What if it were me?"

JOSEPH

A Man Who Stands Up for Women

Joseph is the name this peace advocate requested as a pseudonym for his own protection. He is a very passionate and generous person, and he is a fierce advocate for peace. The seemingly unending cycle of violence in Congo has left a very personal mark on Joseph. His parents were shot and killed by soldiers during the war a decade ago. Then, three years ago, his two cousins were kidnapped as sex slaves in the forests near Walungu. When they finally escaped, he took them in to his own home in Bukavu. It was then that he saw firsthand the stigma attached to survivors of rape in Congo and the unparalleled challenges they face.

A few years ago, Joseph was working as a fixer and translator for an American journalist in Congo when he got the idea to start the Kivu Sewing Workshop. No stranger to the struggles faced by orphans and survivors of sexual violence, Joseph understands firsthand the obstacles faced by all marginalized people in society. So he decided to create a program that would give some sliver of hope to people who often slip through the cracks in eastern Congo.

When he got started, Joseph rented a small shack in the middle of town and invested in a few sewing machines, all on his own meager salary as an interpreter for a humanitarian aid organization. In a small, cramped space no bigger than the size of an average walk-in closet in the United States, Joseph, his wife, and a few other trainers have been teaching women how to sew and provide a support network for people who are on the fringe of Congolese society. Since founding the workshop, Joseph has expanded his organization, Actions for the Welfare of Women and Children in Kivu, to also provide small microcredit loans to women. The organization also identifies children who have dropped out of school for lack of funds or familial support, and help them reenroll in school. He specifically targets war orphans and disabled children to minimize their risk of facing discrimination. Despite the generosity of a few supporters, Joseph funds these programs mostly out of his own pocket.

Though these programs are small, they mean the world

to the people Joseph helps. One such person is Justine (also a pseudonym), a widow whose husband was murdered, leaving her to care for their seven children alone. Joseph brought Justine into the workshop and gave her a microloan of $200. With this money, she has been able to sell flour, beans, and palm oil. The money she has been earning is not sufficient, but without it she would have nothing. Joseph's program also helps Sara (another pseudonym), a teenage girl who was brutally gang-raped when she was only thirteen years old and has a baby boy as a result of the rape. Her parents were killed, leaving this new mother—who is still a child herself—without any support network. Sara's child reminded her of the pain and suffering she had endured. Joseph brought her to the workshop, and thanks to the support of the workshop and the generosity of Joseph, she has begun to come alive again and care for her child. She wants to be a teacher one day and hopes that her child will have an education and a better future.

Though he has seen ethnic rivalries tear apart his country and the broader region, Joseph fiercely believes that nationalities and ethnicities should be able to live peacefully, and for that he has paid a steep price. When two Rwandan women were brought to his attention because they needed help, he invited them to participate in the workshop. His generosity to these Rwandan women was not viewed favorably by many Congolese, who blame Rwanda for the violence that continues to plague eastern Congo. One evening in mid-2009, Joseph, his wife, and his six children were sitting in their living room when they heard their neighbors shouting that their house was on fire. They all escaped the house just before it burned to the ground, along with all their possessions and most of Joseph's savings. The subsequent investigation indicated that his house had been firebombed, in retaliation for the generosity he had shown to the Rwandan women.

Despite the challenges he faces, Joseph continues to

support his organization and the workshop, and he continues to dream of expanding his programs so that he can better support those who are most marginalized in society. He is working to build a better future for Congo, one person at a time. He has already helped so many, with so little himself.

CITIZEN UPSTANDERS:
Congo's Champions in the United States

The war in Congo, and the devastating effect it is having on women and girls in particular, only rarely makes the front pages of newspapers or the nightly news in the United States. But a growing and increasingly agitated community of activists throughout America has responded to this horrific reality in eastern Congo by getting engaged—by staying vigilant about the evolving situation on the ground and putting their talent and commitment to use to sound the alarm.

REVEREND DEBRA HEFFNER

"I Knew I Had to Do Something"

Reverend Heffner is the cofounder and executive director of the Religious Institute on Sexual Morality, Justice, and Healing, a nonprofit organization dedicated to advocating for sexual health, education, and justice in faith communities and society. It wasn't until 2008 when Reverend Heffner attended V-Day's tenth anniversary celebration in New Orleans that she decided to address the situation in Congo and fight to end rape as a weapon of war. A tireless advocate for sexual justice and reproductive rights, Reverend Heffner brought her mother and daughter along to learn more about V-Day, and they all walked out with so much more than she had expected.

After hearing the speech of Panzi Hospital's Dr. Denis Mukwege, during which he recounted stories of the violence and crimes against Congolese women, Reverend Heffner recalled, "I was so incredibly moved that I knew I had to do something." Even though it was her first time hearing about the crisis in Congo, Reverend Haffner took it upon herself to find a way to help. She contacted Eve Ensler and shared her desire to help gather religious voices around ending rape as a weapon of war.

She created the Congo Sabbath campaign, an initiative to call on faith communities to respond to the violence against women in the Congo and participate in a "Congo Sabbath" day. Congo Sabbath is a day when congregations might sponsor an educational program on the crisis, raise funds to provide medical services to Congolese women and girls, or include a prayer during worship for the Congolese people. Local communities are encouraged to host Congo teach-ins, film screenings, prayer groups, and anything else they can think of to show their support to help end rape as a weapon of war in the Congo.

Reverend Heffner developed an interfaith dialogue on sexual justice, reproductive rights, and protection of women from sexual violence in the Congo. She personally reached out to religious leaders and organizations and secured over fifty endorsements for the Congo Sabbath from national religious leaders of various denominations and religions. With these endorsements, her institute launched a viral campaign with letter writing samples, religious bulletin inserts, language for newspaper articles, and online resources for its members. She held meetings and workshops with local clergy to discuss the ways faith leaders could support the quest to end rape and sexual violence against Congolese women.

In less than a year, the Congo Sabbath reached 156

congregations across the United States and helped to raise $4,000 for the Panzi Hospital through small fundraisers throughout the country. As a result of the response to Congo Sabbath, the institute received a grant from the UN Foundation, and it will continue to focus on ending sexual violence in Congo.

LISA JACKSON

Breaking the Greatest Silence

Emmy Award–winning producer and director Lisa Jackson had been tracking the horrors unfolding in the Congo for many years, mostly through anecdotal accounts from friends working in the area for the United Nations. She decided to travel to eastern Congo in 2006 to see for herself if what she had been hearing—that Congo was the "rape capital of the world"—was actually true and, if so, how and why this could be happening.

Lisa went with a video camera hoping to find a rape survivor who would talk with her about her experiences. But what she found was not one survivor but hundreds of women who would often wait in lines for hours just to speak with someone who would listen to their stories with compassion and without judgment. She spoke with rape survivors in their eighties and young girls not yet in their teens. She interviewed activists, ministers, peacekeepers, physicians, and even the perpetrators themselves, traveling alone to homes, hospitals, churches, and to remote villages in the jungles of eastern Congo to meet rape survivors who have often been shamed and abandoned.

Lisa realized that no one was covering this story in any meaningful depth and that these women wanted and needed to have their voices heard. So she resolved to make a feature-length film, and she returned to Congo three more times to fill out the story. Jackson was gang-raped in 1976, and she shared her experience with the survivors she interviewed. These women in turn recounted their stories to Lisa with honesty and immediacy.

She traveled and filmed in Congo entirely alone, struggling with language barriers and other challenges. She also encountered incredible resistance from authority figures, and at one point she spent four hours in jail for having an allegedly forged filming permit. Not to mention the terror of interviewing armed rapists in the middle of the bush and the logistical hurdles of traveling through a war zone during a monsoon on some of the world's worst roads.

Lisa distinctly recalls two Enough Moments that she experienced while in Congo. On her first visit to Panzi Hospital, where many rape survivors are treated, she was stunned and sickened by not only the hundreds of women who were in beds recovering from the surgeries required to repair their mutilated genitals but also by the hundreds more who were waiting for beds to become available. She thought to herself, "Why isn't the world tearing its hair out at the horror of this?" She decided that the world had to know and to see.

Her second Enough Moment occurred when she interviewed soldiers in the Congolese army who nonchalantly—and without fear of reprisal—confessed to her camera that they had committed dozens of rapes. Here were men admitting to war crimes, and when the interviews were over, they just melted back into the bush, and none would ever be held accountable for what they had told her. It hit her like a ton of bricks: women in the Congo have no justice. None. Something had to change.

Little did Lisa know how much of an impact her commitment would have. Her resulting film *The Greatest Silence* inspired the U.S. ambassador to the United Nations to vigorously support UN Security Council Resolution 1820, which finally recognized rape during conflict as a crime of war and as a destabilizing force for families, societies, and nations. The UN passed Resolution 1820 unanimously in May 2008. The film aired on HBO, and it has been screened in the U.S. Senate, the U.K. House of Commons, and in the Congolese National Assembly, and it has also spurred hundreds of grassroots awareness and fundraising efforts by individuals and college campuses around the world.

LYNN NOTTAGE

"Because I Had To"

"I am a storyteller by trade. I remain committed to telling the stories of women of the African diaspora, particularly those stories that don't often find their way into the mainstream media. Sexual violence against the women of Congo is one of the great human rights crises in the world today, and I am using the tools that I have at my disposal to raise awareness and draw attention to the situation; those tools are my imagination and my storytelling skills. I feel the onus is on all of us who have the ability to reach audiences to try and bring an end to the scourge. I cannot bear to live in a world where such horrific things are happening to my African sisters without doing whatever I can to help them. Silence is complicity. I believe that. Our silence on this issue sends a message to the Congolese government that it can continue to rape the land and its people with impunity. Our silence on this issue means that every time we use our cell phones, we are inadvertently fueling a war that is being fought on the backs of women.

Why did I go to Africa to collect their stories? Because I had to."

When Lynn Nottage, the playwright of the 2009 Pulitzer Prize–winning play *Ruined*, first traveled to Central Africa to interview Congolese women seeking refuge in Uganda, she originally intended to write a modern version of Bertolt Brecht's famous pre–World War II play *Mother Courage*, about "a wily businesswoman who does whatever it takes to survive a seemingly endless war," as Nottage explains. But when she began hearing the testimonies of women who had survived rape in Congo, Nottage said she realized that she had the makings of a poignant story that deserved being told in its own right. "In listening to the narratives of the Congolese, I came to terms with the extent to which their bodies had become battlefields. I felt that my play had to deal with the reality in a bold and direct way. The subject matter was not easy, but rape had become part of the vocabulary of war in Congo, and thus became a central theme in my play."

Nottage credits her time working at Amnesty International in New York as a young adult with teaching her that shining a focused light on an injustice can actually lead to tangible change. While at Amnesty International, Nottage began writing a book with Filipina author and human rights activist Ninotchka Rosca with the goal of making the case that women's rights are human rights. Over the course of several years, they gathered testimonies and interviewed numerous women from around the world. Although the book was never completed, Nottage says that the intrepid, strong, and resilient women she encountered forever changed her. "I think that *Ruined* exists because of the journey that I took while at Amnesty International," she said. Nottage concluded: "The power of the theater is that it can peel back layers of emotion to reveal human truths that often get lost in clinical human rights reports and detached news stories. In many societies you'll find that theater is at the vanguard of change. The communal nature of the medium allows us to explore difficult and troubling subject matters that ultimately lead to some form of collective catharsis for the audience."

JACKIE PATTERSON AND STEPHANIE JOLLUCK

Social Entrepreneurship for Positive Change

When retailers and long-time friends Jackie Patterson and Stephanie Jolluck decided they wanted to get more involved in the causes they cared about, they focused on what they knew best: selling merchandise to raise awareness and funds. As entrepreneurs, they felt they could use their creativity, initiative, and passion for positive social change in raising awareness with a unique approach to activism.

A few years ago, Stephanie received the book *Not On Our Watch* as a Christmas gift from her sister. As a social entrepreneur working in Guatemala with indigenous populations, she was already involved as an activist in social causes, but reading *Not On Our Watch* opened an entirely new world of activism to her. In reading the book, she discovered the power of using her voice to create change through the media and the power of holding her elected representatives accountable. It was then that she told her friend Jackie that she had to read this book. Wanting to somehow incorporate advocacy into their current businesses, Jackie and Stephanie partnered with NGOs like the Enough Project and created t-shirts with a social message. Soon their activities evolved into spearheading local advocacy and fundraising efforts after learning more about the causes. They realized that to make the kind of sustainable impact they were seeking, they needed to engage people with various perspectives and talents to "start a dialogue" about genocide and crimes and against humanity, as well as other global social injustices.

Since getting started, Stephanie and Jackie have hosted many fundraising and awareness-raising events, and they've sold thousands of activist t-shirts and other merchandise. They hosted a "Yoga for Congo" workshop in honor of International Women's Day 2009 in Atlanta, during which students dedicated an afternoon to the women of the Congo. The participants learned how to "open their hearts, cultivate compassion, and to take their yoga off the mat and into the world." They've also invited experts to come speak at awareness-raising dinners in their hometowns, and they've started partnering with local universities to engage students in their efforts.

As Stephanie has pointed out, "Contributing in this way is not a job for us, and we aren't paid for this work. It's our passion." Jackie added, "We want to dedicate our free time and energy to creating positive social change in the world."

KIMBERLY PINKSON AND CHRISE DETOURNAY

Eco-Moms Embrace Congo

When thinking about the concept of "going green," most people wouldn't automatically think of human rights. But San Francisco natives Kimberly Pinkson and Chrise DeTournay do, and that's what drew these two eco-activists to the cause of protecting and empowering Congolese women.

Raised with a sense of global stewardship and interconnection, Kimberly attended a UN World Environment Day a few years ago and was inspired to build a global network of women working together to create a healthy and sustainable future. Thus was born the EcoMom Alliance, and she brought friend and fellow eco-activist Chrise on board as executive director. Chrise was automatically attracted to the concept, having spent the majority of her childhood summers on a Native American reservation in Arizona, witnessing huge financial disparities. Since then, Kimberly and Chrise have grown the EcoMom Alliance from just a concept to a worldwide movement with Eco-Mom Leaders in communities from Mumbai to Minneapolis.

Fortuitously, fellow environmentalist and friend Robin Wright invited them to a screening of the documentary film *The Greatest Silence: Rape in the Congo* in the winter of 2008. This powerful film hit them both at their core. As they listened to Robin and John Prendergast during the discussion following the film, Kimberly and Chrise both got this strong sense of being in the right place at the right time. The speakers appealed to the audience, suggesting that if anyone had a group that they convened, such as gatherings at homes where information was shared, those events would be the perfect place to raise awareness about the tragedy that had been unfolding for over ten years in the Congo. Kimberly and Chrise looked at each other, and it all clicked—this is what EcoMom does. With the launch of their new EcoMom Market, an online store that offers sustainable, fair-trade, and environmentally sensitive goods, they realized that they could also help women in Congo with skills training to produce saleable items for their members and beyond. The fit was uncanny, and they put the project, which they called Sowing Hope, into motion immediately.

The project moved quickly from an idea to a campaign, in just a few weeks. Following the film's screening, Kimberly and Chrise teamed up with Robin to begin raising awareness about their project and hosting fundraising events. With this newfound sense of purpose, donations have been made, house parties have been thrown, and women have been sponsored through Women for Women International. As Kimberly always says, "There is no force of nature more powerful than a network of women."

LISA SHANNON

A Simple Run

Lisa Shannon's plan was to be in Paris for her thirtieth birthday. Instead, she caught strep throat and had to cancel her trip. About a week before her birthday, she wound up sprawled on her couch watching the *Oprah Show,* where she learned about the conflict in Congo. In her report, journalist Lisa Ling called Congo "the worst place on earth . . . and the most ignored." Lisa was dumbfounded. The deadliest war since World War II had been raging for more than ten years. The same guys responsible for the Rwandan genocide were still out there killing people, and she had never even heard of it? So she did what was suggested on the show: she signed up to sponsor a "sister" through Women for Women International.

But what she had seen in Ling's report continued to haunt Lisa. On her birthday, she was in an airport and spotted *O, The Oprah Magazine.* They had run a companion story with personal accounts of Congolese women. One woman had written about an attack. She was being dragged away to the forest, the militia was about to rape or kill her, so she begged for her life. One of the militia responded, "Even if I kill you, what would it matter? You are not human. You are like an animal. Even if I killed you, you would not be missed."

Lisa just sat in the airport crying, thinking that in many ways the world agrees with that guy. She knew she had to figure out some way to send the opposite message: these people do matter. Lisa tried to rally her friends into throwing a fundraising party or doing a walk . . . anything. But none of them had heard of Congo, and they thought there surely must be a reason no one was talking about it to the extent that they were talking about Darfur. So Lisa decided she would have to do it alone. All she could think of was running. Since many people make fundraising runs, it would have to be bold enough to get the attention of her friends and family. So she set a goal: she would run a thirty-mile trail to raise thirty sponsorships for women in Congo through Women for Women International.

Lisa didn't consider herself to be a good runner, and she had never done any public speaking or fundraising before. But she figured the only qualification she needed was that she cared, and she decided to figure out the rest as she went along. On her first lone run, Lisa raised eighty sponsorships (about $28,000). We asked her, "Did you succeed because you are compelling and charismatic and just so darned good at all of this?" No, she replied. The success stemmed simply from that fact that she had created an opportunity for people to learn about what was happening in Congo, and she had given them a way to do something about it.

Word spread, and before long, Lisa was at the helm of her new organization: Run for Congo Women. In the second year of Run for Congo Women, people participated in the run by themselves or in groups in ten states and four countries. They received press coverage in *Runner's World*, *Fitness Magazine*, and *O, The Oprah Magazine*. And the runs have continued. Thousands have run, walked, baked, swum, hiked, and biked for Congo's women. Lisa's appearance on the *Oprah Show* in 2009 spread the word to millions of new people. Women for Women International's Congo program grew by 100 percent because of the *Oprah Show*, which doubled the number of women being helped. More than 6,000 Congolese women were enrolled in the program as a direct result of the show. Women for Women International's Congo program now serves more than 12,000 women per year. As a stand-alone project, Run for Congo Women has raised more than $600,000 and has sponsored more than 1,200 women in the Congo.

But to Lisa, there has been no greater sense of success than going to Congo and meeting face to face the women her organization has sponsored. She was shocked at how much they depend on personal connections with women around the world. They carry letters from their American "sisters" in pouches, hung around their necks, tucked under their shirts, like their most prized possessions. Just because someone cared and reached out to them as human beings. Of course they had endless stories of the atrocities they've lived through. But they also had endless success stories of the Women for Women program—stories of buying land, protecting their families, building businesses, and becoming community leaders. What Lisa heard in almost every women's group was, "I feel like a human being again."

FAMOUS UPSTANDERS:
Highlighting the Congo Through Celebrity Activism

BEN AFFLECK

Defying Stereotypes

"If I can lay claim to an Enough Moment, it would be in the course of reading a book about Sudan. I had been asked to participate in activism on Darfur, and, insecure about being a dilettante, I hastily began researching the issue. While ticking off the grim statistics concerning western Sudan, the book made brief, parenthetical mention that the number of deaths paled in comparison to the 5 million Congolese who had died since 1998 in eastern Congo. The conflict in Congo, sparked in part by the 1994 Rwandan genocide, has become a maze of militias, regional influences, and mining interests that have continued to catch the people of eastern Congo in their crossfire.

"I was shocked by the magnitude of the tragedy and ashamed that I'd never even heard of it (not to mention that at that time I had difficulty locating the Democratic Republic of Congo on a map).

"I declined the offer to participate in Darfur-related advocacy, gauging that Sudan had a surfeit of advocates dedicated to raising awareness about the war crimes going on there—certainly relative to eastern Congo. Instead, I decided to commit myself to do what I could to raise the visibility of the people and issues of Congo—where the paucity of news coverage, international attention, and general awareness was surely contributing in some measure to the crisis.

"I became acutely aware of the complexity of the situation in Congo—and even more so of how poorly I understood it. If the goal was to raise awareness, the danger was in raising the wrong kind, spreading misinformation or—at worst—fostering a cultural arrogance that has often characterized Western relations with Africa.

"So I set out first to learn. One of the advantages of celebrity is access, and I used it to meet or speak with every Congolese, Rwandese, Burundian, northern Ugandan, and southern Sudanese expert that I could find in an effort to understand the 'conflict matrix' in the region—the way the nations' histories are interwoven and continue to affect one another.

"I read every book that was recommended, particularly on Rwanda and Congo—whose histories and present are thoroughly interlocked.

"Then I traveled—four times over a year and a half to north and south Sudan, Kenya, Tanzania, Rwanda, northern and western Uganda, and Congo.

"On the ground I spoke with hundreds of people—refugees, the internally displaced, doctors, genocide survivors, child soldiers, rape survivors, artisanal miners, aid workers, politicians, Genocidaires, Mai Mai militia, warlords, UN soldiers, Congolese and Rwandese army spokesmen, presidents, dissidents, rebel leaders, think tank analysts, participants in genocide trials, mediators from the Goma and Juba peace talks, and countless others.

"What struck me most powerfully from this collection of experiences—though it ranged from the good and the great to the notorious—were the everyday people. The people I met who had taken it upon themselves to improve their lives and the lives of their neighbors. I suppose when I started traveling to Africa, I carried with me the subconscious image of people lying on their back, flies in their eyes, bodies like sticks tied together with wire, and hands raised waiting for rescue. Nothing could be further from the experiences I have had across the continent.

"Even during the worst of the fighting in eastern Congo, the regional capital city, Goma, was alive with people going about their lives, selling goods, and doing what they had to do to care for their families, make money, and make do. A volcano had nearly destroyed the whole city a few years before—leaving it covered in gray, hardened rock lava—and yet people simply chopped it up, made houses from it, and carved roads through it. I often had cause to reflect on how in the United States, it is common to hear uproarious, riotous complaining at the airport from people whose flights have been delayed or canceled, and yet in Goma there would be a family of five on a motorbike, carrying rocks to build a house with a war going on—and more often than not with a measure of serenity and grace, often even with a smile.

"However, more important than the spirit with which people dealt with their own adversity was how much they confounded the other aspect of the stereotype: no one I saw in eastern Congo was waiting for a handout. And the most effective help wasn't coming from the West. It was coming from their own communities.

"There are amazing community-based organizations in eastern Congo, funded and run by the Congolese people themselves. Whether it's running hospitals or clinics, counseling rape survivors, or negotiating the release of child soldiers and placing them in communities who will care for them, these people are spectacular. They run peace and reconciliation activities and art workshops, start radio stations hosted by women talking about rape and justice, provide job training and support farmers to grow better, more profitable crops . . . the list goes on. You can read more of their remarkable stories by visiting our Eastern Congo Initiative website at www.easterncongo.org.

"The dynamic nature of the way the Congolese are solving their own problems inspired me and changed the context through which I view aid. Western NGOs and governments can do great things, but I believe we would do well to support many of the existing community-based organizations already doing excellent work solving African problems with African solutions. If they can function with virtually no money, imagine what they could do with our support.

"So often the person has been considered wise who, when speaking about aid in Africa, has said, 'Give a man a fish and he will eat for a day, but teach a man to fish and he will eat forever.' I found, speaking humbly from my own experience, that this aphorism doesn't apply to what I have seen in eastern Congo. I never met an African who couldn't fish already. They just don't have any fish to catch. The people of eastern Congo (and in many countries across Africa) need a stocked pond—basic infrastructure to support small and regional business, stable microfinance and community banking, basic health care for families, and the ability for women and children to live without the constant fear of violence. The people of eastern Congo are no less determined or talented or hopeful than you or I. With fish in the water, the people of eastern Congo will have the resources to provide for themselves so that they can focus on peace and stability, growth and prosperity. This means investing in their vision, their solutions, and in their security."

KEN BAUMANN

With True Modernity Comes True Responsibility

> *This is the beginning of true modernity: to experience your own cultural background as ultimately contingent, irrelevant.*
>
> —SLAVOJ ZIZEK

"The quote above, from one of the most provocative thinkers alive, has stuck with me since the first time I read it. Maybe it resonated with me because of my upbringing; my family raised me without instilling any sort of preconceived notion of who I was supposed to be, what I was supposed to believe in, and what groups, if any, I was supposed to belong to. I was left to explore and make independent decisions with their loving support. So now, even though I would call myself American, and fill in 'Caucasian' in the census, I feel I belong more so to an unbound family. I feel that I belong to people. I feel that I belong to the world.

"And the day I learned about the war in the Congo, I was heartbroken. I had failed, was failing, at being a responsible person, as I was totally unaware of a horrendous crime against humanity being committed right now. The scale of atrocity seems unimaginable. I was shocked that I hadn't known about the conflict earlier. And I wanted to help.

"With the encouragement and participation of John Prendergast, Bonnie Abaunza, Patrick Welborn, and countless others, I organized an event in Los Angeles to benefit Raise Hope for Congo and to educate my friends and family about the conflict and what we can all do as individuals, as Americans, and as consumers to end the conflict. But that was only a small step. What is needed now is massive action, massive media pressure on the electronics companies that use minerals mined from the Congo, massive consumer demand for 'conflict-free' technology, and massive support for our brothers and sisters who are suffering, as well as support for those who champion their safety and freedom.

"I continue to help because with true modernity comes true responsibility."

SENATOR BARBARA BOXER (D-CALIFORNIA)

"Help Bring It to an End"

"I have learned the most about the horrible conflicts in Darfur, the Congo, and northern Uganda from the hundreds of individuals who have traveled to Capitol Hill to shed light on these atrocities—many who have experienced the violence firsthand and others, including many young people, who are determined to make sure these crises get the attention they deserve.

"Over the course of my life and career, I have been saddened and disheartened by the cruel treatment of women and children. What we see on television or read about in the news is just a small snapshot of the horrors that many endure each and every day across the world.

"That is why I am deeply honored to be the chair of the first-ever Senate subcommittee to focus specifically on global women's issues. In this role, I am determined to shine a spotlight on brutality against women and girls and help bring it to an end. In May 2009, I held the first hearing of my subcommittee to examine the use of violence against women as a tool of war in Sudan and the Democratic Republic of Congo. Shortly thereafter, Secretary of State Hillary Rodham Clinton announced a new series of initiatives for Congo.

"The voices of these women have been ignored for far too long. Historians and economists on the right and the left will tell you the same thing: no country will move ahead in today's global economy if half its people are left behind.

"With so many problems in the world, it is more important than ever for my constituents to keep up the drumbeat for action. I am proud that my constituents in California have been very engaged in human rights issues at a grassroots level. From holding massive advocacy events to organizing letter writing campaigns to lobbying elected officials in Washington, these advocates do an amazing job of promoting public awareness."

EMMANUELLE CHRIQUI

"My Personal Wake-up Call"

JOHN: What spoke to you about these human rights issues and inspired you to get involved?

EMMANUELLE: I heard you and your friend from Darfur, Omer Ismail, and your level of commitment and passion, and it literally moved me to tears. I think that's what I was searching for. My personal wake-up call. And to be in a space that was intimate enough to really feel and understand what everybody was saying and to be affected by it. That was really the trigger point for me. What was most inspiring of all was the acknowledgment that there was a lot to learn. It wasn't like from one day to the next, I suddenly would become this massive activist. I needed to learn about the issues. I knew that I was moved, but I needed to understand what was going on. I needed to learn how to speak about what's going on. I can't bite off more than I can chew. That was a tough one because initially when you get involved in activism, you feel as though you want to do more, that you're not doing enough.

I started to brainstorm and thought, "My creative side can really help in all of this." So it continues to be this ongoing learning process that ebbs and flows. I'm at the point where I see the impact that we've already made, just in regard to Congo because that's the issue I really stepped up behind. Stopping the violence against women and girls was something that really resonated with me. How fortunate am I to be a woman with so many freedoms?

JOHN: Where does your desire to become involved like this come from?

EMMANUELLE: I come from a great family where spirituality and awareness are really important. When I watched the film *The Greatest Silence*, I remember being amazed by the strength and courage of these women. And I remember that it was initially a massive driving force for me. Like a wake-up call. That feeling that even on a really bad day, I am one of the luckiest people on the planet. To watch the stories of the Congolese women, seeing how spiritual they are, their sense of community, and the support system that they create among themselves in their villages is mind-boggling to me. That's the story that needs to be told.

In the film, a woman told a story about the worst atrocities I've ever heard that can be done to a woman. She was one of the women who started the group of women speaking at that church, almost like a therapy session. Each and every woman spoke about forgiveness and the presence of God in her life. Forgiveness? Presence of God? These women had the worst things happen to them. It was just the biggest strength of character I have ever *ever* heard of. It makes everything else seem so trivial. We learn from these women.

JOHN: In terms of the Internet tools, what has the most potential for spreading the word?

EMMANUELLE: Getting people to sign and pass on the online pledges or letters or petitions is important. This is going to go to the president so let's gather as many names as we can. I know that when we did that a few months back, we got thousands and thousands of names. It was so easy: "Take this and put it on your e-mail list. Write a letter to your representative from your heart." That's what I did. I wrote a letter from my heart basically saying I rarely do this. I am moved to do this. If you would take two minutes to follow these directions, you will be making such a huge step helping humanity. It's so easy. It's already organized for us. We just need to take the few minutes out of our days to start.

SHERYL CROW

The Responsibility That Comes with Knowledge

JOHN: When did you first realize that these issues mattered to you enough that you decided to do something?

SHERYL: My Enough Moment occurred when I traveled to Bosnia with the first lady at that time, Hillary Clinton. She asked me if I would go and entertain the troops, and I have always been 100 percent behind entertaining our soldiers. So I educated myself as to what we were doing in Bosnia and what that war was about. When we went, I was heavily impacted by what I saw in that war-torn area and by our commitment to ending the Bosnian war. But when I came home, there was so much coverage about the genocide in Rwanda, and nothing was being done to stop it. I was ruminating and reflecting on my trip to Bosnia, but everything I kept seeing on TV was about Rwanda. I could not get it out of my head that the perpetrators demolished entire communities in Rwanda—a full-on genocide—and we didn't do anything but turn a blind eye. Yet we were spending all this money in Bosnia. And I didn't understand the difference. In both places, people were suffering, but we were responding only in one place. Here was a whole country torn apart by genocide. And we didn't do anything.

Much later on, I was at a birthday party for President Clinton, and he spoke about Rwanda, about how it was the one thing during his time as president from which he could not escape his guilt. Feeling as though he had had an opportunity to stand up, but instead the issue got swept under the rug. I feel that it's just such a dark spot on our history, the fact that we didn't step up and do something about the genocide in Rwanda. So watching what's happening in the Congo now, I feel we just can't let that happen again. Especially when we know what we know. And I think everyone has that Enough Moment, when you know what you know, and you have a choice to go forward and ignore what you know, or to do something about it. And there is a lot of responsibility with knowledge, but it's what creates the urgency to act.

JOHN: What brought you back into these issues a dozen years after that trip with Hillary Clinton?

SHERYL: I got the opportunity to hear a Congolese refugee speak at an event we did at the House of Blues in Los Angeles. Her name is Rose Mapendo, and she spoke about her experience there, which was devastating. And you talked that night about the electronic gadgets we use every day and their connection to the violence in Congo. And I couldn't feel good about carrying a gadget that is causing someone else's pain or devastation unless I was prepared to do something about it.

JOHN: Many people can hear about these things, or read this, and say, "Yeah, the world's a messed up place, so sorry to hear that," and then turn away. But other people say, "Oh, wow, really? Okay, I want to try and do something." What do you think—in your family, your character, your past—made you actually become an Upstander on this issue?

SHERYL: I think there is a huge commitment that goes along with trying to reconcile spirituality and consciousness and the everyday living experience. This is why I think there is a grander interest in issues among people from all walks of life. This is why we go buy t-shirts from The Gap that make us feel good about where our money is going. It is entering our consumer culture. And people are starting to take responsibility for the things they buy and the things they support. And maybe it's because of all of the images we see on TV, or maybe it's the amount of product saturation that we are hit over the head with. This phenomenon in the Congo is different because it's not something that has been a huge issue despite the numbers of dead. Living the kind of life I am living, I generally feel that I have a responsibility to people who do not have as much as I do. I have a family, I have food, I have transportation. I think that there is a movement across the board where we are feeling much more conscious about the fact that millions of people are suffering and we have a responsibility to respond.

JOHN: It's an incredible concept because it becomes more possible that these kinds of issues and activist activities and social awareness become more integrated into our daily existence than they ever were in our past.

SHERYL: Yes. Integration of our spirituality into our everyday living experience.

JOHN: So it is spirituality that plugs you into a larger ethical or moral universe?

SHERYL: It's compassion-based decision making. I read this great article by George Harrison. He felt that spirituality was really simple: that one must manifest peace within to manifest peace throughout. I think that once people start becoming conscious of goodness with compassion, then it becomes very difficult to not factor that in when making decisions. If you know wrong from right, then you know when you are making a wrong decision. And people are becoming much more conscious about what it means to live in spiritual alignment. It becomes not only motivating but also a part of the way you choose to live.

JOHN: I love that. People can take meaningful action within the context of their daily lives that impacts people halfway around the world. They can actually make a difference in opposing genocide or mass violence against women. And the actions you take will not be outside the framework of your daily life but rather, integrated thoroughly into it. If that idea can be sold or internalized en masse, we could build a much bigger movement of people who would advocate for compassion as a basic element of our foreign policy.

SHERYL: I think it is being sold. Look at the RED campaign, which is a great example of marketing—even consumerism—

that is actually doing good at the same time products are being sold. And I think people are much more aware of where they spend their money, and what effect their purchases can have. And that's why I keep thinking that something's got to happen on the conflict minerals front in the Congo. If I can buy a cell phone that is conflict free, then I am going to opt to do that over buying the one that is going to cause someone else distress. So it's just got to happen. We gotta make it happen.

JESSE DYLAN

Organizing for Change 101

"It is a fallacy to think you can dictate a top-down approach to community organization. People don't want to do what you want them to do. So you have to give people tools by which they can come up with their own ideas about how to do it. You need to elucidate a very clear problem, a very clearly articulated plan about how to solve that problem, an organizing principle to get people to participate with really specific goals, and then an action on a specific day. A specific goal.

"So you go to the people in your community, you get them on a list, and you ask, 'What are some ideas that we can do?' Give them the power to choose in the same way that the *Yes We Can* video was a small part of a bigger movement. Find new ways of arranging information. People can record themselves performing a song. That's an idea that can bring people together because people can take their piece of the song and put it in there. You need to have places for people to go because they want to be there. I don't think you need millions of people. You need a group of people who are really dedicated. They will find you if you have a place that's welcoming.

"You've got to ask people to participate initially, and then all the technologies and all the other stuff can be built on top of it. But it's got to start that way. In the Sudan 2 million people are being slowly starved to death, over a long period of time, in order to kill them a little bit at a time, and the most effective thing that was said about that was not throwing numbers at people. It was, 'If it were your family, what would you want to do about it?' That's a very powerful thing because you're creating empathy. You want to make the world smaller. How do you get people to care about Africa if they are really far away?

"So there are ways of doing it. Simple things. Like a book club with women in Michigan and women in Rwanda reading a book and talking about it. So it's not about aid—it's about making the world smaller. The website is the greatest democratizing tool ever invented. That's the power of smaller communities banding together. It's all about people who care most about this issue finding each other. If they can find each other, they can change the world. The question is how you make the tools that make it possible for them to do it. The answer is not to think of the answer but for you to give people the tools to come up with their own answers. It's how you get people to participate in these things. It's how you get individuals to decide that this is their issue and then work for it. Because there are so many things that need help. You need a clear, stripped-away message, and then you need to get people involved to help you tell that message. Give people a way to sign up and give them the way to come up with ideas for what they want to do.

"You have to organize an army of people who are really passionate about this issue. That requires superclarification for them and a network that has rules but allows personal expression. Get computer programmers and challenge them to actually build programs and applications. Create small prizes and Facebook and MySpace applications. That information can spread all over the world. A song can spread all over the world like that. Give prizes for creative ways to educate people about these issues and to activate them. Create five different strategies of innovation at the same time, and one of them may work. I think if you have materials that make it possible for people to understand what the issue is in the shortest number of sentences possible with the least amount of the extra stuff, that goes a long way.

"It's really good old-fashioned organizing. So it's short content; it's not an hour-long documentary. It's literally a one-minute film that says, 'This cell phone that you have in your hand came from this mine, and that money went to this person and this person hacked to death these other people. . . . Are you Okay with that?' How outrageous do you want to be? Because you follow the value chain right back up and you make that transparent. They *will* address it because it's a big fat stain. You can take those videos and just have a meeting with a phone company and say, 'Listen, I just want you to know, this is what I'm putting out. It's going to go to a million people on Friday. Are you cool with that?' And you will see change. Because corporations don't want those things out there; transparency is what they don't want. But it's not one thing; it's lots of little pieces of content that are just knocking at their door. And you have to make it entertaining enough that people will actually watch it and it doesn't feel like it's a wooden 'public service announcement.'

"Corporations have to still make money. You can't say to them, 'Listen, we're not going to buy this stuff.' What you are going to say is that you have to be a good corporate citizen and make sure that people are protected. You'd like them to have business ethics. You know corporations have to be beaten to have any ethics at all. You have to make it an anvil.

"When you have a strategy, simplicity is sophistication. The simpler the message is, the easier you make it for people to understand what it is and really make it clear. Boil it down. When you're going to tell people stuff (I make content all the time), if you try to say six things to somebody in a commercial, you're lucky if you can get one idea across clearly.

"Who's going to tell you that you can't do it? Is this the same person who's going to tell you that Ghandi would never make it in India? Social movement isn't about people telling you what's possible. It's about your seeing the vision of what you want to do."

MARISKA HARGITAY

"Your Healing Is Our Priority"

"Rape never played a significant role in my life before 1999. That's when I started playing a sex-crimes detective on *Law & Order: Special Victims Unit*, and the worst of what people do to each other became the vocabulary of my days. The show operates in the world of fiction, and I am fortunate that I can close my dressing room door at the end of those days and go home to comfort and safety. But the show's fictions are based in facts, and the facts are terrible.

"When I was preparing to shoot the appropriately titled episode 'Hell' in the spring of 2009, I encountered a category of facts far beyond terrible. Comparing suffering—'This experience is worse than that experience'—is complex territory. I can say, however, that the realities my research revealed were some of the worst I have ever encountered. The story revolved around an eleven-year old girl who had been held as a sexual slave by the Lord's Resistance Army, one of the militias that has brought terror and suffering to Central Africa.

"I read and watched films about the atrocities being perpetrated in Congo, Uganda, and Sudan. I learned of gang rapes, internal mutilations, amputations, and rape as an instrument of war. I learned of women who had been raped so violently and left so internally destroyed that they can no longer control their bowels. I learned of government, military, and social systems that not only fail to prosecute those committing these acts but fail to condemn them and, worse still, harbor, protect—*and sometimes include*—the perpetrators. I learned of hundreds of thousands of women imprisoned in a silence of fear and shame.

"Holocaust survivor Jean Améry titled his book about his experiences at Auschwitz, Buchenwald, and Bergen-Belsen *At the Mind's Limits.* Reading and seeing the stories of Central Africa's women, that is where I found myself: in a realm of facts that were beyond what my mind could comprehend.

"Améry describes how his most terrible wounds, more enduring than the physical ones, came from the experience of having been in the presence of people who were impervious to human suffering. That, he states, is what makes survivors lose 'trust in the world.' He concludes, 'Whoever has succumbed to torture can no longer feel at home in the world.'

"I remember my shock when, in my research for my role, I first encountered the U.S. rape statistics. In response, and because of survivors who began reaching out to me through my work on the show, I started the Joyful Heart Foundation.

"It was my moment of saying Enough to the shame, suffering, and isolation of rape survivors. Joyful Heart runs retreat and community programs to heal, educate, and empower survivors of sexual assault, domestic violence, and child abuse. We are also seeking to engage in a cultural conversation that will shed light into the darkness that surrounds these issues.

"What we envision is a community that seeks to reverse Jean Améry's conclusion. Such a world community says to the women of Congo, 'We are not impervious to your suffering. We will not add our indifference to what you have suffered already. We will give you our ears if you wish to speak of your anguish, we will lend you our voices if you cannot find yours, we will give you our most courageous and informed action to advocate on your behalf before those who have the ability to bring about an end to your plight. We will hold you within our hearts and our minds. Your healing is our priority.'

"In my work on behalf of rape survivors, I am sustained by the experience of seeing courageous souls find their way back to lives of hope, possibility, and joy. Or, in the words of Judith Herman in *Trauma and Recovery*, 'Something in herself that the victim believes to be irretrievably destroyed is reawakened.' A participant in one of our programs once said it was the first time her body hadn't felt like a crime scene. I have the same ambition for the women of Congo: their bodies are not only crime scenes but war zones. And they have suffered enough."

EMILE HIRSCH

Into the Congo

JOHN: What got you involved in Congo in the first place?

EMILE: I got a call from Oxfam America, and they asked me if I wanted to go to Congo. Immediately my pulse just went racing. I had worked on the film *Into the Wild*. And in the movie, Chris McCandless gave his life savings to Oxfam America before he went on his journey into Alaska. I was supposed to go with a couple other actors. And I was on my way to the airport when I got the call that everyone else had dropped out.

I knew almost nothing about Africa. At the airport, I met Liz from Oxfam, and I asked, "How safe is it?" and she said, "Well, there was this little incident last week in which these people were attacked at one of the refugee camps, and thirteen people were killed." This was when my pulse really started to go. The danger of what I was about to get into hadn't really sunk in until then.

The whole time I was on the plane, I was reading the packet over and over again, and just trying to learn. It is just such an incredibly complex situation in Congo—you have the 1994 Rwandan genocide, and all these people from the genocide going over and crossing the borders and the militias are staying there. And raping and looting. And then you have other militias trying to take these militias out, and they are raping and looting. And everyone is getting rich off the mines.

We went to the Synergie clinic, one of the main women's health clinics and rehabilitation centers in eastern Congo. I learned that over 7,000 rapes had been reported, but only sixty-three people had been convicted of the crime. How many people do you think served a day in jail? She said zero, and I would believe it. We went into a room with two little beds, totally dark, and there was this girl named Kamani. She had been there about a month, and I don't think I had ever seen someone as skinny as this girl, in person, in my whole life. And she told us she had been out in the fields one day with her two-year-old son, and these two soldiers came out of the bush and raped her at gunpoint, in front of her kid. Afterward, she had to take her kid and walk home. And there, her husband found out she had been raped, and he rejected her. And then she was basically an outcast, and she got really sick. This woman was right at death's door. I would be surprised if she weighed more than sixty or seventy pounds. But she was beginning to recover at the clinic.

The Synergie clinic gives these women the chance to hope. They band together, they build baskets, which is one of the activities that they do. I was walking through the compound, and I saw all of these women sitting, because most of them have had fistulae, where the tissue between the vagina and the rectum gets ripped when they are raped, and they can't really walk for a month. So most of them are sitting and weaving baskets. And they sell the baskets. And it's productive for them.

The women nursed Kamani back to health. I was just blown away that Kamani was able to recover. She hadn't stood up in a long time. She was so excited, with our presence and talking to her, that she actually stood up.

You can be cynical and tell yourself that you can't change the world, but at the end of the day, for most people, that's not reality. That's just your own cynicism or personal baggage. Because at the end of the day, you know, if you support these kinds of causes, you can really make a difference. And even if it's just affecting one person like Kamani, I think that is a really big deal, and really important. Especially from a place like the United States, where we are all so fortunate, it's not hard to help these people, it's really not. It doesn't take that much effort. So, that's just a little piece of when I was there.

JOHN: Where are you gravitating toward in terms of your efforts?

EMILE: People are using rape as a weapon of war, but the perpetrators are just the pawns. Who is really the master chess player? We need to find who is responsible. And the violence is really fueled by these mines. All of the money and wealth that is in the Congo, and the government and militias are making that money by keeping the country in a state of chaos.

JOHN: It's not just shady unknown corporations. It's the companies we all know.

EMILE: Yeah, like the ones that make our computers and cell phones.

JOHN: The minerals that come from the Congo are inside all the electronics products we use. That's just the way the market is structured. They all go in one big pot until the companies change it. And they won't change it till we demand that change.

EMILE: I think that we are obligated to try and help the Congo and all the people suffering because we are directly implicated in their suffering. And I think the first step really is raising awareness. Just letting people know what is even going on. And from there, people can think creatively and work through their own ways. But until they know what's really going on, they can't do anything. They're in the dark. It's sad to think that we live in a world where that happens. But we also live in a world where that doesn't have to happen if people act.

JOHN: It's not like we have to sell everything we have.

EMILE: Though we could! We could move to Congo! Drop everything!

JOHN: All right, Chris McCandless. Alternatively, you can accomplish a lot just sitting in your living room and writing to these companies, and writing to your senators, and to President Obama, and asking them, "What are you doing about this?"

EMILE: There is so much that we can do.

JOHN: Like that incredible organization Run for Congo Women. People all over the country sponsor runs and raise money for women like Kamani.

EMILE: Or a jog.

JOHN: Very reasonable. A jog for Congo's women.

EMILE: Or a power walk. Then you have an alliteration: a walk for women.

JOHN: What else, Mr. Innovator?

EMILE: Just regularly search Congo on Google news and learn about what's actually going on. This is something I've started doing since I got back. I think that when you start to learn more and more about the current situation and it's not like you're flipping through a history book, you'll see stuff that's happening that day or yesterday, and it will seem more real for you and you will get more invested in it.

IMAN

"Because I Am One"

JOHN: You have this extraordinary beginning that no one else could possibly compare with because of where you came from. As a refugee from your home country of Somalia, how did it feel? What was it like to be separated from your home and then from your culture, and then from everything that you knew?

IMAN: I could never forget how dehumanizing it feels to be helpless. To see my dad in that condition as a refugee literally broke my heart. He didn't know how he was going to be able to take care of us, so my brothers and I tried to pretend to be so strong, so that he didn't feel that we were so upset. There were six of us in one little hut. Stand in line for food, and you didn't get three meals a day. The humility and the loss of everything—my parents left with one picture of each of us. One picture. We left our families, we left our friends, we left our heritage, culture. I didn't go back to Somalia for twenty years, until the civil war started. And to be in a foreign country where, most of the time, people look at you as if you are looking for a handout, or you are lazy and you just want to take what the government gives you. They think you don't want to work or you don't want to do anything.

Most refugees don't ever want to leave their countries. Ever. They leave because of persecution, they leave because of fear for their lives. They don't live in a happy way. . . . Nobody willingly leaves his or her country and walks and lives in a hut and asks for a handout. Most refugees try as best as they can to become really productive members of the societies that take them in. So I've always tried to really make people understand what refugees are. Because I am one.

JOHN: Where did you sleep?

IMAN: On the floor.

JOHN: Was it in a building?

IMAN: No, no. It was homemade, like a hut.

JOHN: And how did you eat? Did you have some supplies with you?

IMAN: No, we didn't have any supplies; they were given in the refugee camp. But it was an eye opener to not know. And mind you, we had left only with the clothes on our backs because we had to cross the border by foot, so we couldn't take anything with us.

JOHN: After your own personal experience as a refugee, what struck you about the Congo that compelled you to do something, even with all your other charitable commitments?

IMAN: It goes back to how I feel about women and children. It's not lost on me that what sustains the continent of Africa really starts with women. And the fabric of that is being destroyed. The Congolese conflict, and what it's doing morally—the sexual violence, the rape of women and children—is the rape of a whole continent. When families and communities are destroyed in that way, there is a moral issue at stake. We need an Enough Moment for Congo. We all need to say, "Enough of this now." Whether we say it as an international community, or whether they say it in Congo, family by family. It's a front line.

JOHN: There are various elements to the response—such as the empowerment of women who are not just people to be saved but agents of their own destiny, and the transformation of the Congolese culture and society.

IMAN: Exactly. And taking care of themselves. Congolese women know what they need. It's not for us on the outside to decide what they need. We can structure for them what is available, so they can start again their communities. Obviously, one thing is to stop the violence against women and children. But also, it is building communities, infrastructure, small businesses for themselves, which has been shown to be life transforming, especially for women.

JOHN: I think so many people don't understand—no, it's not that they don't understand. It's that they don't know this because it's presented that these women are victims, that they're beaten down, that they have to be saved. But the truth is that every woman I've met in Congo is fighting for her family, fighting for her community. And as you're saying, it's just a small little support that we can provide that can help her blossom.

IMAN: Exactly. And most of the time it is asking them, exactly, what do they need. Because what's needed in Congo definitely is not the same thing as what is needed in South Africa or Kenya.

JOHN: Another aspect of the situation, beyond empowerment, is protection. I think we would agree that protecting women and children ought to be the number 1 priority of the United Nations in Congo.

IMAN: To rape women and children is actually the destruction of a community. It's how to morally and emotionally destroy people. And that's what one group uses against another. So protection is entirely warranted, as much as it would be in a situation of ethnic cleansing.

JOHN: It turns out that inadvertently our thirst for consumption of electronics products like cell phones and laptops is fueling the war in Congo.

IMAN: This is the kind of issue that needs a people's movement. I was part of something close to this. We all have heard about blood diamonds. I was asked to be under a contract as the face of De Beers. I went to South Africa, and I talked to Mandela to find out exactly what I would be representing. How come I didn't know anything about these blood diamonds? But I knew I would have a clear conscience if I wasn't part of it—so I terminated my contract. So what I'm saying is that it's very easy for everybody, if they really want to utilize their consciences, to just ask. Make that call, and ask that we want our phones to not be part of the conflict in Congo. It takes a conscience. And singularly, one person's conscience. I couldn't live with myself. Can you? Pick up the phone and tell companies you want a conflict-free phone.

JOHN: One of the amazing things that I've found is how meaningful it is to refugees when they learn that there are people back in the United States who are working to try to help them go home. That is a direct lifeline to people surviving in these situations.

IMAN: I cannot stress enough the importance of writing letters to our representatives. Whether one is a celebrity or not, it doesn't matter because of the direct impact you can make on somebody who is stuck, somewhere far away, to help them and give them hope that either they can go back home or start anew where they are. It is beyond amazing. Because it has happened for me. I saw it myself and continue to see it.

ANGELINA JOLIE

Finding Hope

In the fall of 2003, Angelina and John traveled together to Congo. After they returned, the U.S. Holocaust Memorial Museum produced a web-based photo exhibit of their trip. Below are excerpts from Angelina's journal of their trip that remain relevant today.

Bunia Internally Displaced Persons Camp
I am introduced to a woman who is starting a committee in a camp. She thanks me for coming so far away to see them. In that statement, I think how much a simple

gesture, just visiting, means. No one here knows what I do for a living, my name, or if I have money. They just know that I came from a more fortunate country. That I'm a foreigner who cares how they are and wants to hear what they have to say.

Bunyakiri, a town in South Kivu

We enter a room of all women. It is dark inside the cement room. Many hold babies, and some are breastfeeding. Most of them are in their early twenties. We ask them to speak freely about what they have been through during the war. No one speaks. No one moves. We say, "You can tell us your story in general, if you wish. It does not have to be very personal."

[They say,] "We are the women of Bunyakiri. We have suffered a lot. We thank you for hearing us. Our homes were looted and burned. We slept in the forest. Many women died, and many were killed. It feels as if the war was against us. The rape was the most shocking. They made us cook, then stole our food and brutally raped us. We had to plant in areas, and we worked hard; they would steal all our crops. If we got sick, we had no way to get to the hospital. We had no funds. We are displaced. We have nothing. As a result of the violence, many of us have STDs. Our families after the rape have banished us, and we cannot afford to send our children to school."

What is interesting here is that the Congolese people on the ground are working toward peace themselves. The local people and the local NGOs, with no outside help, are brokering their own peace deals in their areas. It's amazing, and they deserve support.

As we fly out of the Congo, I think of the hundreds of thousands living in the camps on the border dreaming of one day being able to live at home in Congo. I believe I am right in saying that peace here would not just stop the killing but begin to give hope to all of Africa.

JOEL MADDEN AND NICOLE RICHIE

Integrating Activism into Family Life

JOHN: What was it that made you two decide to stand up for the women of the Congo?

NICOLE: First of all, I just want to say that it is very easy nowadays to kinda turn it all off. So I don't think it is necessarily ignorance that is the problem here. I just think there is a lot going on, lots of competition for our attention. Between computers, television, and cell phones, it is so easy to just become distracted. But if you just take ten or twenty minutes to listen to someone's story, like the stories of some of the women from Congo, I think it is absolutely impossible to turn away.

The first time that I became aware of these issues was when I actually met a refugee camp survivor. I was at a small gathering of about forty people at someone's house, and I listened to a Congolese refugee named Rose Mapendo speak. Rose lives in Arizona now. She spoke of women being raped. It was overwhelming. Children being killed in front of the mothers. And when I looked into her eyes, she was a complete hero to me. And she is right here among us. And she is alive, and she is strong. And she wasn't asking for pity. She was just telling us about the reality she lived through in Congo. And it's unacceptable that this situation exists. Completely unacceptable. She wasn't saying, "Feel bad for me." She was saying, "This is my reality. This is what I go through.

This is what my friends go through." I just can't imagine what that's like.

JOHN: Anyone who heard that would be horrified, but what actually led you to do something about it? What chord did it strike?

NICOLE: It is so easy to complain about the hardships of your own life. I can't imagine what it's like for Rose. Rose talked about the things that had been done to her body, without her consent, and she just had to live with it, her womanhood being just stripped from her. It was completely taken away. And I wasn't okay with just letting that happen. I wasn't okay with hearing about the young girls who are getting raped as well. I still can't even really think about. I still have to separate myself to even be able to get involved with something like this because I cannot imagine it fully.

JOHN: So how did your caring about these issues actually lead you to doing something about them?

JOEL: Actually, meeting you. Most people care when they hear about these things, but they don't act on their concerns. But if they are presented with the opportunity to do something about these things, they will. I think many people don't feel self-empowered. But if you present them with the opportunity, or the moment, to say something or do something, they will.

NICOLE: Most people just need someone to walk them through it—how to get involved, what they can do.

JOEL: I also think that people need to be held accountable in some way to connect how they feel to how they then act in response. And that's what people like you do, and what I have started to do. We help hold people accountable. We are obligated, and we are responsible for our children, our brothers and sisters, and mothers and daughters. When you become a parent, you start to realize not only the value of human life but how precious all people are. It's like the old saying, "There but for the grace of God go I." We are here in our shoes, and not theirs. There is no explanation for why we got dropped here and they got dropped there, why we were born here and they were born there. So we aren't talking about aliens or people without real feelings. We are talking about real human beings, with the same needs, the same feelings, the same happiness, and the same sadness as us. And I think the important thing for me is showing the human side to it all. This is your mother, this is your daughter. These are your children. One problem is that when people hear the numbers of dead, of displaced, they turn away. I hate the way it's being presented to people on TV, because . . .

NICOLE: It seems too big.

JOEL: Millions of faceless beings. We are talking about the deadliest war since World War II, and it's almost invisible because there are not enough faces to it. What made me want to make a difference there, or just try to raise consciousness, or decide to go there? You know, I don't think I would have ever ended up in Africa if I weren't a parent. When you shake people's hands, and you hang out with them, and you live with them, you can feel what great people they are, and how they are living in these difficult situations. And I wanted to bring that back with me. And when it became that to me, it became something I will not ever let go of until it's solved. Until that war is over.

JOHN: When did you first hear about these issues?

JOEL: I met a group of guys from the Invisible Children organization a couple years ago. It was the first time I ever even looked into what was going on in Africa. And that was what sort of sparked my interest. Someone said, "Hey, some friends of mine are doing an event for children in Africa, and you should come." And I went and checked it out, by chance.

I met this little boy who had been a child soldier. They brought him over to LA, to the event. And the kid was like twelve years old. And he was one of the children that had been a child soldier and had escaped, and he was hiding out. He was one of these kids that the group was supporting and fighting for. I love it when I see people who have made it their life's mission to make these kids' lives better. So I said, "Hey, why don't you bring the kid over to my house this week," and my brother Benji and I got to hang out with him. And I fell in love with him. He was such a sweet kid. And I had no clue about the causes. I was utterly clueless. There were all of these different steps along the way, and we met you, and it's just been this journey that's been really cool.

What Nicole and I have tried to do together is to integrate these issues into our lives. It's very important that you pace yourself. And you have to, just like anything else you do in your life. It's just gotta become a part of your lifestyle, that you commit this amount of time and energy to whatever you want to change. Like the work I do with UNICEF and the work I do with Enough—I try to find a way to make it all work together, make it all a part of my life. So that you stay the course. So that hopefully in ten years, we can turn around and say, "It's cool that I got to see that change happen firsthand, and I was a part of it." But it's important for people to understand that we aren't going to solve it overnight. It's more about joining the momentum of something, and spreading the word, raising consciousness.

It's important for us as a family, not only for Nicole and me but for and with our kids, to integrate these issues into our family life. So it becomes something that is normal. If you can raise your kids to be the opposite of ignorant, the opposite of unaware, and the opposite of unconscious, then they are going to be, hopefully, part of the solution, as opposed to part of the problem. For us, it's been more about a lifestyle, integrating it into our family and lives. And now it is very normal. Our kids are going to know what's going on, and they are going to know how to respond. It's already normal for them to hear us talking to other people about it. We have the opportunity to change what we are putting out there to the world, and consciousness is everything.

I'm not an intelligent or elegant speaker at all.

JOHN: Are you kidding? You should write a book, not me.

NICOLE: Our kids are also fortunate enough to be born and raised during a time when these issues and opportunities are so out there in the open. So they are not going to have the same experience as our generation, where we have been so shocked and taken aback by some of the world's problems. They will have the access to address these issues and reach out to people thousands of miles away. That is going to be part of their life. They are not going to be shocked the way our whole generation was.

JOEL: When I was in Africa, I was with these volunteer doctors, people with PhDs, giving their entire lives to live in dirt-poor conditions and to do something. That's where my heart has led me, because my faith holds me to do the right thing as well. This work is an expression of my faith because it's the only place I feel like my actions and intentions are received purely.

CONGRESSMAN JIM MCDERMOTT
(D-WASHINGTON)

"One Has to Be a Stone Not to Be Moved"

"Tragically, I've known about rape as a weapon of war since my days in the State Department in the 1980s. After seeing it firsthand, how could you not be moved to action? I visited a hospital in Goma and saw the wounded. I walked through the refugee camps in the Chadian desert and had letters with pleas for help placed into my hands by innocent people who had lost everything. And I met towering heroic figures—men, women, and children—who were unwilling to yield to the finality of death even as they clung to life. One has to be a stone not to be moved by this. There's a world war going on in Central Africa that most people are unaware of because there is no television coverage by and large and most people get their information from television. These are far-off places and not often covered on television.

"The group in Seattle that reached out to me also reached out across the community to close the information gap. So my advice is straightforward: Get people together, and show one or more of the many excellent documentaries that have been made. One picture is worth a thousand words, and one person can make a difference."

ROBIN WRIGHT

"We All Deserve the Same. Justice. And Life."

JOHN: Why did you say, "I'm going to do something about this"? Why Congo?

ROBIN: Well, it was meeting you. You brought to my attention the gravity of this issue. The violence in the Congo involves a direct attack on women, this weapon of war the armed groups are using. It's that unacceptable Enough Moment in us, in humanity. We as individuals have had enough of feeling that unacceptable moment. And that's what triggered me to be proactive. I feel like I can help get the word out to the public. Society needs to understand where this is coming from. Where are we positioning ourselves as individuals so that we can help?

JOHN: In your own background, history, view of the world, how did you gravitate to this?

ROBIN: Ever since I was four or five, I had this dream that I would work in a refugee camp. I would be a doctor, saving people's lives. Bringing people to safety and sustainable lives. A few years ago I read a script by Erin Dignam. And in that script, you have two people that have the same core beliefs, which are that unacceptable suffering must end, and we must help it end. I felt aligned with one of the characters who wants to get at the root causes of the war in which she is a refugee camp doctor.

JOHN: So you decide to go to Senegal to research the role. What did you take away from your trip to Africa?

ROBIN: It is important that we are able to look at another and say, "We are all one." We all deserve the same. Justice. And life.

Last Word on Upstanders

There are many other Famous Upstanders working on the issues of Sudan, Congo, and northern Uganda who are not reflected in this book. Andie MacDowell does film screenings all over her native North Carolina. George Clooney is an indefatigable advocate for Darfur. Ashley Judd has traveled to Congo and stays closely engaged in developments there. Matt Damon and Brad Pitt work with Don and George on the board of Not On Our Watch in support of Darfur. Julianne Moore, Julianna Margulies, Sandra Oh, Mary-Louise Parker, Saffron Burrows, Jeffrey Dean Morgan, and Brooke Smith have all done videos on Congo. Rosario Dawson and Kerry Washington have worked closely with Eve Ensler on Congo. Forrest Whitaker has visited Uganda and supported schools there. Mira Sorvino has spoken at numerous events and lobbied Congress on Darfur. Sonya Walger and Wim Wenders were judges on a major YouTube contest on Congo. Damien Rice, Mos Def, Norah Jones, and other musicians have contributed songs for a CD in support of the women and girls of the Congo (see www.raisehopeforcongo.org). If top-rated television shows could be Upstanders, *60 Minutes* (thanks to Scott Pelley and his all-star producers) and *Law & Order: Special Victims Unit* (thanks to its creator Neal Baer) would qualify for their ongoing programming focused on these issues.

If you want to learn more about the work of many of these Upstanders, you can visit www.enoughproject.org and go to the celebrity activism section.

CHAPTER NINE

The Menu for Change

Renewing Our Enough Pledge and
Helping You Make Yours

JOHN: This concept of an Enough Moment at the individual level isn't just a one-off deal or a one-time affair, clearly. We all have different challenges or issues that pop up constantly that allow us to recommit and reenter the fray. There are multiple moments when the opportunity arises to be an Upstander again, and we have that choice, over and over again. Look at the last few years of your life: you were in *Hotel Rwanda*, you took a trip to Africa, and then another one, you did all kinds of public events, you helped start the aid organization Not On Our Watch, you helped found Ante Up for Africa poker tournaments with Annie Duke and Norman Epstein, you did the film *Darfur Now*, you designed a boot with Timberland to "Stomp Out Genocide," you are writing your second book with me—hey, didn't we swear never to write another book together?—the list goes on and on. Basically, it comes down to renewing your pledge, your "Enough Pledge."

DON: Hmmm, what makes us continue to renew our pledge? I like that, great way to say it. Your responsibility doesn't end with one action. Like Ante Up for Africa, it is an annual event, so we come back every year. You and I continuously come back to each other with questions—what are we doing now to move the cause forward? What should we do now? It's what you have dedicated your life to, and it's what I continue to recommit to in various ways. During the year when these various events are coming together, every time I'm on the phone with these guys, Brad and George and Matt, it is often a subject of discussion. Mainly because the Sudanese people aren't yet dancing in the streets of Khartoum saying, "We're free."

JOHN: I remember when I was working for President Clinton and we were working closely with Nelson Mandela on the Burundi peace process. People would get discouraged, and President Mandela would remind us—sometimes sternly—that no situation, no matter how bleak the snapshot may look, is actually hopeless. He would tell us stories of his own experiences, being in prison for decades and then coming out and becoming president, to demonstrate how things can change. We just have to stay positive because the worm will turn. One of my favorite stories in our previous book is about your visit to UCLA's campus when you had that torn ACL in your knee, and you had to limp all the hell over the campus all day. You guys started with about fifteen people, and you were like, "Oh no, this is a bust," but the word kept spreading throughout the day, and by the end there, you had well over a hundred students, and you all went in to the hearing room and convinced the university regents to sell all the stocks in the university portfolio that are related to Sudanese investments. That was invigorating. At the end you wrote, "Sore as I am, my battery has been recharged. What's next?" That's an example, if there ever were one, of renewing one's Enough Pledge.

DON: Don't remind me. I still can't beat my man off the dribble because of that injury.

JOHN: I can't beat my man even if I didn't dribble and just ran with the ball. It has all slipped away so quickly.

DON: We had our day. At least we can still walk.

JOHN: Oh, that's what that is called, when you painfully move under your own power from point A to point B?

DON: Speaking of pain . . . I had to write a lot more of my personal stories in the last book, my Enough Moments. I thought you got off a little light. I think it's your turn to really spill the beans and tell us more about how you've stayed in the game for over twenty-five years now, how you've been able to keep renewing your Enough Pledge, fighting the good human rights fight.

JOHN: I'll admit, I've had my share of disappointments and hopes, failures and successes, narrow escapes and lucky misses, lost friends, and found allies . . .

DON: What, are you gonna sing a song or answer the question?

JOHN: Sheesh, tough crowd. All right all right. I was born in Indianapolis, Indiana, to a frozen foods salesman and a social worker.

DON: Please fast forward.

JOHN: Okay. I can't even count the significant forks in the road I've encountered, but it all really started when I was twenty-one years old, sitting in my favorite old Archie Bunker Lazyboy chair with my ankle in a cast from yet another basketball injury, and in the middle of the night, footage comes on from the famine in Ethiopia and Eritrea. I had a choice. I could have given a few bucks. I could have changed the channel if I had a remote control clicker. I could have maybe tried to learn more about what was happening there. But I decided in that instant, when confronted with pictures of human misery like none I had ever countenanced before, I decided to just go to Africa and see for myself and figure out where I fit into the whole thing.

A couple years later, another fork presented itself to me. I was in Somalia and witnessing how a U.S.-backed dictator was destroying his own country. I had started down a career track that was focused on the delivery of humanitarian and development assistance, and it promised to be a fascinating life full of adventure and meaningful work. But as I watched the American government—in its pursuit of cold strategic interest—help inadvertently underwrite the destruction of a country and its people, I decided to go another way. I decided that I needed to come back to the United States and use my one comparative advantage, my U.S. citizenship, to help re-form American policy in Africa so it wasn't solely designed to use Africa and its people to achieve U.S. foreign policy and economic security objectives.

Don! Don! Wake up!!

DON: I'm listening! Whaddya want, minute-by-minute valida-tion?

JOHN: Okay, just checking. Another fork came a decade later. After years of rabble rousing as a long-haired outsider activist, content with making bold pronouncements about U.S. policy in Africa to anyone who would listen, I was presented with the opportunity to put my time where my mouth was and come join the U.S. government to help make its Africa policy. So I went to the barber, got a genuine haircut and not just a "trim," bought one suit from a great thrift store, reinvented myself as a diplomat and peace negotiator, and showed up at the White House the next day to work for Susan Rice and the president of the United States, Bill Clinton.

After I left government, I reinvented myself again as a policy wonk. I spent a few years just working inside the system, inside the Beltway, doing think tank conferences and presenting long and probably boring papers to like-minded people in a circular process that had little effect on actual policy making and the broader public's role in shaping it. I realized that if anything was going to change STRUCTURALLY in terms of U.S. policy toward and interest in Africa, it would only be through a much more informed citizenry shaping those changes. So I reinvented myself again and became a populist campaigner.

In all these years of working on these issues, I have never had a boring day or even a dull moment. And the various paths have been so incredibly unpredictable.

I couldn't have imagined so many of the things that I have since experienced when I had my first Enough Moment at the age of twenty-one.

I was utterly petrified of public speaking when I was younger. I couldn't have imagined that twenty years later I would be doing over one hundred speeches a year, sometimes in front of crowds in the thousands.

I have been a tech phobe all my life. I couldn't have imagined that one of the main things I am doing now is focusing on how to build campaigns using the latest social networking functions, even though I myself don't have any idea how to use them.

Sitting in that Lazyboy at the age of twenty-one, I had never read a book on Africa, or peacemaking, or even foreign policy for that matter. I couldn't have imagined then that fifteen years later I would be helping to broker peace deals in different parts of Africa, including contributing to an end to a deadly war involving Ethiopia and Eritrea, the places that had originally brought me to Africa.

I watched in awe of what musicians led by Bono, Bob Geldof, and Sting were able to do to generate attention for the cause of the Ethiopian and Eritrean famine shortly after I went to Africa the first time in the 1980s. I couldn't have imagined then that twenty years later I would be regularly working with musicians and other artists to raise awareness.

During my college years, as I bounced from school to school, I had been an amateur student of the civil rights movement. I couldn't have imagined that a couple decades later I would be sitting in a D.C. jail cell with John L. Lewis, one of the original Freedom Riders in Mississippi, as we were arrested together for trespassing on the property of the Sudan Embassy and refusing to leave during one of our protest marches.

When I was in my early twenties, no one would hire me full time because I had no experience because no one would hire me, a vicious catch-22. I couldn't have imagined that a decade and a half later I would be sitting elbow to elbow with Nelson Mandela strategizing with him on how to bring peace to some of Africa's war-torn countries.

I moved to Washington, D.C., at the age of twenty-four to take an internship, and I was living in a condemned building because I couldn't afford rent. I couldn't have imagined that sixteen years later I would be traveling around Congo with Angelina Jolie, or that I would move so quickly from renegade outside critic to director for African affairs at the White House, or that I would get the chance to help shape U.S. policy in Africa.

I loved watching the Ben Affleck and Matt Damon movies like *Good Will Hunting* and *Rounders* in which they would team up using their real-life chemistry. I couldn't have imagined that I'd eventually be working with them—and you—raising money for Darfur and awareness for Congo.

DON: What, you don't like my movies?

JOHN: I'm sorry, were you in *Good Will Hunting* as well? Well, what I'm saying is that part of the process of renewing my Enough Pledge has been remaining open to all possibilities and being willing to take less traveled paths. By being an Upstander for others and dreaming big dreams, some of them actually have come true on the road to trying to make the world a little bit better. But it hasn't been all Bill Clinton, Angelina Jolie, and Emmy Awards for *60 Minutes*. Over the years, my mind and focus have been concentrated by some near misses, some real close calls:

- From the side window of a small plane I was in over southern Sudan, I watched a shoulder-to-air missile get launched in our direction, and after evasive measures, I saw the rocket fly a few dozen feet past our plane.
- In a long convoy of trucks in Angola, I watched the vehicle ahead of me explode as it drove over a land mine planted in the road.
- In one of the most dangerous neighborhoods in Mogadishu, the capital of Somalia, a mortar round hit the building I was in, and half the building collapsed (but not the half that I was in).
- On the border of Rwanda and Congo after the genocide, a child soldier all drugged up by his superiors stuck a gun in my mouth and threatened to kill me at a roadblock, but then ended up walking away muttering to himself.
- In both Zimbabwe and southern Sudan, I was arrested and detained for human rights reporting. In the former case I was roughed up and deported. In the latter, I was left in a hut that doubled as a jail for four days in a remote village with little food and water until I was released after having been "taught a lesson."

- In Congo I was stopped at a roadblock, and a couple dozen machine gun–wielding militia emerged from the woods and began threatening my travel companions and me, poking guns in my stomach and simulating a throat slash. We were taken to the militia barracks in the middle of the night, and a debate ensued about what to do with us. We finally were released when we convinced the militia leader we'd put in a good word for him with the U.S. military.

DON: The grim reaper is camped outside your doorstep permanently, it seems.

JOHN: It comes with the territory. Luckily, not everyone who wants to be an Upstander has to experience these kinds of close calls to make a difference . . .

Your Enough Moment Is Calling: How Do You Answer?

DON: So now we're at the point in the book where people hopefully are like, okay, we got all that. Now tell us what we can do. How can we get involved in a way that might really make a difference? And I think at the core of this is the recurring theme of the importance of creating connections. Finding the personal connection between us and them, you and me, so that these artificial barriers dissolve.

JOHN: And I think there are some road-tested ways to do that. One way is by telling personal stories of survivors. People connect to individuals, all the research shows that. It is much harder to connect to 6 million dead in the Holocaust than it is to connect to Anne Frank.

DON: Another way is creating these school-to-school or student-to-student ties. Like what your Darfur Sister Schools Program has done. When young people in the United States get the chance to personally connect to young people in Darfur or another far-off place, the distance between them gets a lot shorter, and you start to see concepts of mutual responsibility play themselves out right in the classroom.

JOHN: I wish every school, every classroom, could have these kinds of connections. Yet another way to establish connections and invest people in activism is by demonstrating the economic linkages. That is why we focused on the conflict minerals in the Congo, to demonstrate to people that this wasn't some ancient tribal feud that led to the highest death toll since the Holocaust. The war there is fueled directly by our demand for electronic products. By demonstrating the links, we show people that there are solutions, and we can even use these electronic devices themselves to catalyze change through texting, call-in, and e-mailing campaigns.

Making a Difference in the Twenty-First Century

The incredible thing in the twenty-first century is that you can raise your voice and fight genocide, mass rape, and child abductions right from your laptop in the comfort of your living room. And that's good because now, more than ever, our voices are needed if we're going to help bring about the change we'd like to see.

Americans are a generous and pragmatic people. We've seen that over and over: Haiti, Hurricane Katrina, the tsunami. When someone is in need, they will help, but usually only if they can see a chance for success or that their help can actually make a difference. We want to help people wade into some of the most difficult issues and broken societies of our time and find the hope, the humanity, and then connect it back here to us, to America's rightful place in the world as a beacon for peace and human rights.

Here's a menu you can choose from, a menu of fourteen (nice round number) life-saving and life-affirming actions, all of which can make a real difference in the battle for a more just and peaceful world. We've learned a lot since *Not On Our Watch* about what is needed to influence policy makers and build a genuine people's movement, so this menu is more elaborate and offers more choices than the one in our earlier book. All of the actions below can be found updated on www.enoughmoment.org. Just start with one of them!

1. **First, Join the Movement!** Get off the bench and get in the game, and recruit your friends and family members as well. It turns out that the most effective tool for inspiring action isn't a fancy ad campaign or a huge rally. It isn't a celebrity endorser. It's when a friend or family member asks a friend or family member to help him or her solve a problem that matters personally. Everyone has social networks and communities both online and offline that are much bigger and more powerful than we might realize. So join an organization like Enough, STAND, Invisible Children, V-Day, Amnesty International, Save Darfur Coalition, or other groups in this movement that stand up for what you stand for. Get involved in one of the ongoing campaigns, like Enough's Raise Hope for Congo, Humanity United's Sudan Now, or Invisible Children's How It Ends. Sign up for action alerts and newsletters, and get your friends and family members to join you and take action.

2. **Contact Your Senator or Representative.** The bedrock of our democracy lies in the fact that your elected officials work for you. Despite all of the new tools at our fingertips, and despite all the special-interest money, policy is ultimately changed the old-fashioned way, and it is a supply and demand system.

If you demand it, our government will supply it. If you don't vote, and you don't write to pressure your elected officials, you don't count. But if you do those things, then you count disproportionately to the one body you inhabit because of all the other complainers who are sitting it out. So get in touch with your elected officials by calling, writing, e-mailing, or even going to meet them when they come to your hometown looking for votes. You are their employer. Tell them what you want them to do for you as their constituent. Thank them when they do what you ask, and hold them accountable when they don't. And in the age of technological protest, where members of Congress can be overwhelmed by huge amounts of electronic communications from large-scale well-financed campaigns, there is no substitute for sending your representative a handwritten letter (neatly written; don't be a loon!) or putting together a unique coalition of folks at the district level and making an appointment to see your representative personally when he or she is holding office hours. Our issues are ones where the greatest political opponent we face is usually apathy, but apathy can easily be overcome with enough concerted political pressure.

3. Call the White House. It takes only a few minutes to let our president know that it matters to you as a voter that he (or in the future, she) makes fighting these human rights crimes a priority. It's easy; you may not even have to write this number down anywhere. The Genocide Intervention Network has a number that you can call to get a short briefing and talking points before forwarding you to the White House switchboard. The number is 1-800-GENOCIDE (1-800-436-6243). Use it, recruit your friends and family to call it, and call back often. They don't have caller ID so don't be shy about calling multiple times. One single call to the White House or your elected officials might not make much of an impact by itself, but a community or constituency can make a world of difference by calling regularly and keeping the pressure on until progress is made.

4. Get Local Media. In the world of newspapers and local television and radio, it is again a supply and demand equation. If a producer or editor gauges that people are interested in a particular subject, he or she will provide that content. So write or call your local radio and television networks, and urge them to cover stories about these human rights crimes in Africa, and the positive stories as well. Ask for a meeting with your paper's editorial board, and make a compelling case for an editorial on Sudan or the conflict minerals trade in Congo. Write a letter to the editor about a newsworthy item related to these issues. Media networks need our help too with content to cover these issues. There are lots of good people who care about these issues working in the media, and they need popular, quantifiable support in the form of letters, phone calls, and e-mails that demonstrate that there is an audience for stories about war and peace and human rights beyond Iraq and Afghanistan. At a time when broader foreign media coverage is rapidly declining, it is often up to us to keep these issues in the news by creating the need to cover it.

5. Get Involved in Corporate Campaigning. Although governments are usually the main players in supporting solutions to complex international problems, private sector entities can also be influential. We currently have two big opportunities here. In the case of Congo's conflict minerals, the Enough Project is spearheading a campaign to influence the behavior of the top electronics companies. We want them to stop buying from suppliers that get their raw materials in a way that fuels war and atrocities, and instead produce conflict-free phones, laptops, and other electronic products. They produce the technology that we all use, but we can use that same technology to organize and raise our collective voices to change their behavior. Visit www

.raisehopeforcongo.org and find out the latest initiatives in which to get involved.

Another great opportunity for corporate engagement comes through organizations like the Conflict Risk Network (CRN) and Investors Against Genocide (IAG). In the case of the Darfur genocide, the Sudan Divestment Task Force (now CRN) forged a campaign to get big institutional investment funds to sell the stock of companies doing business in Sudan in ways that strengthened the government there. Congress passed the Sudan Accountability and Divestment Act, which authorizes and encourages state and local divestment. Twenty-seven state pension funds, over sixty universities and colleges, twenty-three cities, the retirement fund TIAA-CREF, and even Warren Buffett's Berkshire Hathaway have divested from these targeted stocks. Thirteen international companies have ceased operations in Sudan or have developed exit plans as a result of divestment efforts. Get involved with these organizations, and stay informed about how you can influence corporations to do their part to help stop the violence.

6. Join the Darfur Dream Team's Sister Schools Program. This initiative links middle schools, high schools, colleges, and universities in the United States with schools in the Darfur refugee camps and helps fund the refugee camp schools. Video links between schools there and here will allow students to get to know each other and build connections to people directly affected by the atrocities in Sudan. NBA players act as spokespersons and supporters of the program, and they are helping to carry this new program to a wide audience. The more human linkages that can be established connecting good-hearted people with those for whom they are advocating, the more sustainable the movement will be to ensure that the Darfurian students and their families can one day go home in peace. Go to www .darfurdreamteam.org to sign up or donate.

7. Get on the Bus and Attend an Event! Enough, Invisible Children, the Save Darfur Coalition, STAND chapters, Resolve Uganda, V-Day, Jewish World Watch, and many other organizations regularly organize local events to galvanize support, educate the community, and publicly demonstrate that this movement's strength is not just in Washington, D.C., but in grassroots actions carried out across the country. Attending or organizing an event is one of the most important things activists can do because these demonstrations get local press and show our elected officials that their constituents care about these issues at a local level. So get on a bus! Attend an Invisible Children movie screening, support a local STAND chapter, or go to a conference or a lobby day!

8. Use Your Social Media for Social Good. The tools of social media are undoubtedly important in their ability to make us all neighbors in one interconnected global marketplace of ideas and actions. However, the connections made on Facebook, the knowledge gained through tweets, and the opportunities uncovered in communities of interest are only the first step. For social media to mean social good, you must go further.

Start using your online identity to make a footprint on the issues in this book and that you care about. Use your virtual soapbox on Facebook to promote news articles covering the stories that need to be told. If you care deeply about issues like the ongoing violence against women in the Congo, tell somebody! Start a blog, and cover the story in ways that the mainstream media are missing. Write your favorite bloggers like Daily Kos or FiredogLake and ask that they start providing more coverage of these crimes against humanity. Use whatever platforms you can to raise the profile of these tragedies. We can all work to highlight the issues that otherwise aren't getting enough attention.

Finally, make the online world count in the offline world. Use easy and lightweight tools like TweetUps or Facebook groups to bring people together in the real world for viewing parties, discussion groups, or other events that can help promote the importance of making an impact with those less fortunate. Check out social media platforms like TakePart.com, SocialVibe, and Causecast as ways to get further involved and become part of a larger online community.

9. Make a Video! With the popularity of video-sharing websites and an abundance of affordable, easy-to-use cameras on the market, spreading your message via video has never been easier—or more essential. In the past, presidents made weekly addresses on the radio. But President Obama posts his weekly address on YouTube. And there's a reason for that: it's where the eyeballs are.

Creative video doesn't necessarily have to be time-consuming or elaborate (although that doesn't hurt either!). The beauty of video is that it allows you to add your face to a movement simply by firing up the camera, looking into the lens, and speaking your mind. Share your video online, and encourage your friends to join you. A visual chorus of people calling for change is difficult to ignore.

10. Get Off Your Ass and RUN! Run for Congo Women is a grassroots run (or walk, bike, swim, bake, pray . . . you get the point, just get creative!) fundraiser for Women for Women International's Congo Program (www.womenforwomen.org). So far, the group has raised more than $600,000, and it has sponsored well over 1,200 women in Congo. And those women are raising more than 5,000 children. You can visit www.runforcongowomen.org to find out if there's a run scheduled near you or to get tips on organizing your own run. Who knew that exercising could be so meaningful?

11. Host a Movie Screening. Consider hosting a screening of one of the amazing films that have been produced about the issues addressed in this book: Don Cheadle's *Darfur Now*, George Clooney's *Sand and Sorrow*, Tracy McGrady's *3 Points*, Brian Steidle's *The Devil Came on Horseback*, Emmanuel Jal's *War Child*, Lisa Jackson's *The Greatest Silence*, and Invisible Children's various films. Whether you host something at your house or a local venue, this is a great way to get your friends and community more informed and passionate about taking action.

12. Organize a Teach-in at Your School or Your Child's School. V-Day, Enough, and STAND have teamed up to create materials to teach a class about the conflict in Congo. Facing History and Ourselves has a curriculum for Darfur based on the film *Darfur Now* and our book *Not On Our Watch*. Use one of these existing resources or create your own to educate those around you. Let's make sure no one can say he or she did not know about these issues as a reason for inaction. We have to get out and educate our communities and schools about what we know.

13. Involve Your Local Faith Community. Faith-based groups have a great history of being powerful forces for change in areas of human rights—from helping to end slavery to pressuring the U.S. government to lead in creating the Comprehensive Peace Agreement for Sudan in 2005, which brought the twenty-year civil war to a halt. Two great resources for the Christian community are a Bible study series called the *Not On Our Watch Christian Companion* (a resource by Greg Leffel and Bill Mefford, whose inspiring Enough Moment is captured in the Internet companion to this book) as well as a version specifically based on Catholic Social Teaching. (See www.enoughproject.org for these materials.) American Jewish World Service has developed

Jewish prayers and Passover materials to incorporate into Jewish services (www.ajws.org). These tools are just an idea to get you started. Regardless of your particular denomination or background, people of all faiths are called to speak out against injustice. Help organize your local faith groups, and call them to action.

14. Make a Difference on the Ground. While there are many actions we must take to urge our own leaders to take steps toward bringing peace, we must also support and connect to the people we are fighting for. Omer Ismail's and Suliman Giddo's Darfur Peace and Development Organization (www.darfurpeace.org) is a Darfurian-run group that provides education and life-saving aid to those displaced by the genocide. Organizations like Women for Women International work to empower women in conflict and postconflict environments to transition from victim to survivor to active citizen, through programs that address their unique needs. Enough's RAISE Hope for Congo campaign partners with local Congolese organizations that work at community, national, and/or international levels. Together they work to provide a wide range of services, including medical and psychosocial support, child soldier demobilization, skills training, political empowerment, grassroots organizing, and legal counseling. You can find out how to contribute to these organizations by visiting www.raisehopeforcongo .org/partners.

JOHN: Ultimately, all the greatest policy ideas in the world don't mean squat if we don't have a permanent constituency of people behind the ideas, demanding that our elected officials do something about some of the world's worst human rights abuses. I think that the deepening of a popular movement against mass atrocities could literally help change the fate of millions of people.

DON: The truth is, I have doubts all the time about whether we can succeed. I know I drive you crazy with my questions and my skepticism as to whether change can occur in the face of difficult odds. But what I do know is that we can get involved and do something. And there are many things that we can do if we do an inventory of our own skills, our own networks, our own areas of creativity, our own communities. So hopefully this book can provide some examples, some knowledge, some tools, and some inspiration.

The crises in Sudan, Congo, and elsewhere in Africa may seem unresolvable. But real leadership from the Obama administration in Washington—applying lessons from previous success stories of hope, and supported and prodded by the continuing development of a people's movement focused on these issues—provides great hope that the crimes focused on in this book can be ended in the places where they are occurring now and eventually prevented from ever occurring again.

There was a small meeting in New York in early 2004 at which Elie Wiesel and John spoke. This group of people were outraged by the reports of mass slaughter beginning to trickle out of a place few people had ever heard of, and they had gathered in order to discuss what to do. The group didn't seem like much at the time, but the members pooled their resources and the Save Darfur movement was born from that little meeting. Now over a million people are working to end the suffering in Darfur, and it is front and center on the Obama administration's radar screen. Little meetings like that occur all the time on important issues, and you never know what is going to catch fire within the larger population when a small, creative, and committed group of people are backing it. Don't forget what Margaret Mead said:

*Never underestimate the power of a small group of com-
mitted people to change the world. In fact, it is the only
thing that ever has.*

Well, here we are.

And if that quote doesn't do it for you, how about the pre-
eminent historian Howard Zinn:

*If there is going to be change, real change, it will have to
work its way from the bottom up, from the people themselves. That's how change happens.*

And now it is up to you.

It took ten years to build a successful blood diamonds campaign that helped end the wars in Sierra Leone, Liberia, and
Angola. People on the receiving end of genocide, rape as a
war weapon, and child soldier abduction don't have another
ten years to wait. Your friends, your networks, your school-
mates, your sorority or fraternity, your family members, your
union, your club, your team, your church or synagogue or
spiritual center—all these are the small groups that are part
of world-changing movements. We have a chance through
our efforts to support the peace that the survivors of these
human rights crimes so desperately crave. How lucky are we
to have the chance to do this together.

Standing up is key. You will have so many opportunities
in the years ahead to seize an Enough Moment. To be someone who

- takes the road less traveled,
- dives into the deep end,
- loves being an Upstander,
- takes the chance,
- goes for the cake AND the icing,

- trusts yourself and believes anything is possible, and finally
- just goes for it.

When you live like this, especially on behalf of other people less fortunate than you, incredible things can happen. Remember the words of John Donne:

Any man's death diminishes me because I am involved in mankind. Therefore never send to know for whom the bell tolls, it tolls for thee.

Let's remember: Smart, solution-oriented policies plus people's movements together are the answer. They are the indispensable elements of change. But the people's movements, a veritable legion of hope, can't just wish that their good intentions are translated into effective policy responses. Activists must pursue coordinated messages that are more nuanced than just "stop it." A degree of sophistication in the campaigning is required, to gain the attention and respect of policy makers as well as to foster inevitability toward the correct policy choices. And Internet-based mass advocacy requires different approaches that go beyond the old-school notions of sending a prepared postcard to your representative in Congress. The new media have created new opportunities for much wider and deeper education and more creative and participatory mobilization than ever before on issues affecting people halfway around the world.

This is the Enough Moment for us as individuals, as communities, as constituents, as voters, as church or synagogue or mosque members. This is the moment to stand up and be counted as someone who has had ENOUGH with inaction in the face of the world's greatest human rights crimes. In the words of Paul Hawken, "Don't be put off by people who know what is not possible. Do what needs to be done, and check to see if it was impossible only after you are done."

If we fail to get policy makers to stand up, hundreds of thousands, maybe millions, more lives will be extinguished. On our watch.

But if we are successful, if we can make the wheel squeak loudly enough, if we can make enough noise:

- Millions of people will NOT remain homeless in desolate camps.
- Hundreds of thousands of women and girls will NOT be raped.
- Tens of thousands of children will NOT be abducted to be soldiers or sex slaves.

Throughout our lives, we will constantly have choices and opportunities to either become Upstanders or bystanders. If ENOUGH of us choose to be Upstanders, we can help change the course of history. That is the Enough Moment. ENOUGH of us, with ENOUGH commitment, will lead the change.

This is a people's movement worth building. The truth is, it takes fifteen minutes a week to become a full-fledged, card-carrying member of the people's movement to end genocide, or child soldier conscription, or rape as a war weapon. Or all three.

Here's what this all means for you: if the world your own children will inherit someday will NOT be engulfed by environmental destruction, violent wars, preventable diseases, racial and religious discrimination, human rights abuses, and other scourges of our age, it will be because YOU organized, YOU led, YOU believed in yourself, YOU didn't sleep through the revolution, YOU were an Upstander, and YOU made sure your life was a beacon that lit a path for all those seeking a better world!

Epilogue: One Last Word Before We Go

DON: I think often if you look at the totality of it, if you look at the level of despair and inequity that these people are experiencing, it can sometimes feel overwhelming to the point of paralysis, where it is maybe easier to just look away than to try and address in it any way that is substantive. We may be doing the issues a disservice in some strange way when we frame them as massive, complex problems. There is so much noise to cut through and have people say, "Oh, I see you." We are talking about issues that are very difficult to try and get your mind around, and maybe even harder to figure out how to solve them. So it's vital that the movement continue to generate innovative ways to attract attention and draw people to it. And no, it's not about telling people what the answer is. It's letting them know that you need them for the answers and for spreading the word. But even to come up with that, as you guys have come up with on Congo, even to frame it in that context, you have to have a person, a group of people, say, "This is what we need from you." We have done a lot of the heavy lifting in terms of research and policy solutions, but we need you to plug into that and help push in the right direction.

JOHN: Damn, that's so interesting. And it's so contrary to what so many campaigns and causes do, which simply tell people to send this letter now or sign this petition without giving their members or activists any room for creative input. With the issues we're addressing, at the end of the day, it's such a tantalizing and frustrating moment because we have all the pieces in place for a winning campaign. We have policy initiatives or legislation on Sudan, the Congo, and the LRA, we have the knowledge of what has worked in the past in response to mass atrocities—the three P's of the solution: peace, protection, and punishment—that once they are together will help produce a transformed situation. And we have millions of people who have manifested themselves as desirous of becoming activists on these issues. We have Famous Upstanders who care about these things, who show up and do something. We have committed legislators in D.C. and all over the country and even in some other countries. We have corporations that have made changes in regards to divestment. All these pieces, but what appears to be missing at the very core is a way to organize the innovation, the creativity, the challenge to people's initiative that will allow for the most important element of the whole thing: the people's movement applying political pressure and offering political rewards for doing the right thing, for solving a problem. I think what's missing is the level of organization that allows, in some sort of decentralized way, for real creativity on the part of the movement to grow and support the leadership of local activists from Portland to Little Rock to Kansas City, and somehow reward that innovation and local leadership.

DON: And I believe that there ought to be a lot more of "What can you do?" as opposed to "I have something for you guys, do this."

JOHN: Yeah, we need that, we gotta encourage that. The way the world works with issues and causes that are in our direct interest is much easier. Take the National Rifle Association or the American Association of Retired Persons. They send their message out to their constituents with very clear directions: write to this senator with this specific message, and do it this way, or don't bother. It's a very top-down hierarchical thing. And they have the built-in constituencies because they are dealing with things that matter personally to people, so these organizations can just tell their members exactly what to do and when to do it. But as you said earlier, if it doesn't affect your daily life, you better come up with a different model that inspires people to become involved. You have to come up with something that allows them to have a stake in it through their own creative involvement. And I think that the Darfur efforts, for example, probably lost a lot of time by not fully comprehending this necessary way of maintaining momentum and commitment.

DON: People want to feel like we felt with the Obama campaign. You sent the five bucks in via text or e-mail, they hit you back with a creative thank you, and you're like, "Damn, I really did something. I didn't think doing that would have an impact." We usually don't get that kind of feedback. You kind of feel like your action is out in space. "What happened with that money? What did my action do?" There is a "disconnection," which results in a kind of "dis-concern" about the result. So if the feedback part isn't happening, you feel like you might be throwing your time or money into the ocean. You don't feel like there is much more required of you other than "Just give us more money." You still have to somehow figure out a way to make the activist or concerned citizen feel validated, feel necessary.

JOHN: I saw a fund-raising envelope with a starving baby on it recently, and frankly I didn't even open it. You know where they are coming from. It's the same Pavlovian response they are looking for. But if you get a message that gives you some way to be part of the solution, then it becomes interesting. From ground floor construction, to opening the front door when it's finished. I care about schools in refugee camps, but I think more is required to make a connection with someone here. If I met a kid through a video profile or video blogging in his school in the refugee camp he lives in, and I took responsibility for textbooks for his class with my own classmates, then sooner or later I'm gonna want to make sure that this kid has a chance to be able to go home some day, which then would lead me to take action politically. How much more compelling is it going to be for me to be a part of seeing change happen if I have a personal link to someone there, rather than just seeing e-mails that tell me to stop the genocide by giving $5. We need to invest in these folks who have survived these crises, make connections with them, and then ask people here for their ideas on how to make sure these solutions are implemented. I think that's the future of advocacy.

> *I do not pretend to understand the moral universe, the arc is a long one, my eye reaches but little ways. I can calculate the curve and complete the figure by the experience of sight; I can divine it by conscience. But from what I see I am sure it bends toward justice.*
>
> —THEODORE PARKER

We think the speed with which that arc bends toward justice can be dramatically influenced by people getting together to try to make a difference. That is the point. There will always be injustice, driven by greed, bigotry, power. But the degree to which injustice is thwarted and countered and reversed is up to us. The battle is joined. We hope you will choose to be part of it. Millions of lives hang in the balance.

See the interactive companion to this book on the Enough Project's website at www.enoughmoment.org for up-to-date ideas for getting involved in your own community.

Resources

Here's a list of the great Upstanding organizations we discussed throughout the book. We thought we'd put them all
in once place for your reference.

Africa Youth Initiative Network (AYINET), www.ayinet.or.ug

American Jewish World Service, www.ajws.org

Amnesty International, www.amnestyusa.org

Ante Up for Africa, www.anteupforafrica.org

Central Ohioans for Peace, www.centralohioansforpeace.org

Christian Communications Network, www.ccn.tv

Darfur Dream Team, www.darfurdreamteam.org

Darfur Peace and Development, www.darfurpeace.org

Eastern Congo Initiative, www.easterncongo.org

EcoMom Alliance, ecomomalliance.ning.com

Enough Project, www.enoughproject.org

Facing History and Ourselves, www.facinghistory.org

Grassroots Reconciliation Group, www.grassrootsgroup.org

Humanity United, www.humanityunited.org

i-ACT, www.i-act.org

Invisible Children, www.invisiblechildren.org

Jeunesse et Droits Humains, www.jdhrdcongo.unblog.fr

Jewish World Watch, www.jewishworldwatch.org

Man Up Campaign, www.manupcampaign.org

Massachusetts Coalition to Save Darfur, www.savedarfurma.org

Mia Farrow's website, www.miafarrow.org

My Sister's Keeper, www.mskeeper.org

National Association of Evangelicals, www.nae.net

National Council of Churches, www.ncccusa.org

Not On Our Watch, www.notonourwatchproject.org

Raise Hope for Congo Campaign, www.raisehopeforcongo.org

Religious Action Center of Reform Judaism (RAC), www.rac.org

Resolve Uganda, www.resolveuganda.org

Run for Congo Women, www.runforcongowomen.org

San Francisco Bay Area Darfur Coalition, www.darfursf.org

Save Darfur Coalition, www.savedarfur.org

STAND, www.standnow.org

Stop Genocide Now, www.stopgenocidenow.org

Sudan Divestment Task Force, www.sudandivestment.org

Sudan Now, www.sudanactionnow.com

Sudan Social Development Organization, www.sudosudan.org

The Elders, www.theelders.org

V-Day, www.vday.org

Voice of Uganda, www.voicesofuganda.org

Women for Women, www.womenforwomen.org

Youth United for Darfur, www.youthunitedfordarfur.org

Acknowledgments

We are very grateful for the contributions of the following people to moving this book from a vague concept to a reality: Bonnie Abaunza, Nikki Alam, Semhar Araia, John Bagwell, Victoria Bosselman, Hacer Bozkurt, Zack Brisson, Rebecca Brocato, Molly Browning, Summer Buckley (ESPECIALLY Summer Buckley), Katherine Carson, Maggie Fick, Elissa Grabow, Laura Heaton, Alex Hellmuth, David Herbert, Corrine Irish, Omer Ismail, Stella Kenyi, Candice Knezevic, Sasha Lezhnev, Daniel Maree, Ellen McElhinny, Will McElhinny, Russell Moll, Robert Padavick, Larissa Peltola, Gitanjali Prasad, Dylan and Michael Prendergast, Meghna Raj, Eileen Read, Jenny Russell, Sia Sanneh, Courtney Schoenbohm, Barb Scott, Julia Spiegel, Jason Stearns, David Sullivan, Andrew Sweet, Whitney Williams, Meg Whitton, Lindsey Wood, Nate Wright, and Katherine Wycisk. Finally, Heather Lazare was an incredible editor, and Sarah Chalfont ably agented us to the right home at Random House.

Endnotes

1. *Newsweek*, January 25, 2010, p. 20.

2. *BBC Profile*, "Liberia's 'Iron Lady,'" November 23, 2005, http://news.bbc.co.uk/2/hi/world/africa/4395978.stm.

3. *CBC News*, "Ellen Johnson Sirleaf: Liberia's 'Iron Lady,'" March 28, 2006, http://www.cbc.ca/news/background/liberia/sirleaf.html.

4. Integrated Regional Information Networks, "Sierra Leone: Still Last on Human Development Index," December 18, 2008, http://www.unhcr.org/refworld/publisher,IRIN,,SLE,494b62d427,0.html.

5. *BBC Profile*, "Graca Machel," July 18, 1998, http://news.bbc.co.uk/2/hi/africa/135280.stm.

6. Headliners, "Don't Call Me Mrs. Mandela," 2001, http://www.headliners.org/storylibrary/stories/2001/dontcallmemrsmandela.htm?id=33728183847079258416978.

7. Times Online, Interview, Graca Machel, September 2, 2007, http://www.timesonline.co.uk/tol/news/world/africa/article2367072.ece.

8. David Birmingham, "Angola," in Patrick Chabal, *A History of Postcolonial Lusophone Africa*, Indiana University Press, Bloomington, 2002, p. 138.

9. Rufino Satumbo, "Testimony from UNITA Deserters," in William Minter, *Operation Timber: Pages from the Savimbi Dossier*, Africa World Press, Trenton, N.J., 1988, p. 111.

10. In 1983, twenty-four-year-old Satumbo was captured by the MPLA and forced to testify during a series of public hearings in Luanda. William Minter, *Operation Timber: Pages from the Savimbi Dossier*, Africa World Press, Trenton, N.J., 1988, p. 110.

11. Samantha Power, *A Problem from Hell: America and the Age of Genocide,* Basic Books, New York, 2002, p. 269.

12. Human Rights Watch, http://www.hrw.org/sites/default/files/reports/ANGOLA94N.pdf.

13. http://www.africaaction.org.

14. *PBS Wide Angle,* "Lord's Children: Aaron Brown Interview with Betty Bigombe," July 29, 2008, available at www.pbs.org.

15. *O Magazine,* Interview, available at http://www.greenbeltmovement.org/a.php?id=114.

16. Green Belt Movement website, http://greenbeltmovement.org/c.php?id=6.

17. Harriet Martin, *Kings of Peace, Pawns of War,* accessed through Google books.

18. Samantha Power, "Bystanders to Genocide," *Atlantic Monthly,* September 2001.

19. Jimmie Briggs, *Innocents Lost: When Child Soldiers Go to War,* Basic Books, New York, 2005, p. xiii.

20. P.W. Singer, *Children at War,* University of California Press, Berkeley and Los Angeles, 2006, p. 58.

21. Ibid.

22. E-mail correspondence with Enough Project staff, April 2008.

23. For a profile on Olwal, see UN Office for the Coordination of Humanitarian Affairs, "Uganda: Humanitarian Challenges of the Northern Crisis," *IRIN News,* 2006, available at http://www.irinnews.org/InDepthMain.aspx?InDepthId=23&ReportId=65777/.

24. For more on Jacob's project, see Grassroots Reconciliation Group at www.grassrootsgroup.org.

25. Jeannie Annan and Chris Blattman, "Survey of War-Affected Youth (SWAY) Research Brief 1, The Abduction and Return Experiences of Youth in Uganda," April 2006, available at www.sway-uganda.org.

26. *See* Catherine N. Niarchos, "Women, War, and Rape: Challenges Facing the International Tribunal for the Former Yugoslavia," *Women's Rights: A Human Rights Quarterly Reader,* edited by Bert B. Lockwood, 1995.

27. *See* Ruth Siefert, "War and Rape: A Preliminary Analysis," *Mass Rape: The War against Women in Bosnia-Herzegovina,* edited by Alexandra Stiglmayer, University of Nebraska Press, Lincoln, 1994, p. 55; and

Joshua Goldstein, *War and Gender: How Gender Shapes the War System and Vice Versa*, Cambridge University Press, Cambridge, United Kingdom, 2001, p. 363.

28. United Nations Development Fund for Women, "Preventing Wartime Rape from Becoming a Peacetime Reality," June 24, 2009.

29. Beverly Allen, *Rape Warfare: The Hidden Genocide in Bosnia-Herzegovina and Croatia*, University of Minnesota Press, Minneapolis, 1996, p. 57.

30. Sierra Leone Truth and Reconciliation Commission, *Witness to Truth: Final Report of the Sierra Leone Truth & Reconciliation Commission*, 2007, ch. 1, para. 25.

31. Candice Knezevic, "Congo's Courageous Men," blog post, August 6, 2009, http://www.enoughproject.org/blogs/congos-courageous-men.

32. From the *Sydney Morning Herald* special report on sexual violence in eastern Congo, http://www.smh.com.au/interactive/2009/congo/.

33. From John Prendergast and Noel Atama, "Eastern Congo: An Action Plan to End the World's Deadliest War," Enough Project Report, July 16, 2009.

34. Human Rights Watch, "DR Congo: Hold Army Commanders Responsible for Rapes," July 16, 2009, http://www.hrw.org/en/news/2009/07/16/dr-congo-hold-army-commanders-responsible-rapes.

35. Javier Bardem and John Prendergast, "Stop the Vampires in the Congo," CNN.com, October 22, 2008.

36. International Committee of the Red Cross, *Our World: Views from the Field: Democratic Republic of the Congo*, June 23, 2009.

37. Enough Project, *A Comprehensive Approach to Congo's Conflict Minerals*, Enough Strategy Paper, April 24, 2009.

38. Human Rights Watch, "DR Congo: Civilian Cost of Military Operation Is Unacceptable," October 13, 2009, available at http://www.hrw.org/en/news/2009/10/12/dr-congo-civilian-cost-military-operation-unacceptable.

39. United Nations Security Council, *Final Report of the Group of Experts on the Democratic Republic of the Congo*, November 23, 2009, S/2009/603.

40. Human Rights Watch, "You Will Be Punished," December 13, 2009, http://www.hrw.org/en/reports/2009/12/14/you-will-be-punished.

41. President Barack Obama, "Remarks to the Ghanaian Parliament," Accra International Conference Center, Accra, Ghana, July 11, 2009.

42. Ambassador Susan Rice, remarks during an Open Security Council Debate, August 7, 2009.

43. Enough Project, *A Comprehensive Approach to Conflict Minerals*.

Discussion Guide

1. What inspired you to pick up this book? Would you recommend it to a friend or relative?

2. Discuss the thoughts and feelings you had about Africa before reading *The Enough Moment*. Have any of your preconceived notions changed? Why or why not?

3. Have you ever had an Enough Moment? Can you describe it?

4. Did you know anything about child soldier abduction before reading this book? If so, where did you learn about it? How does it make you feel?

5. There are some very vivid testimonials in this book. Which testimonials were particularly moving or inspiring to you?

6. What are the three P's? Do you think this is an effective way to view the problems and resolutions in Africa?

Discuss the Congo, northern Uganda, and Sudan and how the three P's apply to each.

7. Which of the Upstanders did you connect with the most? Were you surprised by any of the testimonials from Famous Upstanders? Who and why?

8. Describe some of the things you might do to become an Upstander.

9. Of the menu of fourteen actions listed in Chapter Nine, which are you most likely to take?

10. Are there actions we haven't thought of?